AROUND
INDIA
IN
80
TRAINS

Praise for
Around India in 80 Trains

"A promising debut from a writer to watch. I am stung with jealousy, not just for the epic journey she makes rediscovering her Indian heritage – on ordinary trains, luxury trains, Mumbai's packed commuter trains, even a toy train – but just for the talismanic power of such a ticket: the idea that you could have one in your hand tomorrow and just go!"
Giles Foden, *Condé Nast Traveller*

"A wonderfully wry and witty debut. Crackles and sparks with life like an exploding box of Diwali fireworks."
William Dalrymple, author of *The Last Mughal*

"A great big lovely shambling train ride of a book, offering wonderful views, hilarious interludes, all sorts of dodgy characters and some very peculiar smells, all for the one ticket."
Giles Coren, bestselling author and *Times* **columnist**

"One can only envy Monisha Rajesh as she embarks on this epic journey through the vast tangle and bewildering extension of India's railways. The ticketing bureaucracy is mad, the travelling companions infinitely varied, the pleasure, discomforts and revelations such that she is guaranteed what even the wriest and most sceptical traveller yearns for: some deeper knowledge of oneself."
Tim Parks, travel writer and Booker Prize nominee

"I love train trips and I love travelling around India. If you do too, then this book is a wonderful companion."
Irvine Welsh, author of *Trainspotting*

AROUND
INDIA
IN
80
TRAINS

MONISHA RAJESH

NICHOLAS BREALEY
PUBLISHING
London • Boston

First published in Great Britain in 2012 by Nicholas Brealey Publishing
An imprint of John Murray Press

An Hachette company

7

British Library Cataloguing-in-Publication Data
A catalogue record for this book is available from the British Library.

Train illustrations by Sroop Sunar
www.sroop.com
Other illustrations by Kriti Monga
www.turmericdesign.com

ISBN 978-1-85788-595-8
eBook ISBN 978-1-85788-948-2

Printed and bound by Clays Ltd, St Ives plc

John Murray Press policy is to use papers that are natural, renewable and
recyclable products and made from wood grown in sustainable forests. The logging
and manufacturing processes are expected to conform to the environmental
regulations of the country of origin.

Nicholas Brealey Publishing
John Murray Press
Carmelite House
50 Victoria Embankment
London, EC4Y 0DZ, UK
Tel: 020 3122 6000

Nicholas Brealey Publishing
Hachette Book Group
Market Place Center, 53 State Street
Boston, MA 02109, USA
Tel: (617) 523 3801

www.nicholasbrealey.com
www.80trains.com

For Baby Rajesh, who is still on board.
May all your journeys be filled with adventure.

Contents

AROUND
INDIA
IN
80
TRAINS

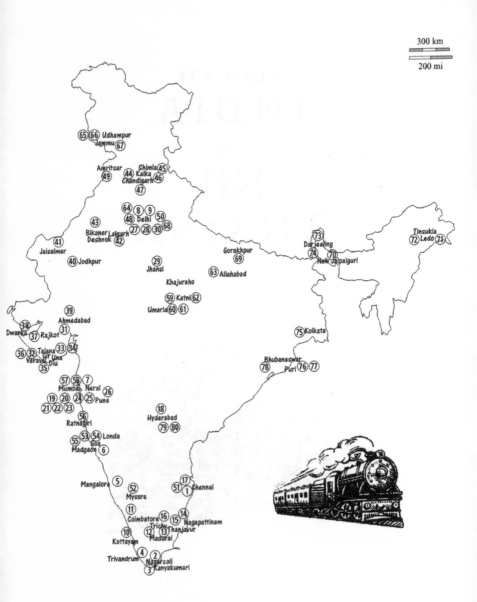

300 km
200 mi

65 66 Udhampur
Jammu 67
Amritsar Shimla 45
49 44 Kalka
Chandigarh 46
47
64 8 9
48 Delhi 50
43 27 28 30 68
Bikaner Lalgarh
Deshnok 42
41 Gorakhpur
Jaisalmer 69
40 Jodhpur 29 63 Allahabad
Jhansi
Khajuraho
59 Katni 62
Umaria 60 61
39
Ahmedabad
38 31
Dwarka 37 Rajkot
36 32 Talana 33 34
Veraval Diu
35
57 58 7
Mumbai Neral
19 20 24 25 26
21 22 23 Pune
56
Ratnagiri 18
55 53 54 Londa Hyderabad
Goa 79 80
Madgaon 6
Mangalore 5
52
Mysore
11 17
51 Chennai
Coimbatore 16 14 1
10 15 Nagapattinam
Trichy
Kottayam 12 13 Thanjavur
Madurai
4 2
Trivandrum Nagercoil
3 Kanyakumari

Tinsukia
73 72 Ledo 71
Darjeeling
74 70
New Jalpaiguri

75 Kolkata

Bhubaneswar
78 Puri 76 77

Outline map © Daniel Dalet/d-maps.com

THE 80 TRAINS

1. Anantapuri Express from Chennai to Nagercoil
2. Passenger train from Nagercoil to Kanyakumari
3. Himsagar Express from Kanyakumari to Trivandrum
4. Trivandrum–Mangalore Express from Trivandrum to Mangalore
5. Matsyagandha Express from Mangalore to Madgaon
6. Mandovi Express from Madgaon to Mumbai
7. Indian Maharaja-Deccan Odyssey from Mumbai to Delhi
8. Visitors' train: The National Railway Museum in Delhi
9. Kerala Express from Delhi to Kottayam
10. Sabari Express from Kottayam to Coimbatore
11. Nagercoil Express from Coimbatore to Madurai
12. Nagercoil–Chennai Express from Madurai to Trichy
13. Passenger train from Trichy to Thanjavur
14. Trichy–Nagore passenger train from Thanjavur to Nagapattinam
15. Passenger train from Nagapattinam to Trichy
16. Passenger train from Trichy to Chennai
17. Charminar Express from Chennai to Hyderabad
18. Hyderabad–Mumbai Express from Hyderabad to Mumbai
19. Local train from CST to Parel
20. Local train from Parel to CST
21. Local train from Churchgate to Andheri
22. Local train from Andheri to Churchgate
23. Koyna Express from Mumbai to Neral
24. Toy train from Matheran to Neral
25. Deccan Queen from Mumbai to Pune
26. Pune–Nizamuddin Duronto Express from Pune to Delhi
27. Delhi Metro from Central Secretariat to Rajendra Nagar
28. Sampark Kranti Express from Delhi to Jhansi
29. Bhopal Shatabdi Express from Jhansi to Delhi
30. Swarna Jayanti Rajdhani from Delhi to Ahmedabad
31. Somnath Express from Ahmedabad to Veraval
32. Passenger train from Veraval to Talana
33. Passenger train from Talana to Una
34. Passenger train from Delwada to Sasan Gir
35. Dhasa–Veraval passenger train from Gir to Veraval
36. Somnath Express from Veraval to Rajkot
37. Saurashtra Mail from Rajkot to Dwarka
38. Okha–Puri Express from Dwarka to Ahmedabad
39. Ranakpur Express from Ahmedabad to Jodhpur
40. Jaisalmer Express from Jodhpur to Jaisalmer
41. Passenger train from Jaisalmer to Lalgarh

Prologue

25 November

London had never looked so grey. From the eighth-floor windows of *TIME* magazine's Southwark offices the city's skyline was spiked with cranes, aerials and chimneys unfurling charcoal plumes. Even Westminster's spires, normally bouncing back glimmers of winter sun, had disappeared under the late-November fog.

Shivering beneath the air vent I turned back to my computer and scrolled through an article detailing how India's domestic airlines could now reach 80 cities. Intrigued, I printed out a map of the country and pored over the airline routes. They were impressive, but nowhere near as much as the railway network, which ran the length and breadth of the country, embroidering the tips of its landmass. I scanned the map, taking in the extent to which the railways covered the country. It was almost 20 years since my family had tried to move back to India to settle, but after spending two traumatic years in Madras we had made a hasty retreat home to England. India and I had parted on bad terms and little more than the occasional family wedding had succeeded in tempting me back.

As I stared out at the skies, sombre at 10 am, India's sunnier climes were an inviting prospect. I had barely stretched a toe beyond Madras and Hyderabad where my extended family lived, and always knew my curiosity about the rest of the country would get the better of me. So far every trip back had involved frog-hopping from one relative's house to the next, having my cheeks pinched, marvelling at my cousins' increasing waistlines while they frowned at my bones, and flying out as fast as I had arrived, with a suitcase full of *murukkus*. But I had never seen India as a tourist. If I was to go back and give it a real chance after 20 years, what was the best way? Leaving a gargantuan carbon footprint behind 80 flights was hardly the right way to go. As I traced the railway lines with a finger, an idea began to form in my mind. I called out to my colleague across the desk.

'Willy-Lee, what do you think of travelling around India in 80 trains?'

He glanced at the diagonals of rain spattering the windows and put on an oversize pair of Dior sunglasses, flipping his scarf over one shoulder.

'You should so go.'

That evening I stayed late after work and trawled Amazon for travelogues on India's railways. While there were almost 3000 books relating to the history, modernisation, finances and, of course, the British hand in building the railways, few were personal accounts. Both Rudyard Kipling and Paul Theroux had covered segments, and Michael Palin had endured a few journeys in his version of *Around the World in 80 Days*. But with the exception of Peter Riordan, a journalist from New Zealand, it seemed that nobody had recently written about a solo journey around India by train. As I gathered my things and waved to Willy-Lee, who was transcribing an interview with Dame Vera Lynn and staring mournfully at the clock, I wondered whether there was a reason for this: were the railways too dangerous? Maybe those who had tried to circle the country by train had fallen ill, been mugged, or died along the way before anyone could hear about their adventures. Still, the thrill lay in the uncertainty of it all.

Of the two years I had spent in India, my fondest memories were of the trains: tucked up in a cosy, curtained cabin aboard the Pandian Express to visit my brother at his boarding school. I could close my eyes to the heat and horrors of Madras and open them as the Palani Hills rose through the dawn haze. Trains were my escape, my ticket out of the city. They allowed me to curl up in comfort as my surroundings slipped away. Unlike air travel, a cramped, clinical affair conducted in recycled air, causing bad tempers and bad breath, train travel invited me to participate. I could sit in the doorway, thundering across rivers instead of pressing a forehead to a grimy oval window, watching them snake silently below. Since 1853 when the British waved off the first passenger train from Bombay to Thane, the network had rippled out across the country, earning the nickname 'The Lifeline of the Nation'. Trains carry over 20 million passengers every day along a route of 64,000 km, ploughing through cities, crawling past villages, climbing up mountains and skimming along coasts. Eighty train journeys up, down and across India would, I hoped, lift the veil on a country that had become a stranger to me.

There was just one issue to address: I needed a travelling companion. India was not the safest place for a single girl to travel alone and although I was prepared to go by myself, some company was preferable. While hunting for the right candidate, I began hankering after books featuring Indian train travel. As I lay in bed one night reading Jules Verne's *Around the World in 80 Days*, I realised that Phileas Fogg only decides to embark on his journey after reading an article in the *Daily Telegraph* announcing that a section of the Great Indian Peninsula Railway has been opened between Rothal and Allahabad, thereby reducing the time taken to circle the globe. The birth of the Indian Railways had clearly been an integral addition to global travel. My eyes began to close as I reached the point where Fogg's manservant, Passepartout, wanders into a temple, not realising that Christians are not allowed in: 'He looked up to behold three enraged priests, who forthwith fell upon him; tore off his shoes, and began to beat him with loud, savage exclamations.'

Yawning, I wondered whether things were still the same. I was not religious in the slightest, but remembered English friends being made to wait outside certain South Indian temples while we nosed around. Slotting a bookmark into the page, I flipped off the light and turned over, suddenly jealous of Phileas Fogg. As much as his hapless companion was becoming more of a hindrance than a help, at least he had someone to accompany him. My search for a travel buddy had proved useless; that is, until the following morning.

By some twist of fate, an email arrived from a friend of a friend. He had recently taken voluntary redundancy and was planning on travelling around Southeast Asia using his pay package. As an added bonus, he was also a part-time wedding photographer, and wanted to expand his portfolio with travel photography. Over scrambled eggs and coffee we discussed the trip. He was easy-going and smiled a lot. Pleased to have a ready-made project to walk into, he offered to accompany me for the full four months. We parted ways and I headed to the tube, confident and happy that I had found the right man for the job.

In *Around the World in 80 Days*, Jean Passepartout claims that his surname has clung to him due to his natural aptness for going out of one business and into another and has abandoned his own country of France for England. Passe-partout – the French phrase for 'all-purpose' – seemed the perfect nickname for my new companion. Twelve years ago he had abandoned his own country of Norway for England, and had now left a job in sales to pursue a career in photography. Less manservant and more travel buddy, his remit now extended to being my personal bodyguard and friend for our journey around India in 80 trains.

A week before Christmas, on one of London's most glorious winter mornings, Passepartout and I found ourselves outside a little office on Wembley Park Drive. Low sunshine flashed off windows trimmed with icicles as we stamped powdery snow off our boots and went in to meet Shankar Dandapani, the UK representative of the Indian Railways. The room was hung with a magnificent map of India and posters of Rajasthani moustaches and pagris. It was furnished with three school desks with flip-up tops, at which the three of us sat in a row sipping tea – Shankar in the middle. He picked up the piece of paper on which I had listed a series of trains and turned it over inquisitively while I sweated under my roll-neck dress.

'What is this?' he asked.

'A list of trains.'

'There are only nine.'

'I know. We were hoping you might be able to recommend some others.'

'Are you doing 80 individually named trains, or 80 journeys?'

Passepartout and I looked at each other like a pair of dunces.

'I suggest you do 80 journeys, or it could become difficult to find individual trains to cover certain areas.' Scanning the list, he recoiled, then turned over the page and began to draw columns that he titled 'scenic', 'toy train', 'luxury', 'Rajdhani', 'Shatabdi'. 'Okay, so you have already organised the Indian Maharaja train yourself, so I suggest the following...'

Within two minutes the list had grown to almost 50 trains long. We leant in, watching with amazement as Shankar annotated a number of the journeys with 'waterfalls', 'beautiful from Goa to Londa' and 'nice interiors'.

'Have you done these journeys?' I asked.

'Many,' he replied, handing over the paper. 'Right, 50 is enough for now. You can work out the other 30, most of which will be connectors between each of these.'

Finally, Shankar issued us with the most important equipment for the journey: two 90-day IndRail passes. They were parrot-green, as flimsy as tissue paper and so outdated that the original price read $300, and now contained a slash across the middle, with $530 written over the top in biro. The passes were only available to foreign tourists and allowed us to travel on any train in second-tier class or below. All we had to do was make reservations at the station or online. Once they expired, we would have to buy tickets for any remaining journeys.

'Take good care of them,' Shankar warned, 'if you lose them, you can't be issued with replacements. And have fun!' he added, as we waved from the doorway.

Outside, we looked at one another and laughed nervously. Passepartout held up Shankar's paper and examined the list. 'Wow, I think he just saved us from turning this trip into a total disaster.'

Christmas and New Year came and went. Despite the high numbers of January detoxers, the upstairs section of The Crown & Two Chairmen in Soho was jammed with well-wishers waving us off. Almost 40 friends crammed in around beer-covered tables. If this had been my birthday, six dependable friends would have turned up on time. Another seven or eight would have arrived in stages throughout the night, while the rest would have texted me with last-minute cancellations. Outside the steamed-up windows it was snowing heavily. Tubes would inevitably be cancelled and buses delayed, yet the overarching possibility that I might die in a train crash had brought everyone out of the woodwork. At least I knew my funeral would have a good turnout.

Beaming at faces I had not seen for months, I clutched a handful of good luck cards and strained to hear conversation over the din. A pair of cold hands pressed my hot face from behind and my friend Sarah clambered over a few bags and coats, unwinding her scarf, and slid into the seat next to me. She sat upright like a meerkat, glanced around, then hunched her shoulders and whispered: 'Is that the photographer over there?'

I looked across to where he was chatting with his friends. 'Yup.'

'Cute.'

'Not my type.'

'What, tall, blondish Scandinavian isn't your type?'

'No, it's not that. I just don't fancy him at all. He's absolutely lovely, but that's it.'

Sarah raised an eyebrow and yanked open a bag of McCoy's. 'Whatever, you'll email me in a month and tell me I was right.'

'I will not.'

'Well, you'll Facebook me then.'

I poked a crisp at her. 'I know everyone thinks that's going to happen, but it's not. I just don't see him like that. In fact, the main reason I'm happy to go away with him is precisely for that reason.'

'Which is?'

'I've saved up, I've worked really hard to figure this out, and I don't want it ruined for something frivolous.'

Sarah gave me the kind of smile reserved for naughty kids. It had a hint of I-don't-believe-you at the edges, but she relented. 'Anyway, you might not have any ideas, but I wouldn't say the same for him.'

'Well, that's certainly not my plan,' I assured her, then changed the subject. 'Anyway, I'm really going to miss you.'

'Yes, I'm sure while you're hanging out of train doorways, your thoughts will be of me sitting at my desk in East Acton opposite Sexist Chris talking about "scones and *jem*".' She finished the end of her pint and gave me a big beery hug. 'Have an amazing time, love.'

As the evening went on, family, friends and old colleagues flitted in and out of the pub depositing large glasses of Malbec under my nose. By the time I and a loyal group of stragglers tumbled out into the snow at closing time, it was safe to say that we were more than a little tipsy. Icy air tweaked the end of my nose as I swayed happily across the road amid the yells, hoots and arguments over the nearest kebab house. The troopers traipsed up Dean Street towards a club where someone claimed to be able to get us all in for free, while others slunk off to the tube. Passepartout decided to call it a night.

'See you at the airport, then,' he smiled.

The snow crunched underfoot and the sky glowed orange as I rocked back onto my heels and reached up to give him a quick hug. Red wine plumped my veins and snowflakes landed on my eyelashes as he turned to kiss me. It tasted of his cigarettes.

Shocked, I pulled back, as he gave me a lop-sided grin before turning and walking up the street. Suddenly sober, I closed my eyes as huge snowflakes fell all around. One word filled my mind: shit.

Shit. Shit. Shit.

1 | All Aboard the Insomnia Express

On 11 January at 5:33 pm precisely, the Chennai–Kanyakumari Express pulled out of Chennai Egmore station and began its 13-hour journey to the southernmost tip of the country. We were not on board.

Having failed to reserve tickets in time, we were sitting at a friend's kitchen table a few miles down the road in Chetpet, nursing two bottles of Thums Up and wondering what to do. Taking trains in India involves a process wholly different from taking trains in England. At home it is not uncommon to arrive at London Euston 10 minutes before a Virgin Pendolino departs to Birmingham New Street, slip a credit card into a machine, grab a ham and cheese baguette from Upper Crust, and hop onto the train with a saver return ticket in hand. The booking system in India opens 90 days in advance and is instantly flooded with reservations, building up endless waiting lists – particularly during festivals and through the wedding season.

This, we knew.

But our plan for the next few months was to have no plan. India is not a country that lends itself well to organisation and punctuality, so to try to incorporate any system to the contrary is like trying to force a square peg into a round hole and will only result in frustration or an arterial embolism. However, it was now the festival of Pongal, the Tamilian equivalent of harvest time, and trains in the South had been booked up for weeks. Fortunately Indian Railways has a useful system in place for latecomers, emergencies and the disorganised. It was into this last category that we fell. Two days before a train departs, a handful of remaining 'tatkal' tickets is released at 8 am on a first-come, first-served basis. They include a small surcharge, but are so sought after that people camp out in queues overnight, or lurk online at 7:59 am, fingers poised over the 'Quick Book' link.

The first destination on our list was Kanyakumari, the southernmost tip of the railways – and the country – where the Indian Ocean, the Arabian Sea and the Bay of Bengal all meet. A total solar eclipse was expected by noon on 15 January, and astronomers had indicated that Kanyakumari would be a prime viewing position. Passepartout was desperate to photograph the spectacle, which meant that we needed to head to the station in a few hours to begin queuing for tickets that we had no hope of securing.

We were currently staying in the home of Imthiaz and Sweetie Pasha. They were my parents' closest friends, who were nothing less than surrogate parents to me, so I trusted they would offer some sound advice – without laughing at me for my failure to book the first train. Reaching across the table, I picked up the internal phone and dialled up to their room.

Imthiaz answered: 'Yes.'

'Uncle Imthi, it's me.'

'How are you, dear?'

'We have a bit of a problem, I can't get those tickets to Kanyakumari and I'm…'

'Leave it with me, dear.'

Click.

The next morning, over a breakfast of papayas and egg dosai in the garden, I spied Subbu, the resident Jack-of-all-trades, hovering in the corner. He approached as though trying not to wake a sleeping dog and handed over two tickets to Nagercoil, a short train ride from Kanyakumari. He saluted and crept backwards, shaking his head, then ran down the driveway. It turned out that after I had spoken to Imthiaz, he had made a phone call to Subbu, who cycled to the station. There, he paid an opportunistic auto rickshaw driver to stand in the queue while he came back home and slept, returning at 8 am to buy our tickets. Since my last dealings with India, it seemed that the more things changed, the more they stayed the same.

In 1976 my parents left Madras and arrived in South Shields in the north of England as a couple of newly married junior doctors. Two children and

15 years later, my dad was lured back by unfulfilled promises, returning with us to Madras in 1991. Leaving behind a life of semi-detached suburban comfort and a bay-window view of the Derbyshire Dales, he now awoke to a balcony view of Elliot's Beach and rats eating sandalwood soap in the bathroom. He drove to work in a borrowed 1960s Fiat, taking a packed lunch of Amul cheese sandwiches in a kid's Virgin Atlantic shoulder bag, once filled with my crayons and colouring books.

Thrilled by the sunshine, beach apartment and mangoes for breakfast, I joined an elitist school, aged 9. Mocked for having an English accent, laughed at for wearing the wrong shade of blue school skirt, and walloped for contesting the Indian penchant for mugging and vomiting up reams of text, I soon realised that the honeymoon period was over. One day, while waiting outside the staff room, I overheard the teachers discussing my mum – 'that *firang* woman who wears T-shirts and jeans and drives her own car'. It made me sad.

I was sad when Pal-Ma, the old milk lady with red-rimmed teeth, was beaten up by the drunk man upstairs and when posters of Rajiv Gandhi's blown-up body were plastered all over town – a collage of his bald spot and Lotto trainers. I was scared when a man tipped a severed human head out of his lungi onto the local police chief's desk, and when the retired colonel across the road – who had offered to rig a cable at night to steal the neighbour's Star TV connection – watched us through a blind on his balcony when my mum was out. I missed home.

I missed getting out the wooden sledge in winter, which our neighbour had carved when we were tiny. I missed drinking water from the tap. I missed the warm hamsters we had left behind. I missed watching *Simon and the Witch* after school. I missed the taste of McVitie's Chocolate Digestives. I missed seeing my parents smiling. But most of all, I missed my big brother. Too old to catch up on nine years' worth of Hindi lessons, Rahul, aged 13, was soon sent to an American international school in a desolate hill station, where clouds came into the dorm rooms, and anybody's parents could turn up and teach. One morning he awoke to find a rat had chewed off the sponge from his Sony headphones to line its nest. But we were not the only ones struggling to acclimatise.

My mum paid bribes to have a gas cylinder installed in the kitchen, waited eight months for milk coupons and endured Hollywood car chases around the city, tailed by men wanting to buy her Mercedes or borrow it for their daughters' weddings. And across town, my dad faced his own battles.

At work, during moments of quiet, he occupied himself by taking swabs of air conditioners in the intensive care unit, the specimens returning from the labs with diseases he had only ever read about as a student. His findings were responded to with little more than a shrug and a *'so what?'.* But after discovering that the hearts of deceased patients were being illegally removed and sold on, and the holes stuffed with cotton wool, he drew the line. This was not a country where he wanted his family to live. In 1993, he repacked his boxes and his brood and left for good.

Returning to Madras was like being reunited with an ex-lover. On the surface we were friends, but while wounds may heal, their scars run deep. We had seen little of each other since 1993 and in that time Madras had adopted a new name, expanded its waistline and grown into a monster of a metropolis that I barely recognised. But like an ex-lover, it still smelt the same. On the drive from the airport, a heady mix of diesel, waste and noxious fumes from the Cooum river was occasionally delivered from evil by top notes of sea air and jasmine swinging from the rear-view mirror. The Honda's headlamps bounced over bundles of bodies asleep by the roadside and my heart tightened. By the time I dragged my bag into my room, my hair was stuck to the back of my neck, my skin was clammy with grime and studded with mosquito bites. India wastes no time in extending its welcome.

To understand India you have to see it, hear it, breathe it and feel it. Living through the good, the bad and the ugly is the only way to know where you fit in and where India fits into you. Once upon a time we had clashed. But we had both grown up and changed. India in particular was now undergoing a seismic shift, swaying in a constant state of flux where everyone who arrived or left – or who had always lived there – was forced to reassess their relationship with the country. India Version 2.0 was now up and running. Indians championed their nation as a global superpower, expounding its potential to overtake everyone as the fastest-growing economy. Yet for all its advances and progression, this was still a country where, in a village in Orissa, a 2-year-old boy could be married off to a dog called Jyoti to ward off evil spirits and ease the bad omen of his rotting tooth.

With Subbu's blessed tickets in hand, Passepartout and I finished breakfast and set off to Landmark to buy a map of the railways and a stack of pins to pepper the proposed route. Landmark was one of my favourite bookshops, which sold embroidered notebooks and jewelled pens and was crammed with shelf after shelf of multicoloured spines. It was where I used to buy Archie Double Digests as a kid. Sweetie had come along in a cloud of Bulgari and was pacing in the aisles, desperate to see a new film called 3 Idiots based on the book Five Point Someone by Chetan Bhagat. It had just come out at the cinema and was enjoying rave reviews, so she needed to see it to keep up with the chat at her bridge games.

'Come, darling!' she urged, waving a frayed map of the railways in my face. 'This will do.'

'It's from 2002.'

'Doesn't matter, all your tracks will look the same.'

'I'm not sure that's a very good idea,' I argued, as Passepartout glanced up over a copy of In Spite of the Gods with a look of disbelief.

'Darling, after one train I guarantee you people will come home.' She tried to stifle a giggle, then gave up and howled with laughter into her dupatta.

With an outdated map of the railways under one arm, a stack of books under the other and a growing sense of nausea, we left Landmark and embarked on our first Hindi film experience.

Sweetie and her friends had arranged to meet for a catch-up. A cinema seemed a strange place to do this; the Madras Club or perhaps a Café Coffee Day would have been a more suitable choice. And yet it seemed that everyone else had had the same idea. Throughout the first half hour members of the audience chatted away to one another, and a few phone calls were made in the row in front. Nobody batted an eyelid. As Kareena Kapoor came floating onto the screen in all her pale-skinned, green-eyed beauty, the audience cheered, clapped and whistled, a few phones reappearing to take photographs. During the interval people disappeared for coffee, spied more friends and began to climb across the seats for a gossip over ice cream. My Hindi was basic at best, but both Passepartout and I had followed the pantomime nature of the film with relative ease until the cast switched from delivering a baby via a webcam, to appearing in Leh, involved in a discussion over mistaken identity. The film ended with a song-and-dance rendition of the theme song, Aal Izz Well!, and we filed out of the cinema hoping that the song title would set a precedent for the journey to come.

❖

The following evening was the eve of departure. I was jittery as hell, nibbling my nails and nipping back and forth to the loo in a panic. I sat down on the lid and glanced around the marble bathroom, taking a mental photograph. It would be a while before I would see toilet-roll holders, embroidered hand towels and old copies of *Femina*. But the more pressing concern was Passepartout. During the flight over I had brought up the kiss.

'Can't blame a guy for trying,' he grinned.

'Look, we've got four months together and a tough job ahead of us. I don't think this is a sensible route to go down.'

'Don't worry, I'll behave,' he promised, fiddling with the seat back.

I raised an eyebrow.

'I promise,' he added, before going back to his book.

Since then he had said no more and I now decided it was no longer worth worrying about. I washed my face, swiped a couple of toilet rolls for the journey and went off to find Passepartout, who was in the kitchen, entertaining the staff with photos of Mishko, his cat. I did not have the heart to tell him that they were more amused by him than by Mishko.

We spread out the outdated map across the dining table as a warm fog of mutton biryani and saffron drifted in from the kitchen. The map gave itself up to a session of slow but determined acupuncture as we stuck pins into areas with subjects of interest: the solar eclipse in Kanyakumari; a classical dance festival in Khajuraho; the rat temple in Deshnok; the world's first hospital train in Madhya Pradesh; commuter trains in Mumbai; the Osho ashram in Pune; temples in South India; tea estates in Assam; and Dwarka, Udhampur and Ledo – the western, northern and easternmost tips of the railways. Just as I poked a pin into Delhi to mark the railway museum, the door opened and a member of staff ushered in my old school friend Bobby, followed by his entourage.

'Hey, we're going to a wedding. Coming?' he asked.

'Whose wedding is it?' I asked.

'I don't know the girl, he knows her,' he said, pointing behind to a friend who was on an unnecessarily loud phone call. 'Come, we'll all go.'

'We can't show up uninvited to a wedding.'

'What's there? We'll go, have some good biryani, then go to one more at the Taj Connemara for a drink.'

'You can't leave in the middle of someone's wedding!'

'That girl's father is a recovering alcoholic, they won't serve liquor at the wedding. Connemara is a Punju wedding, nicely they'll stock the bar,' he slobbered.

Bored friends often wedding hop in the evenings. It is a cheaper alternative to going to a bar, then a restaurant, followed by a club. It does not matter whether or not you know the bride and groom, they are unlikely to know at least 90 per cent of their own guests. Someone among the gatecrashers can always offer a tenuous link to the hosts, even if it is simply that their maid once worked in their house.

'Stinking rich that family, I tell you.' Bobby peered at the map, then pulled a face. 'Assam? Eh! You'll get shot!'

Weddings in India are a place to showcase wealth – for both the hosts and the guests. If generator-run floodlights and the equivalent of a football pitch are required to accommodate your guests, so much the better. People will talk about you – at least until the next wedding. A friend from Norfolk had once accompanied us to a wedding in Hyderabad and observed a guest who had arrived looking as though she had just raided Mr T's jewellery collection:

'They must open their cupboards and think, "Gosh, what a lot of nice jewellery and clothes I own. Let me wear all of it."'

As much fun as it would have been to spend the evening exploiting a stranger's hospitality, we declined Bobby's invitation and returned to the map. It seemed the most sensible way to spend the last night in Chennai.

Thursday 14 January heralded the first of 80 journeys and we were showered, packed and foraging around for bottles of hand gel, paracetamol, pencils, pens, stamps, chargers and adaptors, which would no doubt remain buried at the bottom of a bag to be discovered at the end of the trip. There was too much to remember even to consider having last-minute cold feet. Sweetie had packed dinner for us, making me promise not to eat the food served on board the train. I ducked into the kitchen where I found Govindamma, the oldest member of staff, glowering at me from her corner on the floor, where she was chopping onions like an angry gnome. Her white hair was slicked into a low bun and her nose stud gleamed and glared at me.

'She's very cross with you,' Sweetie explained, shaking a finger in my face.

'Why?'

'Because you're not married!'

'Don't want to do marriage, baby?' Pushpa asked. Pushpa was Govindamma's daughter. She was head maid, perpetually pregnant and wore more jewellery than a temple deity.

'Not at this minute, no.'

She looked through me then turned on her heel, her anklets jangling as she stomped off. I promised Govindamma that I would get married, but that I just needed to take a few trains first. She glared at me and set to work torturing a handful of carrots.

In the driveway I found Passepartout inhaling deeply on a cigarette, the bags nowhere in sight. He shrugged and raised his eyebrows with resignation as Thomas the butler appeared. While looking for a light switch Passepartout had pressed a bell, inadvertently summoning Thomas to his room, and he was still feeling guilty. Thomas had been with the household for over 50 years and had developed immunity to the process of ageing – with the exception of his tufts of ear hair, which had bloomed into great orchards. Now the ruler of the roost, he had delegated the job of fetching our luggage to an apprentice, who staggered behind him carrying both rucksacks like a pair of bin bags. Our send-off involved the gathering of the entire staff, including Govindamma, who hauled herself up from her corner long enough to come outside and smirk. Even the local dogs had sauntered up to the gate and were sniffing around, amid barks that sounded worryingly like laughter. As the car pulled out of the driveway, the staff waved, ominously covering their mouths with the edges of saris as though we were going off to war, never to be seen again.

Chennai Egmore station could be heard before it was seen. A cacophony erupted as we made our way under the arches, running after Subbu who, much to Passepartout's despair, had been instructed to come with us to the platform. Whether this was a display of Imthiaz's diligence in his surrogate role or his lack of faith in our ability remained unclear, though my suspicions leant strongly towards the latter. Indian stations are not designed for running. An assault course lay between us and Subbu, who was winding deeper and deeper into the sea of boxes, briefcases and body parts. We ducked and wove around the slalom of wooden carts wheeled by men with no sense of urgency, strings of hand-holding children, hobbling dogs, stacked hessian sacks, Aavin milk stands, nose-pickers, watersellers, booksellers and red-shirted porters. Subbu now stood by our train, under a digital sign reading B2, his face powder dry, as we bent double, sweat running down our bodies.

Engines hissed and thudded as they began to move, high-pitched announcements singing out in breakneck-speed Tamil, while the smell of dried fish and urine crept up my nostrils. Subbu gently moved me away from the carriage, where the produce from an occupied toilet was spilling onto the tracks and splattering the back of my legs. Passepartout leapt about, clicking away, and I smiled weakly for the camera before boarding the Anantapuri Express to Nagercoil.

Inside, a scene from *Dirty Dancing* was unfolding. The aisles were jammed with a mass rubbing of chests against backs, and thighs against backsides, as passengers' friends and families (none of whom was travelling) refused to move. Subbu had already found our seats and placed our bags on each by the time we squeezed through, drenched and violated. Thanking him, we dug out bottles of Aquafina water, notebooks, pens, toilet paper, flannels and flip-flops, much to the amusement of our companions who had already chained up bags, hidden shoes, plugged in phones and sat down cross-legged, watching us. At 7:20 pm the train jerked. Subbu bowed and slunk off as the train glided out of the station. Through the tinted window he was soon no more than a saluting silhouette.

We were on the move.

Passepartout and I had been allotted the side berths and we now sat face to face by the window with the kinds of smiles that accompany pre-wedding jitters and trips to the dentist.

With a sigh, I touched my head against the glass and pushed back the curtain. A romantic evening haze hung over the treetops that sped past. I soon realised that it was due to a layer of filth on the window and Passepartout pointed out that an insect had laid eggs on the sill. In just under 14 hours we would arrive in Nagercoil. Another short train ride would take us to Kanyakumari, giving us an hour to settle before the solar eclipse began. After Kanyakumari the plan was to work up the western coast of the country through Kerala and Goa, along the Konkan Railway to Mumbai. From there we were due to board a newly launched luxury train, the Indian Maharaja-Deccan Odyssey. Luxury trains were not considered to embody the true Indian train experience, but it was foolish to ignore the one set of trains that so many swarmed to India to enjoy. After ending in Delhi, we would worm our way back down the centre of the country to Kerala, and then temple hop across Tamil Nadu. It was an awkward detour, but the Indian Maharaja had no other availability until March.

'Could I have a look at the map?' Passepartout asked.

'Sure.'

'Where is it?' he asked, unclipping the top of my bag.

'On the dresser in the bedroom.'

'Oh. Useful.'

'Yup.'

The train had now picked up speed and was racing through the outskirts of Chennai. I looked around. It was a comfort, if not a concern, that after 20 years the trains looked no different. Limp curtains shielded the windows, miniature cockroaches flitted across the seat backs and the fan still blew ineffectual wisps of air. A sign on the wall stated that between the hours of 9 pm and 6 am bunks must be put down for the comfort of others and passengers soon began to obey the rules. Paper bags of bedding were shaken out, sheets stretched and tucked in, and cardigans pulled on. Ladies jammed cotton wool into their ears and men stripped down to singlets. They flipped off the lights and soon began to snore. Passepartout, extending his role to valet, had made up my bed for me by the time I picked my way back from the toilet clutching a packet of Sainsbury's wet wipes. Clambering up the ladder, I rolled the covers up to my chin and lay back, staring at the ceiling as the blanket itched my face. A part of me had feared that I would board the first train and instantly regret my decision. What if I hated it? Four whole months within these blue walls lay ahead. My body rocked gently from side to side as a reassuring 'da-dum ... da-dum ... da-dum ...' began to lull me to sleep. It was so peaceful.

And then it began.

At first it was low, then it began to grow. Someone in the compartment was snoring over the noise of the fan. Now the cotton wool made sense. After three sleepless hours I climbed down to check that the culprit was not choking on his own tongue and dying. I now wished I were dead. Tiptoeing in my socks, I stood by his berth and stared at him through the darkness, wondering how such a minuscule man could produce a noise of volcanic proportions. A Korean girl in the berth across from him sat up, her hair spiked like a porcupine, and began rocking back and forth as a baby in the middle berth began to whimper. The compartment was starting to resemble an asylum. Suddenly he rolled onto his side to face me and I ducked. The snoring stopped. A smile touched my lips and I climbed back into bed, just as he coughed and started up again.

❖

Half an hour from Nagercoil I awoke to a polite nod from the Human Bulldozer, who had folded away his sheets, thatched his hair over his bald patches and was now sitting next to his wife, who was painting a large black dot onto their baby's cheek to ward off the evil eye. She had also painted in two eyebrows and drawn around her daughter's eyes, so she now resembled a cartoon character. I glanced in the mirror at my own reflection. I looked like I had slept in a bin. Passepartout had been up since 5 am and was standing in the doorway watching the morning activities with a cup of coffee. As the train rolled towards the town, women dried laundry by riverbeds, boys covered in soap showered under hosepipes hung over branches of blossoms, and a man handed out snacks to a herd of goats, giving a greedy one a quick slap across the face. Our bags were stacked in the doorway and as the train pulled into Nagercoil, passengers pushed the load aside and jumped off while the train was still moving.

The connecting passenger train was empty and took over half an hour to reach Kanyakumari, despite the town being less than 15 km away. Barefooted, bearded pilgrims wearing little more than black or saffron dhotis and beads jammed the roads that led to the seafront. They paddled in rock pools, bathed in the surf, then wandered in and out of the Gandhi memorial, where some of the Mahatma's ashes were once stored. As the sky began to grey, they wound up their dhotis and lined up on walls wearing luminous cardboard glasses. They had come from the Sabarimala Sree Ayyappa temple at Sabarimala in Kerala where an annual celestial fire, believed to have healing powers, glowed over the hills near the shrine.

Passepartout and I perched on a wall and were soon surrounded by a family chewing stalks of sugarcane the size of flutes, carpeting the ground with husk. The toddlers climbed into my lap, pressing sticky palms to my sweating face and neck, and sat down to watch the show. It was now 1 pm and the day had almost turned into night. A hush fell over the crowd as the sea rolled beneath the ball that was now no more than a white ring, blazing against a thunderous sky. A chill raised goosebumps across my arms as I unwrapped the ribbon from around my leather logbook, a gift from Passepartout, and flipped to the middle of the clean-smelling parchment. Here I began to make a list of train names.

Two down, 78 to go...

2 | Guantanamo Chic and the Perils of Wearing Shoes

One in six people in the world is an Indian, yet when Indians spot another anywhere outside the motherland, we stare as though we expect to be the only ones. Rarely does a smile pass between the two teams, but from afar, a mutual screening process is put into immediate effect. Shaved off the moustache? Progressive. Wearing tweed and a flat cap? Overdoing it. In essence, the process is to ascertain: who the *hell* are you? Indians are also the only ones to go out of their way to make each other's lives as difficult as possible, as a visit to an Indian embassy will illustrate. By contrast, Indians living in India beeline towards anyone of interest, curious and keen to offer help. But with the proficiency of a pickpocket they extract details ranging from your salary and star sign, to your brand of mobile phone and any unusual birthmarks. Monesh was no different. He crossed the platform at Trivandrum Central and wandered over to us.

At first a smile shone through the darkness, then a strip of white teeth approached. A South Indian moustache sat above them, like a thatched roof sloping over whitewashed walls. The smile belonged to a man wearing beads, a saffron dhoti and a matching scarf flung around his shoulders, much on trend with what the *Daily Mail* had once labelled 'Guantanamo Chic'. In one hand he held a rolled-up poster in a cylinder, and in the other, a smaller hand belonging to a miniature version of himself. Monesh and his son Ksheetij were also pilgrims from Ayyappa, now taking the train to Mangalore to visit the Mangaladevi temple. It was a boys-only trip. The

Ayyappa temple, although one of the few Hindu temples open to all castes, creeds and faiths, does not permit menstruating women, so Monesh's wife and daughter had stayed at home. He pointed to where two elderly men sat watching our exchange, their ear hair twitching with interest.

'This is my father and wife's father. Where is mummy-daddy?' he asked.

'My parents? In England.'

'Father allowing you being here alone?'

I nodded. He looked appalled, but beamed all the same.

'Why you are going to Mangalore? You are having brother-sisters there?'

'No, no family, but we're catching a train from Mangalore to Madgaon tomorrow afternoon.'

'You are visiting with friends?'

'No, no friends either, we're just travelling through to catch the next train.'

Monesh's look of confusion was now replaced by one of pity. He put his hands on his hips as Ksheetij danced around his feet, hiding between the folds of his dhoti.

'Tomorrow, you come with us. Mangaladevi temple is very beautiful and very special place. I would like to take you around also with Ksheetij.'

Ksheetij paused his dance for a moment and peeked up from the folds. Temple bells rang a warning in my head. Chummy invitations were ten-a-penny and more often than not resulted in the obligation to part with a lot more than a few pennies. Awkward silence swelled in the darkness, then popped as train four, the Trivandrum–Mangalore Express, entered the station, flooding us with relief. Monesh peered at our tickets.

'Your bogie is not coming here. It is *that* side of the platform. Come, we will show you.'

Ksheetij strapped on my small bag as I panicked, struggling with my rucksack. Monesh waved the cylinder in the air like a tour guide and began to weave through the crowd of passengers, porters, dogs and idlers. Ksheetij, whose head barely reached waist height, twirled his way between knees and legs, my backpack twirling away with him. I broke out into a sweat. My laptop, phone, money, passport and rail pass were all winding their way out of sight, but private-school etiquette restrained my instinct to rugby-tackle the 8-year-old.

Harrowing images of trying to call the British Embassy with no phone, and buy a new rail pass with no money, while weeping into a logbook I no longer owned, became too much, and I sprinted the length of the last three carriages, arriving outside our compartment to find Monesh and Ksheetij holding out my things. Sweat dripped down the backs of my legs and collected at my feet in a warm puddle of guilt. The duo checked that we were comfortable and promised to meet us in the morning. I nodded and thanked them both, knowing that amid the morning melee we would not see them again.

❖

'Yeah, Lucy said they dragged him onto t'pavement outside t'club and threatened to lamp 'im. Apparently our Pete were quivering like a shitting dog.'

'What 'appened?'

'Oh he were all right in the end, think they got bored and left 'im to it.'

The delicate nuances of the Lancashire lexicon floated around the corner as I prised the lid off a container of fried rice. Intrigued, I poked my head into the next compartment where two tanned students were chatting. They looked up.

'Hiya, y'all right?'

'Sorry, just eavesdropping. You sound just like a friend of mine from Accrington.'

'Accy?! I'm from Rossendale, me,' the boy replied.

Paul and Claire were from Rossendale in Lancashire and had been travelling around India for six months, about to move on to Thailand.

'You're not from round these parts, are ya?' Paul asked.

'No, we're from London. I haven't seen very much of India before, so we're doing a bit of a marathon train journey for the next few months.'

'They're great these trains, aren't they? I 'ated it when I first got 'ere. I were ready to go 'ome straight away. But you get used to it and you start to love it.'

'Where have you been?'

'We've just come off 'imsagar Express. Sixty-seven hours from Ja-moo to Trivandrum.'

'That's impressive.'

'Yep, jammed into a compartment with this family that had mum, dad, nan, granddad, about eight kids, goats, dogs, you name it, the lot. But I love that. You don't get that at 'ome.'

'Dogs and goats?'

'Families travelling everywhere together. They've always got their nans and granddads with 'em. They proper take care of them 'ere.'

'It's a very Indian thing.'

'I wish my poor nan 'ad that kind of care. She gets so bored living on 'er own that she phones up ambulances to come round. Then when they show up expecting to ship 'er off to 'ospital she'll open the door all cheery, "Hiya boys, y'all right? Fancy a brew?"'

'So where are you off to next?'

'Up to Mangalore and then on to Goa. I know it's dead cliché, but we've proper trekked about and we need a bit of beach. And I think Thailand's a bit wet and mingin' at the moment.'

'Well, have fun.'

'You too. It's a shit'ole, India, but a nice shit'ole.'

I went back to my seat and smiled at my neighbour. Prabaker was dressed in white, like a Gymkhana club waiter, and had blow-dried his bouffant into *Saturday Night Fever* perfection. As he replaced a gold biro in his breast pocket, I noticed that his right thumb sprouted a smaller thumb. He laid his shoes side by side as he got ready for bed and smiled back.

'To where you are going?' he asked.

'Mangalore, and then Madgaon.'

'Very good.' He pointed to Passepartout, who was now reading in his berth. 'Husband?'

'We're not married.'

He shook his head and made a strange, almost apologetic sound.

'Myself I am going to Kozhikode.'

He pronounced the name as though coughing up a fur ball. From Kanyakumari, Passepartout had been desperate to take the Himsagar Express all the way up to Jammu. The train, its name a hybrid of 'Himalayas' and 'sagar' – the Sanskrit word for 'sea' – travels from the ocean to the mountains, and is the longest journey on the Indian Railways. It spans 3715 km, making 66 halts in 71 hours. However, the Vivek Express, due for launch the following year, was soon to outdo the Himsagar Express by 564 km. Three days of non-stop travel would have taken us from one end of the railways to the other, and, presumably, to the end of our friendship. As a compromise we had boarded train number three, the Himsagar Express, at Kanyakumari, but hopped off three stations later in Trivandrum.

Under Prabaker's watchful eye, I looked down at my food and read a few lines of *The Glass Palace*, flicking off grains of rice that flecked the page. I glanced up briefly. He was still smiling, his spare thumb twitching ominously. At the berth-lowering hour, his feet disappeared through the gap in the overhead curtain. Passepartout was now asleep and I wriggled under the weight of the blankets in the side berth and nodded off. At around 5 am a hand crept under the blankets and made its way up my leg. I sat up, my knees retracting into my chest. It was dark and the train was rocking from side to side in silence. Everyone else was asleep. I sat still for a minute, then decided the MSG in my fried rice was causing hallucinations. Sealing the edges of the covers around my legs, I turned over and a hand came to rest on my backside. Ripping the curtains apart, I saw Prabaker standing in the aisle, unchaining his briefcase from under the seats. He made his way to the toilet and I leapt out and shook Passepartout awake. Dazed, he agreed to swap berths, snoring within minutes as I climbed into his bed and pulled the curtain shut, praying Polydactyl Prabaker would try to fondle the tired and grumpy Norwegian.

Playing Musical Berths and Pervert Peek-a-Boo had so exhausted us both that we overslept and were the last to get off the train in Mangalore, but not before spotting an absurd sign nailed to the wall:

'Harassing Women Passengers is a Punishable Offence'

The warning was illustrated with a cartoon of a man behind bars, sporting a wholly unapologetic smile. It looked like an advert for harassment: the offender appeared quite happy to be there, as though his crime was well worth his punishment. In India obscene remarks, wandering hands, singing bawdy songs and staring are clubbed together under the term 'eve-teasing'. It is one of many delightful Indian archaisms, a charming term that suggests pigtail pulling in playgrounds and hiding behind trees, rather than the bum-grabbing, boob-groping action that usually takes place in crowded venues and on tightly packed transport. Were the biblical terminology replaced with the ugliness of what it was, the convict would have looked a lot less like someone had just offered him a bag of sweets.

Mangalore station's platform was empty but for two figures waiting at the end of the train. Twin grins holding hands made their way towards us. Ksheetij skipped around Monesh, baring his teeth in the sunshine, a combination of gaps and wonky milk teeth.

'We are waiting for you to come to the temple,' Monesh explained, 'if you are having time before your train we would like it if you come.'

He was pushy but likeable and we had little else to do for the next few hours but clean teeth, find coffee and file a complaint for harassment, so we followed him out. The Mangaladevi temple was a short auto ride away and I was now intrigued. Monesh had explained that Mother Mangaladevi, the temple's deity, was a useful ally to unmarried women. If fair and pious maidens prayed to her, she would help them fulfil their desires for a suitable husband. I was neither fair nor pious – more wheatish and indifferent – but it would not hurt to pay her a visit if her results were cheaper and more bountiful than a subscription to Shaadi.com, the Indian matrimonial website.

Worshippers were filtered into two lanes of traffic separated by railings. The priest carried out a tray of offerings from the enclosure and several arms stretched through the railings, tossing coins in the direction of the flame and swiping to take a blessing. An elbow clipped the back of my head as I tried to dodge arms in tight blouses, swinging their fatty hammocks of flesh across my face. Claustrophobic, and with flashbacks of the Hillsborough disaster, I disentangled myself and crawled out from under the barrier to join Monesh, who was standing by a statue wearing a beatific smile. He lay down before her and I left him prostrate to wander around on my own. Towards the exit a pot of kumkum sat next to a dish of dull yellow sandalwood, like two bowls of hotdog condiments. I reached forward to take a pinch when the priest hurried over and smacked my hand away, clicking his tongue against the roof of his mouth. He dipped his podgy fingers into the powder and threw it into my palm with an enormous show of self-importance.

Picking my way back through the three silver doorways, I swapped bag duties with Passepartout as he went back into the temple with Monesh, who was only too pleased to explain everything again to him. They reappeared just as my stomach growled and I realised that we had eaten nothing since the hallucinogenic rice. Monesh squatted next to me.

'We are going to take lunch, so you must come with us. We will make sure it is a clean and nice place, but it must be pure vegetarian as you may become sick.'

'You don't have to do that, we can find somewhere ourselves.'

He shook his head, which could have implied a multitude of meanings.

'No, you are our guests. Don't worry, I'll go and come now.'

The little man wandered off in bare feet before returning a few minutes later and leading us to a dhaba filled with men in booths, sucking their plates clean of sambar. Monesh would not allow us to pay for our meals and had finished his idlis, washed up and hailed two autos when we met him outside. Back at the station the family waited with us on the platform until the Matsyagandha Express to Madgaon had arrived. Passepartout was teaching Ksheetij to take photos when Monesh led me away by the arm. He stopped once we were out of earshot from his family and turned to me.

'I must ask you one question now, if I may?'

I nodded.

'You promise that you will be keeping in touch?'

'Yes.'

'See, you both are friends now. Please do not forget us, you will be in touch, no?'

'Of course we will.'

Monesh peered at me, as though searching for a sign that it was all a ruse. His amber eyes swirled with the fear that he and his family would be forgotten the moment we boarded the train – at best they might become a tale to tell fondly around the dinner table. As our train arrived, Ksheetij leapt up into his father's arms. They followed us down the platform until we found our compartment, stacked bags and ordered coffee. As train number five pulled out and the pair waved alongside, I overheard Passepartout mutter into his cup: 'Every child should have a father like that.'

Passepartout was a black-coffee junkie, which upset the natural order of things. Coffee is brewed everywhere, on street corners and unoccupied patches of pavement, on roving carts and in kettles under trees – but brewed in milk that cloys. In South India, cooling hot coffee involves a highly skilled process of pouring the liquid between a tumbler and a metal dish, dragging and stretching the stream into arcs. Preparing coffee is an art form, so ordering it without milk or sugar prompted baffled looks, but started a game in restaurants called Coffee Roulette. When it was ordered all bets were placed on black, but it usually turned up white, extra white, extra sugary; and on those rare occasions when the contents were black, it usually turned out to be tea. At desperate times a Kenco-filled EpiPen would have been useful to jab Passepartout in the arm.

From Madgaon we made our way to our villa, one of a group of four gated villas in Nerul, a village near Candolim, Goa. The other three were taken over by a film crew from Mumbai, who played Lady Gaga at 3 am, smoked in the pool and wore sunglasses at night. Each villa was self-serviced, so the kitchen housed a kettle and a basket of Nescafé sachets. At the prospect of pure coffee to keep himself awake, Passepartout rubbed his hands with glee. He was leaning over the kettle awaiting the rumble of boiling water when our taxi beeped from downstairs. We had decided to leave our neighbouring revellers and have lunch among the Russians and swearing, tattooed people who wandered Candolim's streets in their swimwear. He reached for the cold tap above the basin, opening it briefly to cool his cup and took a sip. The scene unfolded in slow motion and I watched with the sinking feeling that his motions would now be anything but slow.

'Don't drink that, it's not been treated!' I blurted out.

He lowered the cup and frowned.

'But it's a villa, the drinking water will be filtered.'

'But it's an *Indian* villa. The tap's probably connected by a hosepipe to rainwater on the roof.'

That night the coffee kept him awake.

Candolim could have been Magaluf or Benidorm, were it not for the hordes of stray dogs that trotted around licking scraps of egg and chips from under the tables. Indian pye-dogs are a breed in their own right: curly-tailed; itchy; full of personality; full of ticks; and largely forgiving towards any kind of mistreatment, which in India is frequent and harsh. They are also loving and loyal and will adopt anyone as a master should a biscuit find its way between their lips, which in India is rare and laughable.

The main road was lined with cafés and bars serving lasagne and burgers to Russians and Eastern Europeans. It was easier to find Indian food in the Cotswolds. Eventually spotting 'Hyderabadi chikken' on a laminated menu, we settled down at Floyd's. Floyd's was a cosy spot with bamboo roofing propped up by green pillars and red walls slapped with posters featuring malt whisky, smiling babies and a man playing bagpipes. One wall was tiled with a cartoon of fisherwomen dancing while a man suffering with scoliosis played the drums, and a monkey-pig hybrid watched on in confusion. A statue of the Air India maharaja bowed on the bar top, as though apologising for the untidiness of his surroundings. It was a charming hash of tat and colour, enhanced by sunburnt diners. The food took over an hour to arrive, and when it did the chicken curry was as green as the pillars, but delicious.

After lunch we strolled down a lane littered with shacks selling beads, cloth handbags and the kind of shirts worn in a Shakespeare play until we reached Candolim beach. Its sand was toasted golden, the water the colour of emeralds, and the surf frothed and fizzed around teenagers splashing – metres from a gargantuan bulk carrier that had run aground. The *River Princess* looked less than regal, sitting sulkily on the edge of the water, black, rusting and abandoned, casting a sinister shadow across the waves. Ten years ago the 20,000-tonne tanker had drifted in a storm and hit the Goan shore, but was yet to be adopted by shipbreakers. Instead, a politicised salvaging process had begun. Numerous tenders to remove the ship had been awarded and withdrawn and now Goa Tourism, who had taken possession of the ship in 2003, was embroiled in disputes with the original owners over prices for the ship's scraps. That the ship had already caused over 1 km of coastline to erode, encouraged strong and dangerous currents and could at any time break in half and destroy the beach seemed of little importance to anyone involved. After Passepartout had paddled on the edge of the water we made our way back to the villa, preferring to swim in a pool full of fag butts.

Between Mangalore and Mumbai is a 760 km section of railway that constitutes one of the finest engineering feats in the world. The Konkan Railway line contains 320 curves, 92 tunnels and 2000 bridges, including the Panval Nadi viaduct, the tallest in India. The British shied away from constructing this section of the railways, due to its geographical challenges, leaving it to Indian engineers to bore through the Sahyadri hills, enduring flash floods, landslides and the dangers of digging through soft tunnels that often collapsed on engineers. Passenger trains first ran in 1998 and since then sections of the track have succumbed to landslides and loose boulders and a train has even tumbled off a bridge. A daily Jan Shatabdi speed train runs from Madgaon to Mumbai, lopping a good three hours off the normal journey time, while the majority of slower express trains travel at night. Night travel rendered the journey pointless if I could not dangle out of the doorway and watch the waters raging below my flip-flops. The Mandovi Express, however, was the only daily train that took an acceptable 12 hours and arrived in Mumbai at 9:30 pm.

Poor Passepartout was on sick leave and remained foetal in the upper berth, sleeping off the effects of the tap water, while I settled down in a doorway, bathed in the lemon glow from mango groves and palm trees flanking the tracks. During the previous five journeys I had watched in horror as he swung out of doorways, his clothes snapping in the wind, but soon realised it was the only way to travel. As train number six clattered across the Panval Nadi bridge near Ratnagiri, a nauseous thrill swirled in my stomach as I peered between my knees at the drop. A sheet of water stretched to the horizon and I thought of King Thebaw, one of the few characters in *The Glass Palace* based on a real person. In 1885, he and his family were exiled by the British from Burma to Ratnagiri, where he lived out his remaining years in a rundown palace. The palace still remains in Ratnagiri and I imagined the king standing at his bedroom window every morning, looking out through his binoculars across this expanse of grey-blue water, watching for boats and signs of visitors.

'Ma'am, chicken lollipop, ma'am?'

An elderly man carrying a washing-up bowl full of foil-wrapped chicken legs stopped and placed his load on the floor. As he shifted the pile around, steam rose from the centre and the smell of summer barbecues floated up. I bought a couple and the vendor stayed squatting behind me, counting his notes.

'Very beautiful the sea.' He clasped both my hands together and shook them. 'But ma'am, careful not palling.'

He looped his finger up and then down, outlining the path that Wile E. Coyote normally took off the edge of a cliff, and then laughed at his own joke, wheezing as he picked up his load.

'Very punny ... but not safe,' he added, sending a ball of foil out of the door before disappearing through to the next carriage.

We were less than a week into the journey, but I was already beginning to feel at home. Having had my fill of sea views, I gnawed the remaining gristle off the bones and looked around guiltily before tossing them into the water below. Private-school etiquette was already dwindling. It was only a matter of time before spitting and shitting in public would become the norm. Back in the compartment, Passepartout was still bundled up in a pile of sheets. It was warm on board and I began to feel restless, so curled up in the sunshine and dozed off.

❖

'Shoes… they're not good for your feet… don't wear 'em too often.'

An Aussie accent dominated the conversation in the compartment behind us and I sat up. Two Swiss girls were hugging their rucksacks, intrigued by the nymph storyteller sitting cross-legged in his berth, explaining the negative aspects of wearing shoes. Rick was in his late 70s. He was white-haired and wiry, with eyes like chips of blue china that gleamed against his orange skin. His hair was trimmed close to his scalp and he wore a muslin shirt that hung open to his soft belly. Pleased with the growing audience, he patted the seat next to him and continued to describe the origin of the scar on his left leg, which involved a midnight escape from a forest ridden with spear-wielding rebels and what sounded like an allied army of midgets.

'All metal,' he said, running his finger up his shin, 'and a small plate in here too,' he added, tapping the side of his head.

He was the sort of person who revelled in the scepticism shading his audience's faces, but if he eventually revealed himself to be an android, I would feign nonchalance. The train stopped at Thane and the Swiss girls got off. Rick jabbed silently at the window, his face twisted into a ridiculous grin.

'First ever Indian train. Built by you folks. Ran from Bombay to Thane in 1853.'

Rick was travelling up to Mumbai to meet his wife after a three-month stint trekking around India by himself. She was launching a book and had been touring Southeast Asia while Rick rode the railways. A chai vendor clanked past and he raised a finger in the air, fishing a 10-rupee note out of his breast pocket, which hung somewhere around his waist.

'I'll have another please, and one for the little lady, and don't try pulling any of that shit on me again.'

The vendor placed his vat on the floor and allowed two spurts of milky water to fill the paper cups, smiling sheepishly.

'Six rupees, he told me! Six? It's never six. It's always five. Naughty bugger.'

He finished the tea in one slurp, winced and tapped my knee.

'You know how to work out train numbers, eh?'

'Nope.'

'Well, for example, we're on the 0104 from Madgaon to Mumbai. The Mandovi Express that goes the other way is the 0103. Also, the first digit indicates which region you are in. Konkan Railway is "0".'

'How do you know that the one going the other way isn't the 0105?'

'Because they refer to them as going "up" or "down". If a train is travelling away from its home station then you say it's going "down". But if it's going towards its home station, then it's going "up". We're going up, so it has the higher number. But having said that, there are so many exceptions to the rule, so don't take my word for it. Like the rest of this country, don't try to find method in the madness. Anyway, have fun, Pom. I'm getting off here.'

We were just pulling into Dadar Central and Rick jumped off the berth, picking up his canvas bag, and strolled off in bare feet. The Yoda of train travellers had no need for shoes after all. I moved to the edge of the seat and watched him from the window. As the train jerked and moved on, he stopped and fished a pair of loafers out of his bag, threw them onto the ground and stepped into them.

I started gathering my things as we neared Mumbai, when Passepartout surfaced with the confused look of a hamster coming out of hibernation. He tidied up his sheets, lined up our bags and grinned. A new buoyancy took over, the buoyancy of arrival. It brings with it a renewed sense of being that blossoms just before the end of a journey. No matter how long or tiring the journey, the bothersome bits are shelved and forgotten in those final minutes. Impending arrival shifts the traveller's mindset into hopeful optimism that a new and unexplored phase is about to begin.

3 | A Royal Affair

A hairy arm covered in glass bangles appeared by my leg and a large hand tugged at my rucksack. It withdrew, then as an afterthought shot out again to give my knee a quick scratch. Peering over my book, I looked down and saw that the wandering hand belonged to a hijra who wanted some money. While we were buried in our books, a number of hijras had mushroomed around the bench where we sat at Mumbai's Chhatrapati Shivaji Terminus: a carnival of powdered faces, sequined saris, anklets and tomato-red lips surrounded us, covering the platform with handbags, food carriers and bedding.

Hijras are a vulnerable community of eunuchs and hermaphrodites, huddled together in their plight beneath one umbrella of transgendered ambiguity. Many eunuchs within the fold result from forced surgery and, despite claims to the contrary, fewer than one in a thousand hijras are born a hermaphrodite. They flimsily embrace womanhood with garish make-up, cheap jewellery and low-cut blouses stretched around their broad backs. Shunned by society, they are nurtured within their own community, where they survive in bulk as India's third gender. But like a fraction of the country's downtrodden, they have learnt to manipulate their situation to their advantage and impose themselves wherever they go, often on the railways.

Our new friends had parked close enough to make their presence felt, but remained at a safe enough distance that we could watch them combing each other's hair and reapplying kohl, without being asked to pay for the show. Or so I thought. As I dragged my bag out of the Knee Scratcher's reach, she clapped her hands together – rubbing one across the other as she did so – and flipped a curse at me, muttering and pulling out a tiffin carrier from her sack. It was not the most auspicious way to begin a journey.

At that moment a royal blue engine with gilded borders glided along the platform. Train number seven, the Indian Maharaja-Deccan Odyssey, had finally arrived. He paused in silence before heaving a sigh and coming to a halt. Not a soul emerged, but a door opened and a red carpet rolled out like a tongue cooling off on the platform. The hijras' over-plucked eyebrows arched with curiosity. Whispers passed between the group and their earrings swung as they craned their necks to steal a glimpse through the blacked-out windows. Worried that the train might creep away with the stealth of its arrival, we gathered our things, much to the hijras' distress, and picked our way through their outstretched arms, accompanied by their yells. Another door swung open and a head appeared, fitted with a boat-shaped hat, stolen from a mediaeval queen. Benoy, it turned out, was our personal butler for the next seven days.

Air conditioning tightened my skin inside the carriage as the door slammed shut on Mumbai's stickiness and noise. Beaming and bowing, Benoy led us past a gallery of hand-painted miniatures, to cabin B in Salon Verul – otherwise known as the presidential suite. He tried to wrestle the unimpressive bags from our backs, but looked secretly pleased by our lack of matching Gucci luggage that his colleague was struggling with on the platform.

The Indian Maharaja-Deccan Odyssey was a relatively new member to the royal family of trains. His predecessor, the Palace on Wheels, still rolled his old bones up and down Rajasthan's tracks, but had succumbed to age. Reports suggested that his skin was peeling, his insides were damaged and the sparkle in his eye had dulled. Inside the suite, it was clear that the younger model was a picture of health. Fluffy carpet sprouted from the floor and a white duvet hugged the double bed that filled the room. At the head, four pillows puffed out their chests, their corners tweaked into place and a snip of hibiscus lay in the centre of the bed with a note saying: 'Welcome aboard a journey to the depths of your soul…'

After playing with both flat-screen televisions, skin-flaying showers and a forage for appropriate clothes, each of us grabbed a handful of grapes from the living room and made our way to the bar area, passing a gym and a massage room playing Chinese restaurant music. The sound of a Yorkshire terrier being trampled met us at the carriage entrance and a waiter stepped out from behind the bar to hold open the door. A noisy trio sat on a sofa: both men wore beige trousers and deck shoes and slopped their beer with each bark of laughter. The lady wore a linen shirt that revealed a fleshy pink triangle at the neck, adorned with ugly beads that hung like freshly speared testicles. She threw back her head and the canine yelping began again. I checked my ear for blood.

'Oh Roger, you're terrible!' she giggled.

'Well, if I want chicken tikka masala, I shall jolly well ask for it. Although we'll have to get them the recipe from England first!'

Roger laughed at his own joke, spilling more puddles of Kingfisher, which were quickly mopped up by a waiter with a magician's supply of napkins up his sleeves. The trio had just arrived from a week in Panjim in Goa, but lived next door to each other in Bagshot, Surrey.

A sensible distance away sat the couple from the suite next to ours. Cyril was a retired cardiothoracic surgeon in his 80s, with a naughty face and eyes that laughed in place of his mouth. His wife, Marie, had an Audrey Hepburn elegance and wore her dark chocolate hair tucked girlishly behind her ears. They lived in Sydney, but gallivanted around the world, travelling up the Irrawaddy river, playing golf in China, or filming lemurs in Madagascar. Marie and Passepartout clinked their glasses together and sank into conversation, while Cyril chased a king prawn around a plate with a toothpick and winked at me.

'So you two nippers are our neighbours?'

'Yes. Now let me double check,' I replied, not wanting to commit a faux pas, 'you're from Australia...'

Cyril nodded.

'...and Marie's from New Zealand...'

'...and every month we meet in the middle for violent sex,' he finished, clapping his hands and jumping off his seat.

'Oh, Cyril, don't be so silly,' Marie murmured over her wine.

He mock-flinched and his eyes disappeared into crevices.

'I once did a big trip like you. I bought myself a motorbike. Didn't know how to ride it, but where's the fun in that?'

'What did you do?'

'I just got on it. Like anything, you try it first and then learn how to do it later. I went to the shop, got on it and came home. Only I didn't know how to stop it, so as I neared my house I just turned it on its side and stepped off it.' He wrenched both fists across to his right, closed his eyes and went rigid.

A buzz began to grow in the carriage as the remaining guests gathered for dinner, jabbering over the clink of gins and crunch of pretzels. Many ITV reruns of *Murder on the Orient Express* had taught me that a train like the Indian Maharaja was a five-star cruise on wheels, the preserve of retirees, rich grannies and dapper little Belgian men with moustaches. But this was a pick 'n' mix of passengers: a young Swiss couple in matching outfits; three Japanese ladies with an oversized interpreter; Bob and Jane from Devon, who loved tea and *Test Match Special*; Dan and Maisie from New York, who dressed like Don and Betty Draper; and a Russian group made up of two pairs of newly weds and one spare mother-in-law, who arrived in football gear and wore bath slippers in the dining car. The consensus among the guests was that they had won the holiday on a television show. Aside from the staff, I was the only Indian on board. As we made our way towards the dining car, an Englishman with carefree hair appeared in the doorway. James was a journalist from *The Times*. Drew Barrymore had been on board the week before, and he was writing a piece about the resurgence in popularity of luxury trains even though she had apparently left after just two days.

Bob and Jane were already seated at a table, examining a bottle of wine, and waved us over.

'Come on, join us fogies,' Bob smiled. 'We won't bite and we'll try not to bore you to death.'

We slid in as he filled our wine glasses. He peered closely at the bottle and began reading the label, 'herbaceous, crisp, and dry, with hints of green pepper and a touch of spice at the finish'. 'I wish I had the job of writing these blurbs,' he continued. 'I'd have so much fun with them: "a smooth aroma of vanilla and blackberries with an undertone of wet dog". Having said that, this really isn't bad at all.'

My only memory of drinking wine in India was five years ago at a hotel bar in Hyderabad: I had ordered a glass of red wine that tasted marginally better than cough syrup, and when the bill came it had cost more than six Bacardi Breezers put together.

'I'm very impressed,' Bob said, poking his nose into the glass. 'It's very drinkable and apparently isn't produced far from here. Fancy, Indian vineyards, whatever next?'

From across the aisle an Indian man spoke up. Perhaps he had been hiding in his cabin during orientation, but here was a new addition to the group.

Suhel worked in sales for a travel company in Delhi and had reached his target before any of his colleagues. His reward was a trip aboard the train.

'The Sula Vineyards are quite close by.'

'Where is this?' Bob asked.

'A little northeast of Mumbai.'

'How long have they been there?'

'Actually it was started in '99 by a Mumbaikar. He went to Stanford then worked for two years in Silicon Valley.'

'Techies and CEOs are your finest export, aren't they?'

Suhel laughed. 'Yes, but many graduates are going and coming back now.'

'Is there a huge wine-drinking contingent in India? I should think it would only be in Mumbai and Delhi.'

'I think they sell some two, maybe three million bottles each year.'

'Ridiculous, isn't it?' Roger had turned around in his seat and was listening over the booth.

'What is?' Suhel asked.

'Your elite are more bothered about promoting wine drinking than sorting out the masses.'

'But the wine industry is a rural industry. It is based in the countryside and provides employment to rural workers. It's good for us to find resources in India itself.'

'Still, it does seem a bit nuts talking about wine production when half this country doesn't have water.'

Suhel put down his fork. 'And what do you propose. Tell me? Always people want to criticise but nobody gives suggestions. Why should India always mean poverty?'

'And in that case, why didn't you take the Punjab Mail from Mumbai to Delhi instead of the Indian Maharaja?' I asked Roger, then noticed James's pen flicking across his notepad and decided to shut up.

Rolling his eyes, Roger turned back to his meal as Suhel shrugged at me and grinned, poking his biryani with a fork. All around gloved waiters moved like mime artists, twirling plates above their heads and taking wide steps around each other. A thali arrived with a turret of biryani in the centre and a pappadum that opened like a lotus, revealing diced salad. I dived in feeling sorry for Passepartout, who was stirring a bowl of pineapple yoghurt, unable to cope with anything solid. Once the last plate was wiped and the final drop drained, we swayed back to the suite for an early night before the morning arrival in Aurangabad to visit the caves at Ellora and Ajanta. An orchid, damp with dew, lay on the duvet next to a card inscribed in gold: *God bless the inventor of sleep, the cloak that covers all men's thought.* It was a quotation from Cervantes, who had obviously never tried to sleep on an Indian train. For the next two hours we snaked crazily along the tracks, my neck jolting into an early onset of spondylosis. Abandoning sleep, I opened up my book to see if King Thebaw was settling into his new home any faster than I was. Passepartout, meanwhile, had turned the colour of mint chutney.

Sleep must have crept up on me, as I awoke to a tinkling of glass and flipped on the light to find the cabin in the midst of a mutiny. Two wine glasses were rolling around on their sides, a bottle of Merlot was hurling itself against the wall, and the cabin door was sliding back and forth in a rage. After pulling a sock around the bottle and wedging it between the wall and a chair leg, I slid the glasses into a drawer, shoved a screw of paper into the doorframe and flipped off the light. The train chose that moment to glide to a halt. A romantic milky light seeped through the gaps in the curtains and I eased them back in search of a glowing moon, only to find a bent halogen street lamp and a man rearranging himself on the platform. Just before 6 am, Benoy tapped at the door and placed a tray of coffee and biscuits on the bed while Passepartout hugged his toilet bowl.

The breakfast car was as lively as a cemetery. Cyril and Marie were poring over the menu and beckoned me over to explain *chana puri* (chickpeas with fried Indian bread). Intrigued by the bacon, sausages and ham, I opted for all of the above and Zayan, a dreamy-eyed waiter with dimples, flapped a napkin across my lap.

'Eggs, madam?'

'Yes, please.'

'Poachedfriedscrambledboiledbenedictomelettemadam?'

I settled on a scrambled egg flecked with chives and watched as the Bagshot Trio prodded forks at a plate of *usal pav* (spicy sprouts curry with Indian bread). Just outside their window, four beggar children had lined up and were pressing their faces against it.

'Rather off-putting,' Roger's wife Cath moaned, heaping a spoonful of sugar into her coffee.

Roger eyed the row of small faces. 'Just ignore them, dear.'

'I can't, they're staring at me!' she exclaimed, shifting in her seat. 'Do you think they can see me?'

On a day-to-day basis, nobody really notices poverty. People go about their business, chins up, eyes fixed forward, hiding behind tinted windows or in air-conditioned homes. Beggars, pavement dwellers and sick children carrying sick babies are just a part of the landscape. On the other side of the train, a row of ladies with jasmine dangling from their plaits waited with wedding-sized garlands and a silver tray of coconut, sandalwood paste and a pot of kumkum. A flame flickered in the centre on a piece of camphor. Four dancers carried a palanquin on their shoulders on which a bare-chested child was sitting in a dhoti, wearing a papier-mâché head of Lord Ganesha and holding an umbrella above him. He looked like a mannequin. As each passenger descended the steps, bellies like Ganesha, they were draped with the flowers and their foreheads swiped with red, a ritual that continued for the next seven days.

Ellora is like a secret township in the hills. Each wall and pillar, carved with faces and fingers, hips and breasts, pays homage to patience and perfection. The Kailasa cave contains a courtyard and a three-storey gallery and was designed to represent the abode of Lord Shiva. It is also carved from one single rock, and here we found Bob, his Handycam strapped around his wrist, trying to dodge schoolgirls playing hide-and-seek. He stopped, put his fists on his hips and squinted up at a parakeet peeking inside the head of an open-mouthed lion.

'Bloody hell, this is just incredible.'

He ran his fingers over the curves and dips of the carvings, tracing the dents and chips of once gentle faces. His wife Jane wandered over with her binoculars to watch the parakeet, who had found his friends and was flapping around them in a frenzy. She was a round-cheeked lady who adored birds, wore a different shade of pink every day and winced whenever the Bagshot Trio approached. In truth, there was only one main offender. Cath had bleached curls that spiralled around her oversized head and clumped together to reveal patches of sunburnt scalp. She marched alongside the tour guides, from where she could offer a running commentary on her observations. By and large, she seemed not to understand that this was India and not the Peak District.

Mr Gupta, a hollow-cheeked guide wearing a fishing jacket and a look of pure boredom, began an explanation of how the combination of Buddhist, Hindu and Jain caves was designed to demonstrate religious harmony, and led the group across to a wall where Goddess Lakshmi sat cross-legged. A lake of lotus flowers lay carved before her, like a stretch of hungry mouths.

'She is the goddess of wealth and prosperity,' he droned, 'you may know her as she is closely linked to Diwali.'

'Golly, this would have a National Trust tea room back at home,' Cath sniffed. Mr Gupta smiled politely.

'Do you celebrate Diwali?'

'Oh yes, we know Diwali. We do celebrate it as we have a lot of you back at home.'

Cath was oblivious to my presence, but took quite a shine to Passepartout. That afternoon at the Ajanta caves she lingered behind him, following him from one cave to another. She had applied lipgloss and eyeliner, but somehow managed to look worse. After watching him adjust his lenses to the darkness, her mouth slightly open, she wandered over to him holding out her camera and bellowed, 'Can you turn an old woman on?' Meanwhile, quartets of bandy-legged men wound up and down the steps transporting women on palanquins. Their limbs trembled beneath the lumps of sweating dough, perspiration trickling down their muscles. Roger was sitting on a wall as the palanquins passed, watching a crew of langurs snacking on each other's ticks. I ventured over to throw them a few broken halves of Krack Jack biscuits.

'It's amazing, isn't it,' he said, 'that they spent all that time building shrines to what are nothing more than imaginary friends?'

'I wouldn't call them imaginary friends,' I replied. 'Whether or not they're real, they represent virtues.'

'But they aren't real.'

'I know they're not. But I don't think it matters.'

'You don't think it matters that they worship millions of make-believe people?'

'They're different aspects of one entity. If they admire qualities depicted by parables, then so what?'

'It's falsehood. Finding peace without rational, scientific thought is nothing more than self-deception.'

'The stories carved into these walls show human nature in a way that can't be captured by scientific theory.'

'It's just a manifestation of delusion.'

The rock-cut wonders hardly seemed like a waste of time. At the very least, they had created employment for the masses, encouraged artisans and resulted in architecture of ineffable beauty. Roger sat tight-lipped as the langurs began to play with themselves – a pastime they reserved for when they had an audience – so I caught up with Passepartout and relayed the 'imaginary friends' conversation. He looked down at his camera and adjusted the lens.

That night after kebabs and a Merlot, *Octopussy* was screened to set the mood for Udaipur. As Roger Moore leapt out of his gorilla costume onto the top of a speeding train, chased by a sword-wielding Sikh in a blue turban, I wondered why Passepartout had been so quiet. Since the comment about the imaginary friends, he had withdrawn and spent all afternoon with his camera. I flipped off the light, pulled the duvet over my head and dreamt that Bagshot Cath had turned into a gorilla and was throwing blue kebabs at me.

That the Indian Maharaja was a feat of excellence was indisputable. Towels were fluffed and beds laden with nightly gifts, bartenders beamed, crisp wine breathed in crystal and plummy gulab jamuns sweated syrup on silver spoons. But sitting in a lace-curtained window, book in hand, watching the world slip by was a shelved dream. For practical reasons the train travelled at night. During the day he stood quietly in local stations, being fed and watered by his engineers until ready to leave again. Throughout the week the train would jolt during dinner and by the morning be waiting at Udaipur, Sawai-Madhopur, Jaipur, Bharatpur and eventually Delhi Safdarjung. It was like travelling in a luxury Tardis.

One morning I sat in the doorway watching the engineers fill the water tanks, spilling most of it onto the tracks. Benoy appeared and edged his way past in a wide arc, apologising as he did so. I invited him over to chat, but he hovered reluctantly.

'Ma'am, is it permissible that I sit at your level?'

I made space for him in the doorway, but he declined. He rested on his haunches, relaxing a little.

Benoy was a 30-year-old from Kolkata with a wife and a newborn son. He showed me a photograph of them both on his phone, wiping the screen on his sleeve. He would only see them again in three months' time. Benoy was well read, had a degree from the University of Calcutta and seemed over-qualified for his job. He explained that one day he would like to live in England and run his own hospitality business. I asked him why he wanted to leave India just as it was reaching a turning point.

'It is true that India is now doing very well,' he said. 'But this is only true for some people.'

'But I thought Indians who went to university abroad are now coming back to India because this is where it's booming. Even Indians who have never lived here?'

'Yes, ma'am, it is booming, but for people who are low on the scale this makes no difference. The rich are even richer, but the poor are even more poor than before. And now they want many things that they see but can never afford.'

'What do you think will happen?'

'They are slowly learning their rights and they are no longer keeping quiet. The time will come. One day they will refuse to accept this. But it will take some time.'

Another butler appeared from around the corner and Benoy leapt to his feet.

'Enjoy your afternoon in Udaipur, ma'am, it will be very special.'

The day in Udaipur sailed by like the boats on Lake Pichola. A tour around the palace ended with the distribution of traditional pagris for the men and scarves for the women, their vegetable dyes leaving splodges on my neck like angry eczema. A sound-and-light show boomed and beamed before dinner and a tired troop flopped early to bed, as the following morning was Tiger Morning!

A damp chill clutched my chest as I jumped down the train steps. It was barely dawn, the birds were asleep and a handful of crickets was burning the midnight oil. Sleepy talk floated on puffs of breath and a mist curled itself around the carriages. Three tank-like jeeps were parked nearby and the Bagshot Trio squeezed into the front row of the first. Everyone else scrambled towards the other two. Sweeping the pools of dew from the seats with his hand, Raju the driver jumped down and passed a mountain of rough blankets over the sides. He wrenched the gear stick, scraping metal on metal, and the jeep roared off to Ranthambore National Park. A steady blast of wind tugged the skin from our bones and dragged tears down the sides of our cheeks. At the gates to the park the jeep had a seizure, the engine cut out and Raju jumped out and disappeared for 'something'. While we waited, a stack of bodywarmers rose up at the side of the jeep and a row of baseball caps bobbed past. Men in shawls stood around, hands behind backs, eyes shining in the light of their beedis. Each wore a pair of camouflage-coloured earmuffs that clipped around the backs of their heads.

'Bulllllll-a-clawa!' a man called, wearing a holey sweater, a bodywarmer, a tasselled shawl, a scarf and open-toed sandals. He hurled a handful of balaclavas over the side of the jeep.

'No, no thank you, we don't want anything,' Bob said, pushing them back.

'Yes, bullllllllll-a-clawas, very good price, very warm,' the man insisted, standing on his toes and pushing back on the other side. He and Bob engaged in a tussle while at the back of the jeep a selection of baseball caps landed in Marie's lap. She tried to hand them back as Cyril put one on.

'Can we please go?' Bob asked, looking around for Raju, who was sipping coffee between thumb and index finger, nattering to a group of friends. There was nothing wrong with the jeep. It was standard procedure to break down by a group of hungry vendors. By the time Raju strolled back, Cyril was grinning from under a new baseball cap and Bob was sporting a new bodywarmer. He sighed. 'It is very warm, I have to say.'

After a couple of hours the sun had climbed high enough to wink through the trees and warm patches in the jeep. Bob had shed his bodywarmer and the blankets had slid onto the floor. Jane was listing species of kingfisher on her notepad, pointing to a pair of chubby turquoise specimens wearing orange bibs, when a yelp punctured the silence. The guide held up a hand and tapped the driver on the shoulder to stop the jeep.

Silence.

A rustle of wind blew crispy leaves around the ground and the sound pierced the air again.

'This is a warning call from a deer... this means she has sensed a tiger.'

He gave a shoulder tap to the driver, who careered over the bumps in the track and revved up the hill. Startled, two sambar deer jumped away from the road. Another jeep was parked ahead, its passengers standing on seats, leaning on each other's shoulders. All eyes were glued to a movement in the trees where a body was slinking away, his tail flicking behind him. Keen for a better view, the driver strained the jeep up and around the bend, desperate to beat the tiger before it emerged on the other side. As the jeep rounded the corner, a muscular pair of shoulders appeared on the track and the tiger paused, turning to look directly at us. Unruffled by his audience, he leapt onto the road and sloped around the back of the jeep and into the trees. We sped downhill into a clearing, ready to head back to base. But the driver braked sharply.

Less than 20 metres away, a striped body was picking its way through the undergrowth. Sunlight bounced off patches of orange that gently rose and fell. He moved as though a wave was rippling from head to tail. Suddenly his shoulder blades sprang up, his head dipped and his paws lifted with calculated precision. He had seen something. Following his gaze, we saw that hidden in the trees was another tiger, named Machli. Machli was known as the Queen of the Jungle. She was 15 years old and had provided five litters for the reserve, making her the pride of Ranthambore. She was still, watching him with a front paw hovering off the ground, her tail curving like a cobra. When he was less than a few metres away, they bounded towards each other and at the last second leapt up, paws outstretched, and clashed mid-air, sinking claws and teeth into each other's necks.

An apocalyptic roar ripped through the jungle, lifting birds off branches, as the pair wrestled on hind legs, snarling and growling, flanks of muscle and fur merged into one. But Machli was not known as the Queen of the Jungle for nothing. She slashed her claws across his face and gave one final bark as he loped off to lick his wounds. She watched him go, black lips curling around white teeth, shoulders rising and falling, before turning around and picking her way to a tree, where she threw herself down and licked her paws. The guide watched her, a fatherly smile playing at the corner of his mouth.

'The 15-year-old tiger has won the battle,' he declared, before tapping the driver on the shoulder and taking us back to base.

Once the excitement of tiger spotting had died down, the remainder of the week was devoted to ticking off tourist boxes: rickshaw rides through Jaipur; elephant rides up to Amber Fort; and a cockeyed group photo that made the Taj Mahal look as though it were sliding to one side behind us. On the last night, we joined Cyril, Marie, Bob and Jane to toast a wonderful week with steaks and wine, before slipping between the duvets for the last time. From tomorrow it would be five-rupee tea and bedding from brown-paper bags.

4 | 'Excuse Me Darling, I Have a Message for You'

'Pipty.'

'What?'

'One hundred and PIPTY!'

Our stationary auto shuddered in the middle of an angry traffic jam leading to the Paharganj side of New Delhi station and the driver signalled for us to get out. He refused to navigate his vehicle through the mash of metal and bodies thronging at the entrance. Plucking an extra ₹50 from my hand, he swung round and wove off, leaving us standing in the middle of the road to die. A Maruti 800 was approaching from the right, an auto from the left and a cycle rickshaw pedalled in diagonally. The rule was simple: attack, or be attacked. I marched forward and somehow all three swerved to avoid me. Back in Wembley, Shankar had issued precise instructions on how to get to New Delhi station's tourist bureau: don't look left or right, ignore the touts and agents scouring Paharganj's Backpacker Ghetto, and go straight to the IndRail desk. On cue, a skinny man, like a stick insect in flares, appeared at my side.

'Tickets ma'am? I can give confirmed tickets.'

He had the shifty body language of a sixth-former trying to flog poppers at a bus stop. I ignored him and contemplated the least fatal route across the road. Further along, Passepartout was shouting and trying to fend off a group of touts.

'Ma'am, where are you going? … I can get you tickets … how many tickets? Official *government* tickets.'

This last claim confirmed that they were anything but legitimate tickets. Across the road, more touts had spotted us and were winding their way around autos and tripping over bike wheels. A beggar with a withered forearm wandered over and began to flick the useless limb back and forth with his good arm, tapping intermittently at my own healthy arm. To make it to the bureau unscathed, our field position was crucial. Passepartout went into a scrum, holding back the mob. Free to run, I broke out, dodging wheels, bonnets and elbows, and made it to the other side as the touts relented. They had spotted a trio of rucksacks bobbing by and moved on to new prey.

The high-ceilinged hall of New Delhi station was crammed with endless queues, meshed windows and neon signs, few of which made sense. A man wearing earmuffs gripped his nostrils between his thumb and forefinger and blew hard, throwing the contents on the floor, then pointed us towards a staircase. It led up to a landing that looked like the scene of a mass murder. Paan splashed the floors and mounted the walls, one well-aimed spurt obscuring the final 't' on the *Do Not Spit* sign. Another sign pointed to *Refreshment Room* and a pair of blondes appeared from that direction and came down the staircase holding tickets. Both girls wore glittering bindis and Pushkar passports – threads around their wrists. Touts and fake priests often pounce on tourists new to the holy town, offering flowers and blessings in exchange for a few thousand rupees. In return, a sacred thread is tied around the wrist, representing a vaccination against further hassle. Pious passport-wearers preserved the thread for months after they had arrived home in Fulham, and wore it until it smelt, rotted and fell off in the shower. This was definitely the right way to the tourist bureau.

Metal chairs locked into two squares were already filled with travellers clutching white forms, waiting to be seen, while a dispute had erupted at the foreign tourist desk. A Chinese girl, brandishing her passport, was shouting at an unblinking Indian man whose sense of urgency was funereal. A dreadlocked brunette was fiddling with a knitted shoulder bag in her lap and had established an affinity for eye rolling with a hungry-looking teenager whose toenails needed trimming. Two Americans were discussing the Burning Man festival and an Indian man wearing jeans, loafers and a Tag Heuer was watching the scene with amusement. The neon lights and inattention made the bureau feel like the emergency room of a hippy hospital.

Once the Chinese girl had flounced off, with a parting gesture similar to the hijra's curse, we approached the foreign tourist desk and sat down,

laying out our passes for the clerk. He glanced at the passes and looked
back at his computer screen.

'Go to the IndRail desk.'

'Which one is the IndRail desk?' I asked.

The clerk stared at a nail. 'The one saying "IndRail desk".'

I glanced around and he tutted, pointing across the room. Scraping back
chairs, we moved to the unattended IndRail desk. After 15 minutes a clerk
sat down, wrote in her logbook, leant back in her chair to share a joke with
a colleague, changed her glasses and then held out a hand. I handed over
the two rail passes.

'We wondered if we could …'

'Go to the IndRail UK desk.'

Passepartout flinched. 'Where is the IndRail UK desk?'

'That side.'

She pointed to a desk where a head with a smudge in the parting was
bent over a book of train timings and refused to look up when we sat
down. According to the placard, the head belonged to Anusha Thawani,
Chief Reservation Supervisor. The book fell shut with a thud and Anusha
stared at her computer screen. It was about as technologically advanced as
a typewriter. She watched the green numbers on its black screen as though
observing a scene from *The Matrix*. She was in the mood neither to reserve
nor to supervise. Not taking her eyes off the screen, she scowled.

'Whaddyawant?'

So far, we had booked the Kerala Express, a 48-hour journey from Delhi
to Kottayam, leaving in two days' time, but the remaining 72 trains were
negotiable. Handing over our passes, I scribbled down four sets of train
numbers and Anusha screwed up her face.

'Oh God, why have you come so late? I go at 5:30 pm.'

Above her head, the long hand of an Ajanta clock had just pushed past
the hour.

'Then there's still half an hour left and anyway, the door says you're open
until 8 pm.'

She ignored me and snatched the passes.

'Fill in the forms and give me.'

She threw a sheaf of white reservation forms across the table and, as an
afterthought, a broken biro.

I took the lid off the pen and she slapped the table.

'Hurry up!'

I filled in our names and she slapped it again.

'Hurry up!'

'I'm hurrying! For God's sake, let me at least write down the numbers.'

She heaved out her logbook and began tapping train numbers into her computer, muttering half at us, half to herself. Passepartout sank into his chair, pretending to clean his camera lens, shaking with laughter. Since the Indian Maharaja had departed he had wolfed down plates of papaya, been generous with hugs and embraced Delhi with the energy of a dog in an open field, so I put his curious spell down to residual effects of the rogue coffee in Goa.

Anusha shook her head.

'Nothing is available, you need to change the dates.'

She pushed back the forms. Crumbling under duress, I decided it was safer to take away the forms, choose new routes and come back in the morning. Relieved that she could now run off, Anusha pushed back her chair and pulled off her white coat, disappearing into the back as we made our way out.

'Hey!'

It was the young Indian man.

'How come you guys are taking so many trains? You on some charity run or something?'

On the way down the stairs we chatted with Adil, a New Yorker who was spending a few days in Delhi before heading to Mumbai for a wedding. At the exit Adil invited us to his friend's party in Vasant Vihar and promised to pick us up before dinner.

Adil's friend Vik was driving in the middle of the road, touching the steering wheel with two fingers, the rest curled around a glass of Johnnie Walker. His other hand was sending a text. I yanked the seatbelt across my front, only to realise that, like every other Indian car, the clip was wedged deep into the seats. The belt slithered back into place with a clunk. The Mercedes S600 paused at the traffic lights and a child's hand appeared at the window. It was splayed out, revealing missing tips from the third and index fingers. A small boy blew his lips against the glass, puffed out his cheeks and cupped his hands around his eyes. A sliver of dried saliva ran from the corner of his mouth and his lip was split and crusted over. No matter how much time you spend in India or your immunity builds against the dirt, poverty and squalor, some things will always catch you off guard. I reached for my handbag and eased down the window. It hummed, but halfway through the descent, jerked and crawled back up again.

Vik shook his head at me in the rear-view mirror.

'Dude, that fucker's probably had his finger up his nose all day.'

'I wasn't trying to hold his hand, just give him some cash.'

'Don't, they'll just give it to the police or some other bastards waiting to thrash them at the end of the day.'

'But isn't he less likely to be thrashed or have his eye scooped out with a teaspoon if he's actually got cash to hand over?'

'Slumdog gim-dog, you people are so soft,' Vik laughed. 'It's no different from London. You give your money to some fellow in a cardboard box by the tube and he'll buy himself some dope.'

I had no charity-giving rulebook, but if someone was forced to sleep under boxes pilfered from Sainsbury's then they were badly off. Forking out the price of *The Times* and a Twix hardly put a hole in my pocket.

A BMW had pulled up alongside us and was inching its nose forward, putting beads of sweat on Vik's temples. He slammed his foot down as the light turned green, causing a tidal surge of people and traffic in every direction. A few minutes later, we drew up at a four-storey building with a garden on the second floor and a line of cars spilling out of the driveway.

Adil led us through the garden, ducking under trees strung with fairy lights, breathing in the smell of cloves lifting off clusters of Sweet William. Mock Victorian lanterns lined the path and a ring of red dots hovered in a corner – smokers, vigilant to stray aunties who might spot them and tell their parents. Adil made a beeline for the bar, which was propped up by a trio in tight T-shirts, working their way through a stock of Blue Label. The host, a hazel-eyed Hrithik Roshan lookalike, stood behind the bar, his pelvis jutting out in the direction of a light-haired girl wearing turquoise contact lenses. His shirt was undone one button too far, revealing a surplus of chest hair. He looked like a bad Thums Up advert.

Hrithik threw a peanut into his mouth and arched what looked like a threaded eyebrow.

'So you're the train geeks, huh? How many have you done?'

'Seven.'

Less than thrilled that the 'Train Geek' badge was already pinned in place, I changed the subject.

'So, how do you and Adil know each other?'

He poked one of the tight T-shirts in the chest.

'Hey man, these two are travelling all over India... in 80 trains!'

His friend, who was already breaking out into whisky sweats, wiped his mouth and widened his reddening eyes.

'Eigh-dee trains? Fuck... Why don't you fly?'

'Because I don't like airports or peanuts.'

'Those trains are disgusting. I normally wear gloves if I have to take a piss.'

'I clean my teeth with the tap water.'

'You eat the food on the train?'

'Mostly.'

'You'll get a tapeworm or something.'

'You know there's a tapeworm diet?' the light-haired girl piped up. 'I saw it on *The Tyra Banks Show*. You swallow one tapeworm and then you can eat anything at all and you don't put on any weight.'

A blitzkrieg of questions about our train fetish descended and we took cover behind large drinks. Soon enough, Passepartout's veins were plump with vodka, so I went in search of food. Across the hallway, a chandeliered dining room was lined with waiters lifting lids off steaming trays. A quick scan revealed a carved ham, chicken and mushroom risotto, cheese and cauliflower bake and sautéed potatoes. It was a far cry from English party food, which normally included Marks & Spencer onion bhajis, chicken tikka and vegetable samosas.

A busty aunty with a gold necklace lodged in her cleavage appeared wearing leggings, Louboutins and pink lipstick on her two front teeth.

'I hear you're from Hampstead!' she clapped, spooning cheese sauce all over my plate. 'I used to live in West Hampstead in the 1970s when I was an air hostess.' She paused. 'What do your parents do?'

'They're doctors.'

'Oh how lovely, in Hampstead?'

'No, they live in Birmingham.'

She blinked.

'You don't live with them?'

'No, I live by myself.'

'My son is actually a banker in London.' She licked a nail, beckoning over a man in a Jean Paul Gaultier top. His nipples peered through the black netting that stopped a good two inches above his jeans. 'He works for Citigroup and lives in Islington.'

'Oh, that's nice.'

'Where is your family from?'

'A fishing village near Pondicherry.'

Her face tried to collapse with disappointment, but held firm with Botox as she led her son away by the elbow. Something told me I was not what she was looking for; or, for that matter, the gender he was looking for. Adil's train was leaving early the next morning and we were due another audience with Anusha, so we licked a few spoons of Häagen-Dazs and called it a night. Delhi's elite would have to make do without us for entertainment.

A combination of traffic and a visit to the railway museum brought us to the tourist bureau, yet again, at 5 pm. But after much debate, train number eight was now crossed off the list. The National Railway Museum in Chanakyapuri, spread over 11 acres, features a tiny visitors' train. It carries passengers around a sandy rail yard, offering close inspection of vintage engines, coaches and saloons, and a complimentary bang on the head for anyone over 4 feet tall climbing into its child-sized compartments. Passepartout was unconvinced that the Joy Train qualified.

'You can't count it as a train. That's cheating.'

'Are we in India?'

'Yes.'

'Are we travelling on a train?'

'Yes.'

'Then we are, essentially, travelling around a bit of India on a train.'

Tickets cost ₹10 at the turnstile and boarding took place next to a bright yellow station sign for 'Museum Junction', so he gave in and clambered aboard. Among the vintage collection stood the Fairy Queen, the world's oldest running steam train, and also an original rake of the Palace on Wheels. Scrawling the Joy Train into the logbook was satisfying and it added variety.

Anusha would not care.

Anusha did not care. She looked up and her face fell.

'Oh my God, why you are coming so late again? I knew, I just knew you were going to come late again. Hurry up, I have a party to get to.'

Anusha's severe ponytail had been abandoned and her hair spilt down over her shoulders, streaks of henna skimming her temples. Her white coat had gone and she was wearing a pink salwar kameez with purple beading. Her nails were polished pink and her lips smudged with purple. She had blossomed into a vision of pink and purple angst.

'Can we come to your party?' I asked.

Anusha snatched the white forms and somehow processed the bookings within minutes. As the printer strained with constipation, curling the tickets onto the floor, she glanced down the remaining list and began to change our choices to trains that were faster, cleaner, safer, more punctual and with better food.

'Come back when you're next in Delhi,' she said. 'I can find you trains with foreign tourist quotas so you won't have to book so far in advance.'

She shooed us out, fishing her lipstick out of her handbag. I had a feeling that this was not the last time we would see Anusha Thawani.

As a general rule, morning appointments in India take place at one fixed time. Whether it is to meet a friend for coffee, to pick up blouses from the tailor or to discuss business with a colleague, the time arranged is the same: 'leven-'leven-thirty. Between 11 am and half past the hour is a nicely vague 30-minute window that allows for lie-ins, traffic jams and the two parties to arrive in a state of pressure-free tardiness. The Kerala Express was due to depart at 11:30 am and on average was only two minutes late. However, this driver was running on Indian Standard Time and the train was nowhere in sight.

The platform was bloated to bursting point. Passengers pushed to the edges, the odd one occasionally dropping off, like quarters in a casino coin-pusher machine. They simply wandered up a few girders, found a gap and hauled themselves back onto the platform, unfazed by impending death. This was just another one of many contradictions that made India so very curious. At any given time the country is in a hurry, racing to keep up with itself. In every sense Indians are in a constant fight to move ahead. People shove to board buses, push to get off trains and retrieve their baggage from overhead bins while planes are still taxiing. Yet at instances of genuine urgency, there is a distinct predisposition towards nose picking and bone idleness.

As a soft brown goat on the track chewed its way through an empty Monaco biscuits' wrapper, flicking its ears, the train appeared in the distance and the big push began. So far it was a game of chance as to which end of the platform we should wait. Thinking we had cracked the overhead

signs, we had waited towards the top end of the platform, only to watch
carriage A2 flash past. Our compartment was now 17 carriages away and
the platform had turned into a mosh pit of madness. Boxes crowd-surfed,
bodies pushed both ways in the doorways and at least one man lay face
down on the ground, trampled beneath the mob. It reminded me of when
the Foo Fighters had played the Isle of Wight.

Once the rage had subsided, we snaked around the families holding
hands through the bars and arrived at the door to A2 as train number nine,
the Kerala Express to Kottayam, creaked and began to move again. Our
tickets were for the side upper and lower berths, which were ideal for such
a long journey. Passengers in those seats have no reason to share sitting
space with anyone else and can gaze out of the window all day. But side
berths cause issues at night. They are narrower than the main berths of a
2A compartment and leave the lower passenger more susceptible to a face
full of passing backside, and the upper passenger more likely to stay awake
due to conferences that often take place in the aisle at unsociable hours.
Claustrophobics will also want to avoid the upper berth, as the three closed
sides and one drawn curtain create the feeling of lying in a moving coffin. It
was barely midday, so sleep was a long way off.

After sizing up our companions, we unpacked books and iPods, tucked
away bags and settled into what was to be home for the next two days. I slotted
my bookmark into the back of my book and smiled at Passepartout. So far
we were getting on wonderfully well. He had a tendency to get rather ratty
when deprived of nicotine and coffee, and I knew to avoid him when he was
hungry, but otherwise he chatted to everyone, frequently stopping to take
photographs of anyone who wished to pose, and ensuring that he had noted
down each person's address so he could post them copies. When we were not
reading chunks of our books out loud, swapping music or amusing ourselves
with the surrounding oddities, he was content to leave me to go about my own
business while he wandered off to find souvenirs for his nephews and nieces.

A bookseller was still on board and stopped by carrying a pile so high
that only his chin and fingertips were visible. The body of books was stacked
with the usual suspects: Paulo Coelho, Chetan Bhagat, Dan Brown and
Jeffrey Archer. Passepartout scanned it for Richard Dawkins' *The Greatest
Show on Earth*, but on principle I refused to buy photocopied books. A man
in the adjoining compartment had chosen *The Monk Who Sold His Ferrari*,
which the boy was trying to slide out from the bottom of his pile, when
another boy came past jingling luggage locks, followed by a high-pitched

vendor selling 'chackobar' and 'badderscatch' ice cream. All three pushed to get past one another in the aisle. It was like a scene from a Peter Sellers film. The vendors vanished and I went back to my book, eager to find out Dolly's fate.

'*Excuse me darling, I have a message for you.*'

A syrupy voice purred from behind me. It spoke up again.

'*Excuse me darling, I have a message for you.*'

I looked around.

'*Excuse me darling, I have a message for you.*'

Wondering if the hallucinogenic rice was still causing aftershocks, I spun around in confusion. In the compartment behind us a boy was slouched against the wall tapping at his mobile phone. He had chosen the creepy voice to alert him to text messages and it stayed with us for the next 48 hours. The recipient enjoyed her attentions far too much, judging by the number of messages he must have sent to encourage the multitude of replies.

A head poked around the limp bit of curtain keeping out the sunshine. It had an IRCTC (Indian Railway Catering and Tourism Corporation) baseball cap on backwards, a bashful grin and a vague effort at a moustache.

'Lentz?'

Shyam was taking lunch orders, scribbling on a small notepad with a well-chewed pencil.

'Weg? Non-weg?'

'What's the non-vegetarian option?'

'Yegger biryani.'

'Sorry?'

'Yegger.'

Passepartout put down his book and leant forward.

'Sorry, what kind of meat is that? Chicken or mutton?'

'Yegggggggger biryani,' he repeated, pulling at his cap.

'Egg,' said the book buyer from across the aisle.

Feeling rather stupid, we ordered two portions of egg biryani, which arrived, in the end, without the yegg – and without spoons, even after three reminders. At one point Shyam appeared wielding two plastic spoons, one of which he dropped before he reached us; the other disappeared between the door and a conversation with the book buyer.

Outside the tinted windows, the outskirts of Delhi began to slip away. Within minutes, BMWs had morphed into bullock carts, shopping malls into shacks. Tying up the remainders of our lunch in an eco nappy-bag, I worked my way down the carriage and squeezed the rubbish into the slot beneath the sink, which actually had a bin bag in place. At this point I was unaware that the bag would simply be thrown out of the door at the next possible opportunity. It was bright and warm outside and the train was yet to pick up pace, so I heaved open the door and sat down on the step. Behind me the carriage door opened and a lady wearing a tennis shirt and bootleg jeans leant out and tossed a plastic bag full of food straight over my head. Rice, dal and pickle came loose mid-air, the open bag landing on a bush already strung with blue and pink plastic ribbons. Every inch of the foreground sprouted plastic bags, foil and bottles, resembling the immediate aftermath of Glastonbury.

As the train slowed towards Mathura Junction, a man in a striped shirt and suit trousers pushed his friend on a broken-down motorbike up the adjacent track, and a farmer with a herd of suntanned sheep squatted at the edge of the lines, watching the duo go past. Suddenly the shacks and huts shrank away and the train trundled past farmland. A lone cyclist pedalled at the edge of a field, a mammoth bundle of sticks straddling his back wheel. Bent over between strips of tall grass, one blood-red sari billowed in the wind, like a single tulip in a field of green. Between Jhansi and Bina, the sun and I became embroiled in a game of peek-a-boo. It darted over rooftops and ducked under trees, hiding behind rogue clouds. But it soon became tired of the game, turning pink from exhaustion and sliding down behind the hills, winking on its way out.

As the hours rolled by, a slideshow of bucolic beauty played in the window. Maize swayed, bullocks wallowed in mud baths and blossoms weighed down branches. On the descent towards the south, a new reel of pictures began to play, touched up with a darker green. Trees clambered for space, pushing for prime location. Houses hid behind bushes and lakes shimmered in the sunshine. The sun was now wide awake, bouncing across leaves and leaping above branches. Gone was the dust and dryness of the north. Kerala had a cool, Colgate freshness and everything felt clean. Everything, that was, apart from me. I had started to smell like an unwashed football shirt. Around 'leven-'leven-thirty, the Kerala Express slid into Kottayam station. We jumped down the steps and toasted forty-eight hours, six states and two stinky people with a short, sharp burst of proper South Indian coffee.

5 | Hindus Only Allowed

For Indians a journey is important, but it is reaching the destination that really counts. In a country where survival is priority, this applies, in a broader sense, to their every undertaking. Lying, cheating, bribing and conning are bad, but if they get you where you want, then their definitions become flexible. Buying medical degrees, flashing red lights with no VIP in the car and inviting an entire constituency to a political wedding in exchange for votes are the norm. Everyone does it and everyone knows. The cancer of corruption and nepotism is in no way unique to India; it exists in every country and within every system. But in India it is structured: condemned on the surface, but accepted as integral to a working society. Theoretically, this clashed wildly with the naivety of our travelling mindset, but the practicality was undeniable.

After the two-day journey to Kottayam, we recovered in a houseboat on the backwaters of Kumarakom, then took train number 10, the Sabari Express, along the Western Ghats to Coimbatore. There we booked tickets to Erode, to visit a man who oversaw the building of temples. I had long been intrigued by the complexities behind their construction and he had invited us to explain the mathematics of structure, positioning and the astrological considerations of each new project. But less than an hour before our departure he failed to answer his phone, choosing instead to fire off sporadic text messages citing a combination of an ill mother and a business meeting out of station. Now, waiting in the chief reservation supervisor's office at Coimbatore Junction, I clutched a white form to my chest, pulled a sad face and prayed that we could exchange tickets for the next train to Madurai. It was due to depart within the hour and the waiting list was endless.

The office was filled with fellow fraudsters mumbling guilt-ridden stories of dead or dying relatives, or pretending not to understand their ticket's dates and travel restrictions. The outcome of their efforts also depended on the discretion of the man in charge. Glaring over his glasses at one poorly rehearsed performance, the supervisor raised his hand and pushed his tongue between his teeth, which translated loosely as 'get out of my sight before I bash the living daylights out of you'. He beckoned me forward. Dewy-eyed and sniffing, I scribbled down the preferred train numbers and handed him our tickets, looking down at the floor while brewing up a plausible lie. Without questioning, he slapped a form for emergency tickets on the table. His pen hovered above the box labelled 'reason for emergency' and he eyed me closely for a moment or two, then wrote 'BRITISH TOURIST'.

He smiled.

I smiled.

He shook his head from side to side.

I shook my head from side to side.

He handed over the new tickets.

I fled.

Two people had been pushed down the waiting list because of our whims and fancies and I felt terrible – but only for a moment. This was India and this was how India worked. Somewhere along the journey, the same would happen to us. That was how karma worked.

Travelling on 80 trains was a tall order, but the number was set to rise in the next week on the Great South Indian Temple Tour through Madurai, Trichy, Thanjavur and Nagapattinam, ending in Chennai. Each city was relatively close to the next and the stretch would include a number of unreserved passenger trains. As the Nagercoil Express slipped into Madurai at midnight, it marked number 11.

Madurai's Hotel Chentoor had been booked on account of the guidebook's description of 'spic-and-span rooms', which were so filthy that the sheets looked as though someone had died in them. A patch of greasy handprints slapped on the wall – just above the pillow – suggested that the room had, however, witnessed plenty of live activity. According to the same book, the hotel also laid claim to 'what surely must be the dimmest lit bar in India'. That much was true. It was a perfect hideout for meetings between hookers and drug dealers, or, more fitting for Madurai, young lovers cowering in corners. The bar was so dark that it was impossible to see whether anyone was in there and it required much blinking and grappling to find a table or a waiter.

Once we adjusted to the darkness and ordered drinks, Sai Baba became the topic of conversation. Not Shirdi Sai Baba, the slight man with a white beard and headscarf often seen holding one foot across his knee, but Sathya Sai Baba, more commonly known as 'the one with the 'fro'. Just before the age of 14 he had declared to his parents that he had come to this world with a mission to re-establish the rhythm of righteousness in the world and to motivate love for God, and had since earned a mass following that included Prime Minister Manmohan Singh, Sonia Gandhi and Sachin Tendulkar. He was famed for performing miracles that ranged from coughing up what looked like golden Easter eggs into hankies to curing illnesses and conjuring up sacred ash, which he then sprinkled into his devotees' outstretched hands. His ashrams were established in over 100 countries, though his image was heavily tainted with allegations of sexual abuse and fakery.

Passepartout looked around and smirked. 'They have photos of him everywhere. It's crazy.'

It was true. Most hotels, restaurants and shops displayed his photo with a stick of incense crumbling in front. Friends had sat in his audiences and were convinced that he was as much a miracle worker as a magician at a 6-year-old's birthday party. Passepartout was on a roll.

'He should be exposed! People like that should be brought down and put away for exploiting the poor.'

'But at least he funds hospitals and schools.'

'These people make the poor spend money on small pictures and trinkets that do nothing!' His voice was rising and a furrow began to crawl down his forehead.

'If keeping a photo of somebody gives them a sense of protection and comfort, and that's all they have, who are you to criticise their choice?'

'Carrying pictures of people who aren't real and placing faith in them is fucking stupid!'

My cheeks prickled. In the cloth purse I had bought at Dilli Haat was a palm-sized picture of Shirdi Sai Baba that my dad had given me the day before I left England. An amusing chat had morphed into an ugly exchange and I was keen to end the discussion over what was essentially a personal choice. I picked up a handful of chilli peanuts as our drinks arrived.

'Anyway, can we please stop talking about this?'

'It's dis-gust-ing!' he enunciated, as though I had learning difficulties.

'Why do you care so much?' I asked. 'It's really none of your business what other people choose to do with their lives. I've already asked nicely if we could change the topic.'

'He's a FUCKING FAKE!' he spat, showing no sign of relenting.

I briefly mulled over the face gurning across the table, then took a small sip of my gin and tonic.

'Talk to me like that again and you're on your own.'

I picked up my bag and walked out, leaving Passepartout, his beer and his anger to stew together. It was nearing 4 pm and the Meenakshi temple would soon be open to afternoon visitors, so I made my way there alone. It was not that I disagreed with his sentiment, but spouting obscenities in the middle of a bar more reminiscent of a dungeon was hardly the appropriate warm-up to visiting a temple.

Winding through a labyrinth of back streets, I spotted the first of the Meenakshi temple's *gopurams* rising above the entrance to the temple town. It was a gaudy, wedge-shaped monumental tower, decorated with radioactive paint and covered with rows of gods, goddesses and demons. They had eyes like Chihuahuas being squeezed at the neck and a confusing mix of beards and breasts. Winged lizards glared outwards, their tongues hanging out next to figures that looked like a mixture between Chinese dragons and angry housewives.

Inside was beautiful. Feminine figures frozen in motion gazed outwards, their sharp nostrils breathing in a combination of camphor and marigolds. The walls were cool to touch and the ground warm from hundreds of pairs of feet padding through. Worshippers had thronged for the evening puja and hurried past carrying ladoos, garlands and restless children. In the heart of the temple, butter-balls, rolled and sold outside, were being thrown at the statue of Meenakshi and her consort and a group had gathered before Parvathi, the temple elephant. If visitors bowed before her, she placed a blessing on their head with her trunk, then swung the hairy tip down to take a coin from their hand, dropping it into the lap of her owner who sat behind. It was a smart, entrepreneurial move, marrying charm and religious servitude for material gain, but ultimately being tapped on the head by a smiley elephant was a rare occurrence and a childish thrill. One afternoon, while being walked to the temple, Parvathi had been scared by a couple of stray dogs and charged into a restaurant, much to the horror of the diners but to the delight of the owner. Overjoyed that the elephant had blessed his establishment, he rewarded the tearaway with 100 idlis and a handful of bananas. Parvathi was a proper little Indian with the right level of cunning to survive.

A short distance away, a man using opposite hands to grip each of his earlobes with two fingers began bobbing up and down in penance. His son was pulling at his pocket, asking for a coin for Parvathi. He ignored him and the child gave one last, fatal tug. He turned, slapped his son on the back of the head and went back to gripping his earlobes. This behaviour was not uncommon. During my Madras days I would often dangle my feet through the gaps in the balcony and watch the Brahmin at the house next door doing his daily puja. Every morning without fail, he would appear, freshly bathed and powdered, then sneak across the road to snap three heads off the bougainvillea tree that belonged to two dancers, scuttling back to place them on his shrine.

'Shameless fellow, as if God can't see you,' my mum would mutter.

Fed up and feeling cynical, I wandered out of the temple and found cynicism personified lurking with his camera. After a stiff exchange, Passepartout and I made our way back through the streets to catch train number 12, the Nagercoil-Chennai Express to Trichy, where the Sri Rangam temple awaited our arrival.

A ride on the number 1 bus brought us to the Sri Rangam temple complex, where the bus braked, slamming my forehead against the woman in front, then banging the back of my head on the railing. The temple sat on a small island formed by two fingers of the Cauvery river and was visible for miles.

Deemed the largest Hindu temple in the world after Angkor Wat, the Sri Rangam complex was almost a town in its own right. Passepartout refused to come in.

'I don't see the point,' he said, kicking at the sand.

I stared up at him, my face flaming from both the heat and my own pent-up anger, and chewed my lip to stop from screaming out: *Well, why the hell did we come all the way then?*

Shrugging, I turned and went inside. He eventually drifted between the columns just inside the entrance.

It was easy to get lost between the carvings and the forest of sandy-brown pillars, many of which provided shade to dozing visitors stretched out across the paving slabs. Being within the compound calmed me immediately, and my breathing soon went back to normal as I moved with the crowds, stopping briefly to take aarathi and allow the priest to press a finger gently to my forehead. A rapid tinkling drew me towards an enclave where another priest was bringing out an aarathi tray and I watched from behind a pillar. Several people waited, palms pressed together, shoulder to shoulder. I enjoyed seeing the coming together of strangers, in particular the moment of absolute silence when the bell stopped ringing and many bowed heads closed in around the flame, then moved back and dispersed, carrying on once again with their business.

A man clutching a plate of fruit and prasad saw me examining the carvings and wandered over. His eyes expanded behind his thick glasses and he shook his head with approval.

'If you climb up, you will see Sri Lanka from the tip.'

'Really? From the top of the temple?'

'Yessssssss,' he hissed with excitement, jiggling his plate.

'Is it open for visitors to go up and check?'

He squinted through his glasses at the wall. I tried again.

'Can we go up to have a look? I want to see if it's true.'

He walked off.

Scraping squashed flowers and barfi from my feet, I threaded deeper into the temple maze to where a line of devotees queued to reach the deity. It was like a human pile-up: each nose was pressed into the back of the neck in front. Limbs protruded from all angles and a row of eyes watched enviously as a well-dressed couple walked freely through the empty VIP lane. The pair glanced around with the smugness of business-class passengers watching other passengers traipse through to economy.

To the right and up some steps was a yellow door with a sign scrawled in black:

HINDUS ONLY ALLOWED

It looked rude. Why invite someone into your home if they could not warm their hands at the hearth? Among the candles and carvings that symbolised harmony and love, the words were contradictory and divisive, far removed from the notion of Hinduism as an inclusive philosophy. Despondency was beginning to bore a hole in my stomach, so I found Passepartout and crossed the road to plug it temporarily with food.

Balaji Bhavan was a pure vegetarian restaurant that specialised in bowls of pongal soaked in ghee and foot-long dosai served by Narayan, a 73-year-old delight, smiling with what appeared to be one long tooth peering through his candyfloss beard. He hobbled his way barefoot around the room, ladling hot sambar onto banana leaves and came back to see whether we wanted coffee. Of his own accord he pointed and asked: 'Black coffee?'

Passepartout fell in love. Narayan laughed behind his beard, his tooth wiggling around.

'Foreigners don't always like Indian coffee. Too sweet.'

Narayan had a BA in Hindi from Kerala University and spoke six languages. Here was yet another example of an over-qualified worker: back home he would be working for MI5. Narayan moved around the restaurant on rickety legs, single-handedly serving every diner during the lunchtime rush. He put his health and agility down to the fact that he had never been married. 'But I'm not a bachelor!' he winked, waving a finger in the air before sending us on to the Rock Fort temple and chuckling at his own joke. Hard-working, cheerful and seemingly happy with his lot, Narayan mirrored the temperament of most train vendors, road-sweepers and shopkeepers we had met so far.

Leading to the foot of the hill on which the Rock Fort temple stood was a street jammed with stalls and shops selling everything from saucepans and lampshades to adult nappies, baby dolls and 'dictionerys'. At this early point in our travels we had already collected an inordinate amount of junk. Much was typical tourist tat: postcards of people with mullets, incense sticks, mirrored shoulder bags and cheap jewellery. It was a complete waste of money: the postcards slipped into books only to be rediscovered on the flight home; incense sticks broke; the bag was far too kitsch to be used outside Asia; and the jewellery left grey stains on the skin. Determined to stop being wasteful, we emerged at the other end of the street with jasmine flowers tied in twine, a bag of masala popcorn, an *Archie* comic and two cages of live birds. For the bargained fee of ₹450, ten birds – the colours of the Meenakshi temple – had been purchased with the intention of releasing them at the nearest patch of green, which in dry, brown Trichy was no mean feat.

Embarrassed to be seen carrying the cages, we hurried towards the temple and found a clearing inhabited by one elderly goat with infected udders that swung like two footballs in a bag. She glanced up briefly, but went back to chewing her Amul butter box. By now the birds were throwing their multicoloured bodies around the cages. Feeling like Mary Poppins, I sat on a bench, opened the door and waited for them to soar into the sky, before swooping back to place a flower behind my ear. Instead, they fell out one by one and rolled around in the sand. Their wings had been clipped. And that was not all. On close examination, the source of their colouring also became clear – they had been coloured in with felt-tipped pens. Fortunately for Passepartout, his birds were in better shape and zoomed straight out of the cage like doves at an Olympic opening ceremony. With a little effort, my breadcrumbed stragglers managed to hop into the bushes beneath the watchful eyes of a pair of hawks who were circling.

Panting, I faced the last stretch of 437 steps that led up to the top of the Rock Fort temple and winced as a pocket-sized lady, older than God, sped ahead of me holding up her sari in one hand. She flashed a gummy, toothless smile on her way past. Eventually I reached a levelled platform where two little girls slept peacefully in an alcove beneath a series of notice boards educating visitors on the marvels of the temple: 'It is a proven fact that those who worship the God will be blessed with children and that pregnant ladies will have an easy delivery' and 'according to geological research this mountain is 3500 billion years old'.

It was hard to determine which of the two was more impressive. It was not unusual to come across tremendous fabrications. To their credit, Indians are extremely quick thinkers, but rather than admit to a lack of knowledge they have a tendency simply to make things up on the spot. The Sri Rangam temple management confirmed that the Sri Lanka story was a myth and for safety reasons visitors were not allowed up to check. Harbouring a constant sense of incredulity made every day in India a new adventure.

Once again, non-Hindus were not allowed into the Vinayaka temple at the top of the hill – though a greased palm sometimes waived this rule – so I cut the visit short and we stumbled down the steps and arrived back at Trichy Junction for Chinese food, before boarding train number 13, a passenger train to Thanjavur. Indian Chinese food, or 'chindian' food, was of hakka origin and tasted little, if nothing at all, like authentic Chinese food, but it was delicious. Dishes often came in gravy and were flavoured with typical Indian spices like cumin and coriander and the key ingredient, a healthy dose of chilli, which catered specifically to Indian taste buds. Chinese was fast growing as the most popular choice for dining out in India, and London's Yauatcha was soon to open a second branch in Mumbai, after Alan Yau noticed that a large chunk of his dim sum diners were Indian. Trichy station's upstairs restaurant was a few grades off the Soho teahouse, but did great 'Schewzen' noodles, vegetable 'chowmin' and American 'chopsaucy'.

'*Neenga engirundhu varinga?*'
I blinked.
'*Neenga Tamil pesuvingala?*'
'I'm sorry, I don't speak Tamil.'
'*Amrika?*'
'No, I'm English.'
'*Yingland*, ah? *Appadiya?!*'
Thrilled to bits, my interrogator clapped his hands above his head and the entire row sitting opposite us hooted with delight and clutched each other's elbows. Apparently I did speak Tamil. The passenger train to Thanjavur was jammed with workers on their way home and our compartment housed a group of eight co-workers, an elderly lady and her two granddaughters, three students and a sticky baby with limbs like sausage links, whose parents had dumped the big-eyed bundle on my lap. This was a large number of people for an area that could comfortably take eight, but four dangled from the luggage racks and one man sat happily on his friend's knee, stroking his leg. If I so much as touched Passepartout's arm every pair of eyes would stare at me, but jiggling around in another man's lap was perfectly acceptable.

The rest of the group squashed against one another, holding briefcases on their laps, tickled by the intruders in their compartment. I felt like the new kid on the school bus. Nobody spoke much English and my limited understanding of Tamil went back to one long and boring summer holiday when my brother and I would call up the speaking clock and pretend to order soft drinks from the automated voice. We would let her finish her tongue-twisting spiel before clearing throats and replying 'Mmm, *rende* Pepsi, *rende* 7Up, *romba* thanks', then collapsing into giggles.

Memories of this early role-play helped when it came to buying things in twos, but at this moment verbal communication was stunted, though gestures were fully operational.

From the mass camaraderie it was evident that the group worked at the same office and this was their regular commute. It was unclear what they did, but they were firm friends despite their ages ranging from early 20s to late 60s. There was also a clear hierarchy. My interrogator, an elderly man with buck teeth, was head boy and sat in the centre of the row. His loyal prefects flanked him and the juniors sat in the overhead racks, open to good-natured bullying, which involved the odd pinch and name calling. Having established that I did not understand Tamil, they combined forces to elicit as much detail as possible, poking at the cameras and pointing at my diary, which I readily handed over.

'Writingwriting,' said one of the prefects.

'Yes, journalist,' I replied, adopting a suddenly ridiculous accent.

'Jhurr-nalist?' said the other prefect. 'Oh-ho.'

A combination of photographs, hand gestures, sketches and passing around the stack of train tickets revealed the nature of our travels to the group.

'*Aiyyo!*' exclaimed the head boy, slapping his palm to his forehead and then thrusting it up at me. It was an elegant expression that meant 'you moron'. The whole compartment broke out into laughter.

'*Appa* name?'

I knew that asking my father's name was a disguised attempt at finding out my caste, which I could not help them with. I had never known it, nor did I care. But in India it is important to establish certain facets early on in a conversation, as it sets the dynamics for the ensuing relationship. To most visitors to India, this is just the Indian way of making conversation, in the way that the English cannot resist discussing the weather, or Americans discussing themselves. In truth, this is often a more measured process. Each question establishes where the other person sits on the social spectrum: surnames give away caste and social standing; jobs indicate earnings and therefore power, as does revealing where you live. Once they have all the answers, they can assign people to categories and gauge how useful the acquaintance will be in the future. In this situation, our new friends were simply having fun with us and I loved their unabashed game. But I, too, could play the game.

'Rajesh,' I said, knowing full well there would be confusion. There was. The head boy frowned and shook his head.

'Monisha...?'

'Rajesh,' I repeated, bringing out my passport to stir things up a little. Four people leant forward, grabbing its corners. Rajesh was indeed my surname, but it was actually my father's first name. Our surname should have been Naidu, but trying to explain why would have been futile. After a few minutes of playing dumb, I conceded.

'Naidu.'

'TELUGU?!' shouted the head boy, his eyes like saucers.

I nodded.

Elated, the entire group cheered. It turned out that we had come upon a compartment of Telugus in the middle of Tamil Nadu. We had also just pulled into Thanjavur. Miserable that the journey was over, I gathered my things, wrestled back my passport and clambered over everyone to the doorway. On the platform we turned back to wave. Three of them had come to the doorway and were taking photos on their phones, while the rest poked heads through the barred windows and waved.

The sun was still asleep when we arrived at the entrance to the Brihadishwara temple, bats flitting overhead. In the damp morning air, the enormous Dravidian structure loomed majestically through the darkness. Known appropriately as the 'Big Temple', the Brihadishwara temple was commissioned in 1010 by Rajaraja Chola, who established the Chola Dynasty that reigned across South India, as a show of his devotion to Lord Brihadishwara, an incarnation of Lord Shiva. The UNESCO World Heritage Site is considered one of India's architectural marvels and was celebrating its 1000th birthday.

Unlike most other temples, the structure is built of granite, using stones that interlock without cementing. It had rained the previous night and the stone was cold under my fingers as I worked my way around a pavilion that housed a serene but hefty, 25-tonne carving of Nandi, Lord Shiva's bull. Above his head was a series of midnight blue and yellow frescoes, scratched and fading, depicting details of the Chola lifestyle.

There was a notable elegance to the temple and its surroundings. It was quiet in colour and demeanour and reflected the majesty of its founders. But like many other Indian sites of wonder, it was home to yet another myth. A favourite story told to visitors was that the shadow of the Vimana, the 66-metre, pyramid-shaped tower above the inner sanctum, never touched the ground, but this also proved to be untrue.

As Passepartout watched the reflections of the tower in the puddles filling the compound, a bell beckoned me into the sanctum that housed Lord Shiva. I reached the front in time for the puja and joined the queue to receive prasad. The priest handed over a ladoo and some dried fruit. I took it with both hands and he held out his hand.

'Ten rupees.'

Bags were forbidden inside the temple and I had no money on my person. He took the prasad back from me and placed it in the hands of the woman next in line, waving me along. To my knowledge, the Vedic origins of prasad were explained as an act of generosity and this was the first time I had ever seen a fee demanded. The hole in my stomach had started to grow again and I jumped down the steps, dragged Passepartout from his puddles and left.

Train 14, the Trichy–Nagore passenger train, arrived late into Nagapattinam, a small fishing town in Tamil Nadu that had been badly hit by the tsunami. There was no particular temple of interest, but I had heard they did the best prawns in South India. It was also home to an old house belonging to my dad's family, which sadly, along with the prawns, I could not find. Across the road from the station was a string of stalls selling fried chicken wrapped in sodden newspaper. It was deep-fried earlier in the day, then refried in a smoking karahi, flavoured with car fumes and garnished with grime from the cook's nails. Clutching a steaming bag and a bottle of Thums Up, we found the hotel and flopped down in front of a Tamil film featuring a man with big hair and red eyes wielding a pole at a man with small hair and red eyes. Passepartout was sulking.

'Is anything the matter?' I asked, fishing out the burnt crumbs from the bottom of the oily bag and wondering whether I should go out and buy another. 'You've been rather quiet for the last couple of days.'

'I'm just really surprised, that's all.'

'By what?'

'You. I never thought someone with your intelligence would be as closed-minded as you are.'

'What the hell is that supposed to mean?'

'I'm shocked that you could condone someone like that fraud and think that it's okay to exploit people.'

'Oh God, not this again.' I scrunched the bag into a ball and hurled it against the door. 'I didn't say I condoned him, just that if someone chooses to believe in something it's not your business to criticise.'

'Yes, and I'm shocked that someone with your intelligence can't use your brain to think, rather than believing in what you do. If you hadn't stormed out of there, I would have.'

'I was pissed off with you for swearing in my face, shouting in public and not being decent enough to just stop the conversation when I asked you nicely. We have very different views about religion and clearly won't see eye to eye, so for the rest of this trip I don't want to talk about it.'

His reluctance to comment on the 'imaginary friends' conversation on the Indian Maharaja, and his constant search for *The Greatest Show on Earth* by Richard Dawkins, now made perfect sense. He was what he called a militant 'devout' atheist, a description that even A.C. Grayling, a renowned atheist, had likened in its impossibility to 'sleeping furiously'. I was not. I was born into a nominally Hindu family, enjoyed rare steak and would have liked to see proof of the existence of a higher power, but that was where it ended. Rites, rituals and following religious doctrine meant nothing to me. Religion was a personal affair and an individual's choice as long as it brought no harm to anyone else. Passepartout demanded that I justify my faith, which was none of his business, and that led me to the conclusion that he and I should no longer discuss religion and sour the rest of the journey.

The morning train journey from Nagapattinam to Trichy passed in silence. The passenger train journey from Trichy to Chennai also passed in silence, as did our time on board the overnight Charminar Express from Chennai to Hyderabad and the Hyderabad–Mumbai Express. At this stage, I no longer cared about the journey, it was the destination that really counted. As the white dome of CST came into view, we arrived in Mumbai on 15 February, on the morning of my unhappy 28th birthday.

6 | Super-dense Crush Load

Mumbai was like a thousand cities poured into one. Stepping onto the platform felt immediately different. You could sense it on your skin and taste it in the air. This was India in its most concentrated form. Delhi was teeming and vast, but its pockets of green offered space to breathe and time to stroll. Mumbai raged unharnessed: if you strolled you would be trampled, or at least knocked over by a cyclist. Even the tendency towards idling was noticeably absent. In Mumbai, everyone meant business and the feeling was addictive. This was our second visit to Mumbai and as the tide of commuters swept its way through the halls of CST, dragging us with it, a familiar thrill heated up my blood – or perhaps it was just an early symptom of malaria. Mumbai was a city of dreams and a city of nightmares, of hopes and of horrors – and I hoped to find the latter on the spaghetti trails of its commuter trains. After a month of smooth rides and few delays, it was time for a journey that would spice things up a little.

So far everyone we had met had issued the same warning: 'Do not in any circumstance attempt to ride the local train, it is not for novices', which we interpreted as an open invitation to do just that. Mumbai's commuter train network, or the 'locals', is notorious for passengers compressed in the open doorways, grazing the roof with their fingertips, inches from certain death. During rush hour, a nine-car rake designed for 1800 standing passengers can often carry up to 7000, known as a super-dense crush load. It was a suicidal exercise in survival that seven million of Mumbai's workers were forced to endure on a daily basis – almost the population of Greater London. The vulnerable nature of their close proximity had made commuters the perfect target for terrorists, who attacked in 2006, hiding explosives in pressure cookers that killed at least 180 people and injured more than 800 in a series of seven coordinated blasts at rush hour.

Mumbai's local trains were certainly not for the fainthearted. Footage of locals floating around on YouTube included a man falling from the doorway, as the cameraman yelped in shock but continued to film. Other clips showed passengers riding on the roof or stretched across windows, like Spider-Man in flares and flip-flops. On two separate occasions, unidentified luggage left behind had been opened up to find, not explosives or forgotten aloo parathas, but the body of a woman: one pregnant, inside a suitcase on a platform; the other tied up in a sack and wedged under a seat. Discovering dead bodies was low on our list of priorities, as was falling out of the door, or falling victim to pickpockets and eve-teasers. But ultimately it was just a ride on public transport. How bad could it really be?

While flicking through a magazine left behind on the train from Hyderabad, I had come across an article about a spa in the suburbs that had recently begun offering a form of icthyotherapy. This was just one paradox of Mumbai. Most of its residents could not afford shoes, while the remainder would happily pay for imported fish to nibble dead skin from their cracked heels. The spa was in the High Street Phoenix shopping mall near Lower Parel, which presented the perfect excuse to test out the trains.

At midday we returned to CST. With its pencil-point turrets, archways and Victorian Gothic architecture, the sprawling structure resembled a cathedral rather than a railway hub. Originally named Victoria Terminus after Queen Victoria, its colonial ties were snipped in 1996 and it was renamed Chhatrapati Shivaji Terminus, after a Maratha warrior, though it was still fondly referred to as VT. It was now also listed as a UNESCO World Heritage Site. Beneath the stained-glass windows, swooping arcs and shitting pigeons we scoured the signs for the train to Parel, from where it was a short walk to the mall. Lower Parel was on a different line, but chopping and changing was a little ambitious for the moment. A driver who had stepped down from his engine to stretch and scratch flashed a smile and pointed to his train to tell us to board.

The carriage was wide and clinically clean, with rows of miniature ceiling fans blowing in sync. Lacquered seats waited patiently to be filled and a woman sat reading in a corner. She looked up, acknowledged us and went back to her book. It was like being on a London tube, but friendlier – and infinitely more hygienic. Train number 19 remained empty until it began to move, at which point a number of men leapt in with ninja stealth, slicked their side partings back into place and sat down clutching carrier bags. This was not how a Mumbai commuter train was supposed to be. Covering the roof was a series of hooked metal handholds that gave the creepy feeling of travelling in a human abattoir. Passepartout stood in the middle of the carriage, swinging from one and gazing at the slums rolling past the doorway. Our cold war had ended after he booked a surprise birthday apology at the Trident in Nariman Point, a victim of the 2008 Mumbai attacks. After five weeks, the first sight of a bathtub, the feel of fluffy robes and a flat-screen TV had calmed all anxieties and we left rejuvenated, taking the tea bags, apples and coffee and lingering in the lobby until the 24-hour internet had run out, along with the receptionist's patience.

Nonplussed by the pleasant journey, we arrived at Parel and made our way through a fruit market, foggy with the warm fumes of jackfruit, and hopscotched across several dug-up sections of road to High Street Phoenix. It was a monster of a multiplex that housed names from Canali and Marks & Spencer to Armani and Accessorize – which sold the same stripy knee socks I had bought in High Street Kensington at Christmas. Clothes shopping in India had come a long way since the mid-1990s trends of Vibe, Weekender and Benetton.

Upstairs, the spa was filled with giggling therapists in loose trousers, tickling one another. Dispersing in an instant, they bowed deeply, taking us into a back room with trickling water, a CD playing bird sounds and a tank of fish darting around waiting to be fed. Sensing food was on its way, they spread back like synchronised swimmers and then shot forward, wriggling their way between toes and clinging to both heels. It was as though hundreds of electrical charges flowed through my soles, which was strangely relaxing, until I realised how insanitary it was to stick my feet into a tank of water filled with numerous varieties of toe skin. I withdrew my now slightly smoother feet. Passepartout was enjoying a foot massage and as one last indulgence we stopped briefly at McDonald's for a McChicken sandwich, which after many weeks of dosai, uttapam and idlis was like heaven in a sesame bun.

❖

It was still bright and there was plenty of time before the evening rush began, when traffic became too gridlocked to cross the roads without ducking dangerously between lorries and roaring buses. We arrived at Parel station, where an overhead clock read 17:35.

Rush hour.

Mumbai's light skies and chattering birds had been misleading. Thinking it was still late afternoon, we were now face to face with the one thing we had been told to avoid. Sickly excitement washed around my stomach.

Hundreds of people swarmed across the footbridge and thundered down the stairs to the platform, but swerved off to the left and right before they reached the bottom. The reason was soon clear. Halfway down the stairs, in the middle of a landing, an elderly lady with her hair pulled into a walnut-sized bun had spread out a square of dirty cloth. Her chappals were placed to one side and she sat cross-legged, cleaning her teeth with one finger. She faced the oncoming masses with an air of enviable nonchalance. In the same manner that cars avoid cows that hold up traffic, everyone curved around her, but not one person raised a question or their temper. Pigeonholing in India is futile; for every rule there are one hundred exceptions. But Indians exercise great levels of tolerance – mainly of each other's idiosyncrasies. Their astounding levels of acceptance go some way to explaining how millions can live in such close quarters without daily outbreaks of civil unrest.

At the bottom of the stairs the crowd was already four people deep. At the back of the platform a man was cutting and serving slices of papaya, the colour of sunsets. Bottles of chilli powder lined the side of his stall, which reminded me of the guavas my grandma used to eat with lemon juice, salt and chilli powder, so I bought a slice and rejoined the crowd. A full 2-metre gap stood between the crowd and the edge of the platform, so we darted in front and parked ourselves in the space. After the Goan coffee incident, this was the second foolish move of our trip.

A 'tick-tick, tick-tick, tick-tick' drew nearer and train 20 came into view. The crowd tensed in anticipation, like a row of runners waiting for a starter pistol. When the nose of the engine reached the platform and the sound of braking and creaking grew deafening, moustaches and sweat-sodden polyester shirts appeared in the doorways, looming larger and higher before they suddenly leapt into the air from the moving carriages and hit the ground running. Before the train had stopped, hordes of men rained down on us with monsoon force, while the rows behind began to heave forward, reaching over our heads to grab the doorways and haul themselves in. The papaya was knocked from my hand and slithered down my leg. Once again the rule was simple: attack or be attacked. Crushed between satchels, stale armpits and wet skin, spitting out mouthfuls of coconut oil-flavoured hair, we managed to push forward and fell into the middle of the carriage.

Bent double and wheezing, I saw that beyond the human barrier at the doorways the carriage had spare seats. The crush was just another one of India's little mysteries. Sitting down, I wiped the papaya from my knee, where a fly was rubbing his legs with glee, and looked around at fellow passengers. Their angst was always short-lived. Moments earlier they had shoved, kicked and elbowed each other in the face. Now they sat, shoulder to shoulder, snoozing, stabbing at phones or staring at me. I stared back. Most became bored and looked away. One brought out his phone and took a photo. It was fair enough. If we could waltz around photographing their daily life, why shouldn't they?

As we neared CST the crowd had dwindled and I was now standing in the doorway, both arms looped around the pole, invigorated by the blast of air. But something looked wrong. The train had come into the station and was already sailing by the platform when pockets of men appeared, inching their way towards the edge, crouched low, satchels over shoulders. Before the train had stopped they took flying leaps into the doors, desperate to bag seats for the train's next journey. Those last seconds became a blur, but Passepartout was rugby-tackled by a mouse of a man wearing bell-bottoms. He threw himself through the doorway while I ducked my head and rolled onto the platform, hoping my skull would not be stamped, if it even survived the impact. Checking for blood and bruises, we brushed ourselves off and gripped hands through the crowds with an air of triumph. So that was rush hour.

After the previous night's bone-crushing venture, I boarded the women's carriage to the airport to collect Ed. Ed was my oldest school friend whom I had known since I was 8. He was passing through India on his way to Australia and I could not wait for him to arrive so we could find a tourist bar, drink Hoegaarden, eat kebabs and gossip. Passepartout was sleeping off a few Kingfishers, so it was a perfect opportunity to experience a women-only carriage. Since our arrival in India I had been stared at continuously as though I had a fist growing out of my head. It did not bother me, as I knew it was out of curiosity, not rudeness, and Passepartout was always on standby as a deterrent to wandering hands. But this time I was looking forward to peace and a chance to read a book without constant questioning and non-consensual frottage.

With a copy of *Five Point Someone* in one hand and a bottle of water in the other, I sat down by a window and a girl in a burka sat down opposite me. As soon as train 21 jerked and moved off, she pulled down the face cover, put her feet up on the seat ahead and opened a copy of *Marie Claire*. Having not quite understood the Hindi dialogue during *3 Idiots*, I was keen to discover the real story. Neha and Hari, the two lovers, were blatantly on the verge of being caught when a scream tore me from the book.

Two women were pushing for the same seat even though there were plenty available further down the carriage. A Punjabi lady, like a pudding in a purple salwar kameez, wedged her buffalo-sized backside into the seat, butting the other out of the way. Her rival, a wiry, dark-skinned hawker with a terrifying expression, had boarded carrying a basket of hair bands, grips and bows, and now used it to bang her on the head. Purple Pudding leapt up and pushed the hawker so her basket fell sideways, tipping the contents all over the floor. I put my book down and turned around to take in the action. As Pudding turned to go back to her seat, the hawker reached forward and yanked her plait. Two other women who had nothing to do with the fight joined in. It had now developed into a full-scale bitch fight, with a couple of offshoot scraps. There was much slapping, along with more hair pulling and jabbering.

Thrilled, but eager not to be drawn into the madness, I turned away and did what any nice English person would have done: I pretended not to notice. Before taking up my book again, I caught the eye of the girl opposite me, who had pulled her burka back over her face and was laughing uncontrollably behind it. The hawker, realising she was outnumbered by angry women with fleshy limbs, squatted down in the middle of the aisle, trying to retrieve bunches of ribbon unravelling across the carriage and ranting to nobody in particular. It was a sorry scene and no one moved to help her gather her things. I caught a reel of pink ribbon as it rolled past and gave her a handful of clips that had scattered under the seat. She smiled and shook her head, revealing a beautiful set of teeth that gleamed like the floral-shaped stud in her nose. At the next station, a crowd had gathered and the women began to trip and fall in through the doorway before the train had stopped. I peered through the bars and saw the stampede stepping over a girl sprawled on the ground. Eventually she picked herself up and adjusted the jasmine in her hair before coming on board. So much for the peaceful journey.

Ed arrived looking far too clean and spruce for a ride on a commuter train and had brought a worryingly high number of bags. As we waited on the platform at Andheri, a dwarf marched past pulling a suitcase behind him, the same height as he was.

'Ooh, can you hire them?' Ed asked.

It was his first time in India and the best method for survival was to throw him in at the deep end. Fortunately, train 22 emptied at Andheri, so we found seats and travelled back into the city undisturbed, with the exception of a troop of hijras who boarded a few stops later and sat in the aisles touching up each other's eyeliner and tapping at Ed's foot.

Struggling with the bags down Colaba Causeway, we passed a restaurant that had placed a sign in the window for the chef's special: 'Roast Tongue in Garlic Potatoes Served Dry'. Ed wretched.

'Love, I was looking forward to proper good curry,' he said, disappointed.

Colaba Causeway was a favourite with tourists and a prime spot for locals looking for iced coffee, chindian food, pizzas and pastries. It was also home to Leopold, the café made famous by the book *Shantaram*. During the day it buzzed with activity: cycle rickshaws kerb-crawled behind tourists buying feathered earrings and browsing bookstalls, art lovers roamed from one gallery to the next and packed dhabas drew chaat lovers from the pavement. At night a different group came out to play. Taxi drivers milled between airport trips, chowkidars dozed on stools and fathers gambled in circles over bottles of dirty spirits, their families asleep on charpoys and mats. Luckily for Ed, we had already scouted out Olympia Coffee House's keema pav and a pair of Indian restaurants near the hotel, called Sher-e-Punjab. They appeared to be run by the same management and were across the road from one another. Both restaurants did excellent keema and parathas. One served alcohol, one did not. The first was popular, the second was not. Above all, they showed the IPL cricket and were jammed full of Indians throughout the day, which was always a good sign.

❖

Before leaving Mumbai, there was one last train to take. Technically it was not in Mumbai and involved taking train 23, the Koyna Express, to get there. A toy train ran from nearby Neral, 86 km from Mumbai, up to Matheran, an unpolluted, woody hill station, the smallest in India, hiding along the crags of the Sahyadri mountain range. It was discovered in 1850 and had originally been used for viewing Mumbai's shipyards. Matheran, whose meaning lay somewhere between 'wooded head' and 'jungle topped', was apparently reachable only by the tiny train that ran on two-feet narrow-gauge lines and had the sharpest curves out of all of India's hill railways. The first fact turned out to be a lie. Matheran was also reachable by taxi, which became our only option after we stopped to feed Marie Light biscuits to a quivering puppy at Neral junction and missed the morning departure.

Taxis only climbed as high as a car park of monkeys leaping from bonnet to bonnet, and then visitors had the option of completing the uphill journey on horseback. None of us wanted to ride, preferring to walk along the rusty red train track in a dutiful homage to *Stand by Me*. From the size of the track, no wider than one side step, the train was minuscule. Matheran had an entry fee of ₹25 per person, to be paid at a ticket hut before setting off on the track leading to the town. I approached the window and handed over ₹30. Reaching down, the vendor snapped up the three tens and pushed back my ticket along with a chocolate bar and no explanation. Confused, I peered down and was about to protest when the puzzle pieced itself together. He had no change and the chocolate was worth ₹5. I wondered how far the bar could move into circulation if I tried to use it to buy a cup of tea on a train. I broke it into pieces and fed it to the monkeys who bounded along behind us, grabbing at our bags, trying to fish out the remainder of the biscuits. Fed up with their stalking, we threw them a bag of Lay's crisps that they tore open, devoured and then licked clean. It only made them keener to stick with us, seeing us now as a mobile tuck shop.

On the way up, a number of single chappals lay buried in the rocks and grass. This was not the kind of terrain for a barefooted climb and we wondered why they had been abandoned. At the top of the hill a baby train sat waiting by a forecourt. A list of timings showed that the last train departed at 16:25, so we vowed to leave an hour to queue for tickets, or, to be precise, an hour to join the scrum.

Breathing deeply in Matheran cleared the fog from my blackened lungs. Although the ground looked like the surface of Mars, trees shaded

the streets and the absence of cars and buses meant that the air was free
from dirt and noise but for the squeals of children on horses and families
running around with ice cream and fudge from Prince Chikki Fudge Mart.
It was more a village than a town, or a giant playground covered in horse
shit. After lunch and a nose through Varanasi Handicrafts, we wandered
downhill towards the public gardens that had a real playground and views
over the valleys. It was evident why the British had used Matheran as a
summer getaway. It was now mid-February and there were no western
tourists, only Indian families and young couples hand in hand.

Worried that the last train would leave without us, we arrived at the
station after tea, where a queue had begun. Blinds were drawn down over
the window and as 60 minutes ticked by, impatient passengers banged on
the glass, then loitered nearby, as though it would speed up the process.
As the crowd grew, so did the width of the queue. Most tickets had been
pre-booked and as this was the last train of the day, there would only be a
handful available. God have mercy on anyone who tried any tricks. In the
meantime, the history on the walls provided valuable entertainment:

BY THE GRACE OF GOD – THE NERAL-MATHERAN
LIGHT RAILWAY –
A BRAIN-CHILD OF THE LATE HONOURABLE
MR. ABDUL HUSSEIN ADAMJEE PEERBHOY
WAS DULY CONSTRUCTED BY HIS RARE
ENGINEERING SKILL
FROM 1901-1907, AT A STAGGERING COST OF
Rs 16,00,000/
FINANCED BY HIS ILLUSTRIOUS FATHER
LATE SIR ADAMJEE PEERBHOY (KNIGHT)
WHO WAS THE THEN OWNER OF THE MATHERAN
RAILWAY.
MR. ABDUL HUSSEIN ADAMJEE PEERBHOY
WAS POPULARLY KNOWN AS 'MATHERAN
RAILWAYWALA'
PRESENTED BY HIS GRANDSON
ADAMJEE ESMAILJEE MOHAMMED ALI PEERBHOY
1983

My own name sounded so boring in comparison.

As opening time neared, people started to slink in at the sides and hand money to those at the front of the queue. Having waited fourth in line for over an hour and with our return home now at stake, I jutted both elbows up and stood firm as a young woman in a salwar kameez appeared at my side. It reached the witching hour and the blind flew up behind the glass. Within seconds the queue broke apart into an angry rabble while the woman next to me edged forward with me, avoiding eye contact. Queuing is a rarity in India but if you are the next in line, you do not stand behind the person being served. You stand next to him. If possible, you stand next to him with one elbow lightly touching his ribs, so that when he moves you are guaranteed your spot.

My turn was next, so Passepartout ducked out of the queue and four people scrambled to take his place. He and Ed watched from the sidelines as a hurricane blew up. Angry Marathi sounded out what could only be the foulest of insults and a man in a baseball cap elbowed me in the back as he grabbed the girl in the salwar kameez and shouted his halitotic abuse into her face. I was beginning to love Mumbaikars. No wonder Mumbai was the centre of the film industry: their natural flair for dramatics was enviable. Even the monkeys had arrived in a group and were pulling distractedly at their tails and watching with interest. Eventually a policeman arrived, blowing his whistle and waving a stick to break up the fight.

It turned out that there were enough seats for everyone in the queue and for the next two hours we wound down the hillside, six to a cabin, touching knees and rubbing elbows. Leaning out of the window, I was horrified to find my view blocked by a row of men hanging from the side of the train, which explained the abandoned chappals seen on the way up. Train 24 was so delicate that I was scared they would weigh down the carriages and pull us all over the verges. A sign in the compartment even warned passengers to 'keep windows open during storms or bogies may get thrown', which Ed loved. Most of the hangers-on had either hopped or fallen off by the time the train was halfway down the hillside, but one passenger had come prepared and was wearing a motorcycle helmet. He had the foresight to bring a helmet, but not to book a ticket.

The ground flattened out and the train rattled its way past a village where mothers pumped water from rusting butts, scraping pans and preparing their evening meal. Kids in khaki shirts wearing no underwear ran alongside waving at the windows, waiting for recognition. It had been a tiring but thrilling few days, and Mumbai had not let us down. Its locals had treated us like family and I knew I would be back, but for now it was time to leave the city and look for a new adventure.

7 | Sexual Healing

As the sun slid down behind the distant hills, the train came to a halt at Karjat and for the next two minutes rocked gently as her bankers were attached. The newly added pusher engines gave the 80-year-old an extra boost to climb up the mountainous route to Lonavala, where she would again pause for breath before continuing to Pune. Her royal highness the Deccan Queen was one of the most well-loved trains of the Indian Railways, known fondly by her subjects as the 'Blue-Eyed Babe'. She sashayed onto the scene on 1 June 1930, as a weekend special service that shuttled horse-race fans from Bombay to Poona. However, she was the reserve of the white sahibs and only by 1943, after Indians were allowed on board, was there considerable demand for a daily service. Gradually, the Queen became known as a husbands' special, carrying commuting men to Bombay and returning them to their families at the weekends. Even today, if her majesty is running late all other trains are pulled to the side to allow her to pass.

Our encounter with the Blue-Eyed Babe was purely by chance. We had planned to take the overnight Mumbai Express from Hyderabad and arrive in Pune on 13 February, but the train was fully booked, so we held back by one day. On the morning of 14 February, over a breakfast of dosai and coconut chutney, I picked up *The Times of India* and read the headline:

Blast Rips Pune's German Bakery; 9 dead, 45 wounded
PUNE: Terror returned to haunt the country on Saturday
when a bomb blast ripped through the city's popular German
Bakery, close to the Osho Ashram and diagonally across from
the Jewish Chabad House, recced by 26/11 suspect David
Coleman Headley, killing at least nine people, four of them
foreigners, all women.

The Osho ashram, now called a resort, was our only reason for
visiting Pune. Bhagwan Shree Rajneesh, or 'Osho' as he later preferred,
was a controversial, self-styled spiritual leader, famed first and foremost
for his fleet of Rolls-Royces and alleged orgy-filled ashrams. He was
born into a Jain family but renounced all religion, developing his own
methods for meditation and cultivating an enormous following, largely
comprising disillusioned westerners. He claimed that his meditational
devices, which included chaotic breathing, dancing and whirling, were
'needed just to clear the rubbish that Christianity has created, and to
bring you to a state of naturalness, simplicity... And from there the only
way is witnessing, which is called, by Buddha, Vipassana.' Vipassana,
which means 'to see things as they really are', had long been on my radar
after a couple of my friends had undergone the 10-day silent meditation
courses and returned in unimaginable states of calm. Why Osho felt
that his forms of meditation were prerequisites for Vipassana was, as
yet, unclear.

On a passenger train from Trichy to Chennai, I had found myself
wedged in next to a lady who had first-hand experience of Osho's talks
from the 1970s. Urmilla wore her hair in a well-oiled plait and smelt
of Pond's Dreamflower powder, the remnants of which greyed the top
of her back. She was working her way through a Tupperware box of
watermelon chunks, pushing seeds out from between her teeth.

'All that he taught has been stripped bare now,' she said, eyeing me as
though it were my fault.

'There's nothing left of his original intentions. These firangi
come here, wear robes for two weeks, then think they've discovered
something.' She paused and eased a couple of seeds out of her mouth.
'All spirituality died with Rajneesh,' she finished, sealing her feelings
with a glob of spit that sailed out of the window, its tail trailing like a
tiny silver comet.

Despite the many stories of Osho's luxurious lifestyle, the brainwashing of his sannyasis and their willingness to be manipulated by his wily ways, I could understand his reasoning behind the abandonment of religion, that being handed a belief system at birth removes an inherent desire to find the truth. Rather than adopting a blinkered belief system about Osho, it was only fair to experience his teachings in person, at his Koregaon Park resort in Pune. In truth, I was desperate to see if it really was a screaming hotbed of sex-fuelled lunacy.

After the detour to Mumbai, the three of us boarded train 25 and arrived in Pune exactly one week after the bombing. During her younger years, the Deccan Queen had been decked out in regal splendour. Her first-class restaurant car was finished in silver oak with zebrawood panelling and glass-topped tables. The second-class dining car was panelled in maple with walnut mouldings. Third-class passengers were not allowed on board. As the British disappeared, so did the Queen's grandeur, and we settled back in the standard chair-car carriage and shivered in the air conditioning. Our fellow passengers were mainly businessmen and office workers, many of whom have asked the Indian Railways to set up wi-fi connectivity and additional mobile and laptop charging points in the dining cars. But despite their gripes, they garland the Queen every 1 June, celebrating her birthday at Pune station without fail. We celebrated our evening journey with the grande dame with a hot veg-cutlet sandwich and a squirt of chilli ketchup, washed down with a couple of cups of tea.

That night, as our auto wound up Pune's North Main Road, we passed a row of figures linking hands like paper-chain people. Their frames were silhouetted against the glow pulsating from a host of candles. It was the remains of the German Bakery and a vigil was taking place to mark one week since the blast. A white board hung from the awning on an angle, painted with the following:

LET US JOIN THE BATTLE TO SAVE OUR HOME
WE LOVE INDIA
THINK + ACT + LIVE & LET LIVE,
THINK BEFORE IT'S TOO LATE…

A wonky black-and-white peace sign had been clipped to the metal barriers that stood shoulder to shoulder, protecting the peace on the pavement from the rage on the road. Four people squatted on the bakery's blackened floor, arms wrapped around their knees. Log-sized candles brimmed with pools of wax until small tears escaped and rolled down their sides as they sank slowly to the floor in mourning. Magenta orchids wilted quietly in a corner, mixed bouquets lay among the wax puddles, and a lily gazed at the photos of a Sudanese student and of a dark-eyed beauty, scrawled with *Rest in Peace, Nadia, My Darling*. Nadia Macerini, a 37-year-old member of the ashram, had been caught in the bombing.

From the latest reports, the Lashkar-e-Taiba (LeT) or 'Army of the Pure' was suspected to be behind the attack, the same terrorist cell considered responsible for the indiscriminate killings at the Red Fort in 2000 and the Mumbai train attacks in 2006. It was almost 9:30 pm and for a moment I considered a world without religion. These crumbled walls would still be standing. The dangling wires would be lighting up the room of Saturday-night revellers, while the Sudanese student and Nadia Macerini would be laughing with their friends instead of gazing out from curling photographs. Perhaps it was not religion but what people did with it that hurt.

At the hotel, Ed and I sat on our bed scrolling through Osho's website while Passepartout washed his T-shirts in a bucket in the bathroom. Ed grinned. 'Is this place gang-bang central or something?'

'Who knows. I've read all sorts of stuff about it, but I guess we can only really know by going there.'

Passepartout walked past and pulled a face as he hung up his laundry. 'I could save you time and money just by looking at that website.'

Ed rolled his eyes.

'That's what we call wiki-journalism,' I replied without looking up. 'Oh look, they have a video showing their whirling meditation.'

'You know me, doll, I'll give anything a whirl,' Ed cackled.

Passepartout snorted, then picked up his cigarettes and walked out, slamming the door.

Ed glanced at the door. 'Babe, how do you put up with that?'

I shrugged. 'You get used to it. And besides, when he's not on his high horse he's actually taken good care of me.'

'Do you know why he's like that?'

'He grew up in a happy-clappy Christian household in a little town in Norway where he and his siblings weren't allowed to read anything other than the Bible or go to the cinema.'

'Unhappy-clappy, more like.'

'It sounded quite stifling and I think he just had an epiphany one day that it didn't work for him any more.'

'Epiphany. Nice choice of words.' He pressed a palm to his chest. 'I've barely been here three days and I can't listen to him. Why don't you go off on your own?'

'I've thought about it. But it wouldn't be fair. We came out here together and I don't want to abandon him. Besides, it's really not very safe for me to travel on trains at night by myself.'

'I'm sure you'd be fine on your own.'

'I would still feel mean. He doesn't have any friends or family here at all, while I'm pretty lucky to have a support system if I need it. It's not an easy country to negotiate alone.'

The following morning we squeezed into an auto to Koregaon Park, the home of the Osho Meditation Resort. Cameras were strictly forbidden, so there was no need for Passepartout to join us. We arrived at the gates and he refused even to get out of the auto, let alone come anywhere near the gates. He sped off to buy train tickets as we approached the reception area, where an Indian man stood behind the desk. He smiled at Ed and handed him some forms, ignoring me.

'We're together,' Ed said.

'Indians register separately,' he replied with a pseudo-Californian accent, refusing to make eye contact. He reminded me of one of my brother's teachers at boarding school, who had spent a short time on sabbatical in Wisconsin and after his return began every lesson with an apologetic 'please eggs-cuse ma yummerican aaaaccent', which he delivered in a heavy Keralan accent.

I pulled out my battered burgundy passport, which matched his robes, and inched it forward under his nose. Flashing a Colgate smile, the autoracist handed over another form explaining that the registration would cost ₹900, which included the bonus of an HIV test thrown in for good measure, and then ₹850 for every subsequent day of attendance. Not to mention ₹5000 per night should we choose to stay on site. After stopping to hug a friend, 'Jazz' (Jaswinder) ushered us over to his colleague to complete the registration. Magdalena was a Bolivian artist with hazel eyes and wide, sloping cheekbones, who had been travelling in India for five months, four of which she had spent at the resort.

'India is so beautiful,' she said, waving a bangled arm at the custom-built waterfalls and the patch of sunshine falling on the potted palms. I glanced at the webcam as it snapped a shot of me with one eye closed.

'I would love to draw your face,' she said, scribbling onto the registration form. 'You should stay for a while and then I can paint you.'

'Why do you do an HIV test on arrival?' I asked.

'Osho encourages free love in the resort so you cannot come in if you are having the disease.' She pointed behind to a small room. 'The doctor is free to do the test now.'

Excited to see a fellow Indian, the doctor broke into a smile, revealing a broken front tooth, and scanned my papers. 'Oh. British.' His face fell and he produced a miniature stapler and clicked the tip of my index finger.

'Are you a doctor?'

'No.' He shooed me out.

Twenty minutes later, declared disease free and fit for fornication, we were now to shed the constraints of our modern vestments and adopt the maroon robes. At first sight the resort's shop looked like a standard grocery store. But beyond the shampoos, soaps and stacks of condoms, it opened out at the back and was manned by a Croatian lady with a crimson snarl and a drooping perm that, like her enthusiasm, had long since lost its lustre. A myriad of maroon and white dresses hung around the room in styles designed to suit everyone – as long as they fell into a category that lay somewhere between slutty Tudor maids and wizards. Trying on a folk dress, I emerged from the dressing room and was pounced on by the Sulking Perm, who deemed it too short to be decent. Her concern was the mid-calf hemline, not that my tightly bodiced chest was struggling to stay within its compounds. Apparently decency only applied to below the knee. Once we had settled on a hippy-skirted sleeveless number, I came out carrying the useless dresses over one arm and Perm started gasping in horror: the hems were touching the ground. Leaping from behind the desk she seized the robes, twisting her hands, muttering something inaudible about dirt and purity and hung them back on the rack. Ed's eyes were shining with delight. Shuffling through a wad of money, I held out a 1000-rupee note to Perm, who recoiled.

'We don't use rupees here. Buy your vouchers at the gate.'

I later overheard that Indian money was considered dirty and germ ridden. Once the vouchers were purchased, the robes collected and our nerves in shreds, all we had to do was return in the morning for a new beginning.

❖

The sun had begun to stretch and unfurl its fingers across the sky and the koels were calling their morning greeting as we arrived for orientation. A comfy-looking blonde woman with smiley eyes and red toenails sparkling from beneath her hemline greeted us at the gates. Tess was an ex-travel rep from Liverpool, who, suffering empty-nest syndrome since her daughters had fled to university, had decided to spread her own wings and come to Pune.

'It's just lovely here, I like it a lot,' she gushed, Scouse scraping the back of her throat. 'I really do think tha' if you wanna get the most outta being here, you should volunteer.'

So the resort ran on free labour. She scrunched her sunburnt nose. 'And it's great 'cos they place you where you're most suited. Having worked in tourism they've got me showing people round and if you choose to work, you get a bit of a discount on your housing.'

Even better. Trained employees paying for the honour of working on site. And they thought it was a great idea. Osho was a genius. Tess and Ed wound their way up the path, deep in conversation about freedom, which involved a lot of hands to the chest and blinking, when a burgundy blur appeared in the distance. It vanished, reappearing again, this time attached to a pair of outstretched arms and a sweep of hair. Through the trees, in a clearing, a handful of people twirled like ballerinas on a jewellery box. Each held one hand to the sky, the other to the ground, their skirts rising and falling in unison. Others were flat on the ground, oblivious to the human tornados twisting above their heads.

'Whirling meditation,' Tess said. 'You keep whirling until you find an unmoving centre in your being.'

Tess brought us to Padma, the group leader, who was handing out leaflets, stopping every few minutes to hug fellow sannyasis passing by. Osho hugs were of a special brand. Not the hearty squeeze and back-rubbing jollity normally shared with friends, but a more deliberate process. Both parties approached with arms spread, placed their heads sideways on each other's shoulders and remained wordless. It was the sort of hug commonly seen at funerals. Others had arrived to join the newbies, including an elderly German man, three pouting French teens, a Dutch couple, two Indian girls with tattoos and two Indian men in their 50s. Padma, a curly-haired nymph from France with tiny hands, a tiny face and a tiny brain, turned to the first Indian gentleman, who was adjusting his robes to hide his belly. Tilting her head to one side, she asked, 'Do you... speak... English?'

'Yes', he replied, 'but I can speak to you in French if it's easier for you.'

During the introduction Padma was joined by Kamini, a Dutch lady with Amy Winehouse eyeliner, who drifted around in a cloud of beedi smoke. She contributed little to the session other than nodding and disappeared halfway through. Satisfied that we were ready to trial the meditation classes on offer, Padma led us, like a line of ants in pursuit of a sugar lump, to the studio across the path.

Slipping off shoes, we went inside. A burst of Bob Sinclar's 'Love Generation' filled the dance studio. *Pum-pum, Pa-da-pum-pum, Pa-da-pum-pum...* and there, alone in the middle of the room, was Kamini, swaying from one bare foot to the other, sweeping bundles of air towards her chest. *Pum-pum, Pa-da-pum-pum, Pa-da-pum-pum...* Those beats were to live on in my subconscious like a Pavlovian nightmare.

'Everyone dance!' Padma called, clapping her hands and raising her arms above her head. Tufts of pale hair peeked out from her armpits. 'Connect with each other with your eyes! Don't smile, greet one another through your eeeeeeeeeeeyes...'

Kamini spun her way over, arms at full wingspan, eyes flashing from under her long fringe. She wore the look of a spider about to eat its young. Halfway through the song, the elderly German gentleman developed a severe cramp and collapsed beneath his weight, his face twisted in agony. 'Feel the looooooooove,' sang Padma, ignoring him as he hobbled alone to the side, clutching his leg.

The impromptu disco was an exercise in shedding inhibitions, which was followed by a medley of music from different countries. As each song played, observers had to copy the native dancers. A tight circle of onlookers formed around the French teens as they struggled to dance to 'La Vie en Rose' and the Dutch couple to a waltz. An iTunes update was in order. Osho claimed that his meditations were scientifically designed for the modern man to allow him eventually to experience the silence of meditation more easily. While dancing, one should become the dance. Just remain alert. Consciously go mad. Be total.

'Anyone English?'

I stayed silent. This time St George would have to take a back seat while I cloaked myself in green and saffron. The four other Indians in the group provided enough mass for me to hide in, while they inevitably threw down some Bollywood shapes. Pushing plugs and changing light bulbs were manageable, but Morris dancing was out of the question. Ed edged his way to the middle of the circle alone, eyeing me with an expression that teetered precariously between pleading and murderous. As the stereo hissed and crackled, John Lennon sang 'It's been a hard day's night... ' and Ed began to move like a dad at a school disco. Riddled with guilt, I broke out of the ring and joined him in the middle to consciously go mad. As the Beatles' voices bubbled on, our dancing became a kaleidoscope of the Mashed Potato, the Shimmy and the Swim – complete with sinking underwater – ending with the Chicken Dance. On the periphery, Padma and Kamini were filled with concentration, holding their noses and flapping their wings. We came to a rest, bowed to one another and slipped back into place.

'You see,' Padma declared, 'we are so conditioned from birth that we are unable to dance like people of other nationalities.'

The grand finale was a video explaining the resort's rules. Gathering cushions, the group settled down together. In one scene, the silent meditation hour is already underway. An Indian man clatters in late, unrolling a giant strip of carpet to sit on. A western woman, to his right, opens one eye in annoyance as he stretches himself out. His feet stink and she curls her nose in disgust. Laughter rippled through our group. He makes a phone call to his mother to ask about the cricket score. Kamini and Padma bent double in hysterics. The message of the skit? Do not disturb others' meditation. It continued in a slapstick fashion, fixated on not touching food with the fingers and leaving the meditation hall should you cough or sneeze.

Free to go, the group disbanded at the end of the video and we wandered around the lush grounds, stopping at an onsite café where we met Tegh, a 24-year-old medical student from Jalandhar, who was training to be an ophthalmologist. Although his matching maroon turban was testament to his faith, he felt no loyalty towards its traditions and was in the middle of his seventh stint of volunteering at the resort's café. He wheeled out the bins, dusted his hands off and straightened up to his full, towering height.

'You know, what Osho says is so beautiful...' He paused and fixed me with a defiant stare. A pair of green ring-necked parakeets landed on the rooftop, edging sideways, nibbling lovingly at each other's necks. '...especially about sex,' Tegh finished.

Bingo.

That his words were so revered by his followers conflicted with Osho's self-declaration: 'My purpose is so unique – I am using words just to create silent gaps. The words are not important so I can say anything contradictory, anything absurd, anything unrelated, because my purpose is just to create gaps. The words are secondary; the silences between those words are primary.' Hanging off words designed to create noise was, at the very least, ludicrous.

'You know,' Tegh said, dropping his voice and glancing into the café, 'when Indian men come here, they are taken to a special meeting at 3:45 pm and given a half-hour talk'.

'On what?'

'The sexual impulses.'

'All men, or just Indian men?'

'Only Indian men. They are so full of sexual impulses they need to be controlled so they don't just grab at all the western women here.'

Anyone would think that western women were a pious bunch, nervous lest they show ankle, chastity belts in place. Together we crossed the grounds and collected in the smoking area by the main restaurant. Ed lit up a cigarette and inhaled deeply. A man I recognised from the video wandered over to the area and approached a slim Japanese girl smoking a slim Marlboro Light.

'Hello, rice grower,' he grinned.

Ed choked on his cigarette.

In the centre of the resort was a general meeting place where a group of helpers sat dotted around to answer any questions from new arrivals. One looked like a younger, gentler version of Woody Harrelson and had a genuine smile, so we introduced ourselves and joined him.

'I'm Narendra.'

'What's your real name?'

'Narendra.'

'Where are you from?'

'I'm from Germany.'

'So what do your friends in Germany call you?'

He paused. 'Helmut.'

Helmut, it turned out, was a camp version of Woody Harrelson who ran a garden landscaping business in Essen. His first trip to the ashram, aged 21, was in 1992 when he came for three days. He left eight years later.

'What are you looking for?' he asked, resting a clammy hand on my arm. His breath smelt of pomegranate. Now we were here, it was worth pulling out all the stops and bending the truth.

'Well, my parents are pressuring me to get married, but I just don't think I'm ready... and it's tough when you straddle two cultures...'

'Oh,' he began, waving his hand round and round as though he had heard it all before, 'you are in the right place'.

He gripped both my hands and jerked them as he spoke.

'You *find* yourself here. *Be* how you want, *with* whom you want, *when* you want. It's a beautiful way of life. You have no constraints, no conditioned expectations. If I wake in the morning next to my partner and I look at her and think, "I no longer want to wake next to you", it is OK. It is so liberating.'

Ed had been listening quietly. He leant forward, touching Helmut on the wrist.

'I just wondered, how much of the fees go to charity or local projects?'

'Well, you know, it's so expensive to run the resort. The electricity alone is a crazily huge bill every month and also to maintain the beautiful grounds is very costly.'

We thanked Helmut, who encouraged us to volunteer and placed a healthy kiss on Ed's neck as we all three hugged and held one another closely.

Across the compound, the Kundalini meditation session was about to begin in the Osho auditorium, a 28 metre-high, soundproof, air-conditioned pyramid, built to house scores of meditators. Keen to take part, we scooped up our robes and raced over, as entry was forbidden even five seconds into the meditation hour. Stragglers were running across the bridge to the pyramid, designed deliberately across a stretch of water to remind people to leave their minds on one side before going in. Just as we reached the door, Perm stepped out from the shadows and, like a Power Ranger, crossed both arms in the air to show that we were no longer allowed in. Spotting another door at the end of the corridor, Ed ran down, wrenched it open and, before she had time to react, we slipped inside.

Two hundred pairs of feet bounced lightly on the floor of the enormous hall, causing the entire room to vibrate. It was a pleasant feeling and the idea was to allow the sensation to enter through your feet, until you eventually became the shaking. This soon grew a bit dull and I was glad when the second stage began, which involved dancing any way your body wished to. As the third stage commenced, which involved 'witnessing whatever was happening' – inside and out – I sensed something behind me. Turning around, I witnessed a blindfolded girl kicking and thumping at the air, wrenching at her blonde hair. She went through a routine of punching to the right, then kicking to the left, before grabbing fistfuls of her hair and yanking her neck from side to side. Ed had moved away from her and was lingering nervously by a pillar. For the last 15 minutes we lay down in silence and I dozed off amid a symphony of farts. As we left the auditorium and wandered back across to the main compound, I felt quite calm, but no more so than when I had first arrived. Feeling peckish, we stopped at a self-service café for a croissant and a cup of coffee. From the varieties of marmalade, fig jam and tahini, I picked out a jar of Nutella and spooned a dollop onto my plate, before licking the spoon clean and looking around for a place to leave it. A server walked past as I waved the spoon, snatched it from my hand and shoved it straight back into the jar, forbidden germs and all. Ed almost had a seizure.

Dusk was falling and the mynahs were muttering quietly to themselves as the sky took on an eerie orange glow. A stream of followers floated past in white, their maroon robes nowhere in sight. It was almost time for the highlight of the day, the Evening Meeting of the White Robe Brotherhood, which the leaflet described as 'a unique opportunity to experience alertness with no effort'. Ed and I arrived back at the main gate and, experiencing alertness to the first auto rickshaw, flagged it down with no effort and sped away as fast as its dinky motor could go.

8 | The Crazy White Man in the Cupboard

Serendipity had so far graced us with her presence when it came to stumbling across quirky trains. First Delhi museum's toy train, then the Deccan Queen and now, as we crossed the overhead bridge in Pune Junction, a multicoloured train awaited our arrival. After the hasty departure from the Osho ashram, we decided to leave Pune earlier than planned and the only train to Delhi running on a Tuesday, with last-minute tickets available, was the Pune-Nizamuddin Duronto Express. It chopped a whopping six hours off the 26-hour journey, which may not have seemed like much, but it was always the last few hours that triggered involuntary rocking and made the compartment feel like a padded cell. We were due to arrive into Delhi just after 7 am, so there was barely time to wake up and get off, let alone wake up and moan. Train 26 was less than six months old and was part of a new fleet launched by Mamata Banerjee, the railway minister. Shatabdi Express trains are currently the fastest trains on the railways, but the Durontos – which meant 'quick' in Bengali – ran a non-stop service between each station, cutting down overall journey times.

Among the row of trains lined up below the bridge, the Duronto was impossible to miss. It looked like a metallic version of *The Very Hungry Caterpillar*. Fuzzy strokes of green, yellow and orange covered its outer walls with a pair of blue runner's legs painted in the middle, indicating the speediness of the new trains. The Duronto Express looked as though a bunch of toddlers had been given licence to scribble all over the carriages with wax crayon, but it later emerged that the vinyl wrap had been created by Mamata Banerjee, based on her own artistic designs.

Ed waited dutifully with the bags while we trawled the list of names stuck by the door to our carriage. Having left it late to book tickets and sent Passepartout to the station to do the honours, we had three confirmed seats but only one confirmed berth. This was no reflection on Passepartout's skills when it came to filling in forms and standing in queues, but his ability to bat his eyelashes and look helpless was largely inferior when compared with what I had now developed into an art form. In too many ways being a woman in India was still an enormous struggle, but I had gradually come to realise that if defiance and feminist force did little more than to make men laugh, then the only way to sidestep difficulties was to manipulate the situation.

Passepartout and I were double-booked into one sleeper, which was not a huge problem, but Ed was sharing seat 41 with a 'Mr Harpal Singh, 61'. This was the first time in 26 train journeys that our waitlisted berths were not confirmed and it came at a time when we were travelling with someone unaccustomed to Indian trains. After cheating someone else out of tickets in Coimbatore, our karmic fate had finally come round.

To his credit, Ed had survived Mumbai's commuter trains, which many Indians refused to take. At rush hour he had stood sandwiched between skinny chests and bouffant hair, clutching his bag. His eyes bulged and he occasionally let slip shouts of manic laughter. It seemed to be the only way to deal with impossible situations, and as a British Airways air steward he had substantial experience in handling obnoxious travellers. Ed's shock absorbers had scored highly, but a 20-hour journey to Delhi was a test of stamina and endurance. Maternal responsibility took over and I felt it only right to ease him into each new situation, especially as he was visiting me in my motherland, so I began a cagey description of how Indian train journeys could sometimes be rather drawn out and uneventful. 'Bit like Chinese water torture, then,' he had said, and gone back to watching *Gossip Girl* on his iPhone. Incidentally, the Duronto Express from Pune to New Delhi proved to be neither drawn out nor uneventful.

Once the train was on the move it seemed wise to find Harpal Singh and stake Ed's legitimate claim to one half of the seat, at least until night time, when the stand off would begin as to who got to sleep in the full berth. Unfortunately his seat was in the adjoining carriage, away from ours, which would make it difficult to shuffle people around. Scouring the numbers on the walls, I arrived at seat 41. It was occupied by a Sikh gentleman sitting cross-legged and picking at his foot. A mound of dead skin sat at the side of one heel and he looked up and fixed me with a pair of bloodshot eyes. An attempt at bartering would be futile. Harpal Singh, 61, was the last person in the world who would fancy sleeping top-and-tail with Ed and I doubted Ed would want to share his makeshift chiropody clinic.

The train ticket examiner, or TTE, came through the carriage and declared that the train was full and no spare berths were available. He flared his nostrils and gave his moustache a tweak before carrying on to the next over-crowded carriage to bear more bad tidings, trailed by a trio of seatless passengers with 500-rupee notes slotted between their fingers. Defeated, we settled into the single berth, which Passepartout had given up so Ed and I could share. He then disappeared to the doorway, where he struck up conversation with Virender Verma, whose nametag read BED ROLL ATTENDENT, in the hope that he may be able to pull a few strings at night.

Outside the open doors, warm wind whipped by as the train thundered past the dry Maharashtrian landscape. Swinging off the edge of the step was a well-built twentysomething wearing mid-calf shorts and sporting a carefully trimmed goatee. Edwin was originally from Cochin, but lived in Pune and travelled to Delhi for work. This 20-hour journey was his twice-weekly commute. Never again would I complain about the Jubilee line. Edwin was one of many regular commuters between Pune and Delhi, relieved by the launch of the Durontos, which made his life that little bit easier. Tickets were also cheaper than the regular Rajdhani trains that normally did the run. Edwin was assigned to the berth directly above us and did not mind sharing his seat with two others during the day, even if it meant putting up with Ed's Europop and the pack of melted Twix bars he had brought over on request, now smeared into the seat.

Five hours had passed since our breakfast of omelette and ketchup sandwiches and Ed had begun to roll the ends of the Twix wrappers, squeezing out the melted chocolate like toothpaste, when a member of staff came through handing out packets of salt and pepper. Neither could be eaten, but they ignited hope that food would soon be along. Moments later he came through again and distributed packets of Amul butter and a couple of breadsticks. A lady in the opposite compartment gnawed through her breadsticks like a gopher, then ate the butter separately, rubbing it along her gums with one finger. On the third occasion, the server brought a box of chilli tomato soup and Ed visibly relaxed as it steamed in his hands.

So far we had mainly travelled on express and mail trains where food was not included in the price of the ticket, so soup and breadsticks were a luxury. A lunch of mutton curry, dal, rice and rotis arrived on plastic purple trays and I pulled out my Osho robe to use as a tablecloth. Ed said his robes had freaked him out and he had refused to pack them into his suitcase, preferring to kick them into a corner of the hotel room. Edwin rooted around the bottom of his bag and produced a bag of fried fish, which he offered up. He then revealed that it had been packed in Cochin and I politely declined. My stomach had toughened, but I knew better than to play with fire – even if it smelt delicious.

Meanwhile, Passepartout had struck up a deal with the bed-linen man. Virender had gone and, with the coast clear, an older attendant had agreed to let Passepartout sleep in his cupboard, setting the ambitious starting price of 500 rupees. He was an unshaven man, with hanging jowls covered in white stubble, and was a shrewd opportunist. Between each carriage was an area with a sink, two toilets – one western and one Indian – and a set of metal cupboards containing bedding. Western toilets housed a porcelain pot and were to be avoided at all costs. The seat was either broken or missing and at least one long mustard stain slid down the side. Indian toilets were classic holes in the ground that were cleaner and much easier to use during train travel, but both stank. Aside from obvious pollution, the open toilets also contributed indirectly to railway collisions. Acid from waste falling directly onto the tracks caused premature corrosion of the metal, weakening them long before their time.

Edwin shook his head, laughing. 'Five hundred rupees? Is he mad? That bed guy is pulling a fast one!'

'I know, but he's letting Ed share with me, and now he has nowhere to sleep,' I replied.

'Five hundred rupees is crazy, he shouldn't indulge that dirty fellow.'

'But he has to sit up all night, at least we get to share one.'

'You don't have to share, you can take mine. I always work at night and I have plenty of stuff to get through, I don't mind sitting up.'

'That's really kind, but not fair.'

'*Cheee cheee*, it's okay, really I don't mind. I have my lappy, I can work.'

Ed was eyeing me with a look that said, 'Shut it, woman, this way we can both sleep comfortably.'

Through the windows the terrain had transformed in the last hour, flattening into a red stretch that shimmered in the heat. White pyramids shot past in succession – salt mounds drying out in the sunshine. By teatime the train galloped past cliff faces and over canyons, where the outlines of once thick rivers wormed their way along, now just streams waiting for a monsoon to restore their health. Since the Kerala Express, few other journeys had included such varied topography, so the Pune-Nizamuddin Duronto Express ranked highly in our esteem. Even the interiors were upgraded. Nifty bottle holders replaced net pockets and LED panels had ousted the rusty metal light fittings that often scraped the back of my head.

At Bharuch, a soft-spoken man with a boyish face came to the doorway with his hands behind his back and watched as the Gujarati town sailed past. Nitin Das was a filmmaker who had made a film called *The Magic Feather*, which featured seven short stories set in Mumbai. Deliberately showing a side to Mumbai that rivalled the pessimism of *Slumdog Millionaire*, his film included short, spunky tales about magic and mischievous kids, revealing a lighter, brighter side to Danny Boyle's city, which reeked of evil. He had released his film online to raise money for NGOs helping street children, many of whom acted in his films.

'Did you visit Mumbai?' Nitin asked.

I described the rush-hour incident and he giggled.

'Did you go to see the slums at all?'

For a few years now, a tour had been running through the Dharavi slum in Mumbai, Asia's largest, which allowed curious tourists to witness the inner workings of the district and learn that there was a lot more to the community than open sewers and despair. From biscuit baking and pappadum making to pottery and leather tanning, visitors could observe the small-scale industries of an area whose annual turnover was approximately £410m. Eighty per cent of the profits after tax from the tour tickets went towards a community centre that provided schooling for Dharavi's residents. It was a worthwhile venture in erasing misconceptions about slum dwellers, but I had personal reservations about paying for the privilege to pry, then leaving in an air-conditioned car.

'So where are you travelling to next?' Nitin asked.

'Well, after Delhi we want to get to Khajuraho for the classical dance festival.'

'You know there's one direct train now from Delhi? Just a while back it started.'

'I was told you had to go via Jhansi, then drive?'

'No, I assure you there is a train, but you may have to check as it might be booked for the festival.' He smiled. 'Have you heard of Orchha?'

'No.'

'You must visit, it's a quiet place on the way to Khajuraho. When you approach it, it's completely covered in green and if you look closely you can see the tops of temples and shrines for miles. It is so beautiful.'

Orchha was now on the list.

Ed was beginning to look restless just as dinner arrived, which proved a timely distraction, and he made his way happily through chicken curry and dal, but made a great show of edging away the tub of ice cream. For his own good, I had forbidden Ed from eating ice cream for fear that he might fall ill. Not ill with a sore throat and cold – which Indians seemed to think were acquired not through viruses, but by drinking cold water and eating ice cream – but ill with a bad stomach. During power cuts ice creams often melted and were then refrozen and melted again on numerous occasions, making them potentially lethal to weak stomachs. On my way back from the toilet, I caught him quietly licking the lid and he flicked it away. 'My tongue needed cooling after that curry.'

Bit by bit, ladies in the compartment began to button up their cardigans and, much to Ed's delight, pull on woolly hats and knee socks. Bedtime was approaching and they were preparing themselves for the 'chilly' night. Outside in the foyer Passepartout was in the middle of his own bedtime shenanigans. The linen cupboards had been emptied of bedding, now distributed to passengers. A few sheets remained, lining the base of the cupboard that resembled the kind of box magicians' assistants were sawn in. His bag was already in one end and now he placed one foot on the edge of the door and tried to haul himself in without banging his head. He slotted one leg in, then carefully pulled in the other and lay down. He looked like he was in a coffin. I drew the door up to his neck just as an elderly man came to clean his teeth. He bent over the sink and cleared the back of his throat and nasal passages before hacking out the contents and gargling. As he looked up in the mirror he caught sight of Passepartout's head poking out of the cupboard, where he was now propped up holding a torch and reading a copy of *A Fine Balance* in Norwegian. The man's eyes flew out on stalks and he began to choke and laugh at the same time. I smiled politely and the man walked wordlessly towards the door, looking back over his shoulder until he was gone. The door flew open a second later and two children came tumbling through, looking for the Crazy White Man in the Cupboard. Once the show was over, Passepartout fished a warm Kingfisher out of his bag and waved me off to bed.

Ed and Edwin were deep in conversation when I came back, trying to work out how three people could take it in turns to sleep in two beds through a period of eight hours. Given that, among three of us, we had three undergraduate and three postgraduate degrees, none of us could work out the answer.

By the morning I had slept for less than an hour. Climbing down from the berth I found Ed, his body contorted into an unnatural coil, his head resting on a copy of *Intimate Adventures of an Office Girl*. Edwin was sliding off the end of the seat, his chin on his chest and one elbow across his face. Passepartout was hunched by the door and looked like he had died during the night and then been frozen. The doors were wide open and the train was rolling quietly past the backs of Delhi's slums on approach to the station. It was nearing 7 am and it was too early to consider complaining. As we hopped down the steps, Ed shivered.

'Bloody hell, Delhi's not warm, is it?'

At least he was still talking to me after his first proper Indian train journey, so I considered the feat a great success.

From the auto we peered between the bags on our laps, watching Delhi's roadside activity. Mothers soaped children under water butts and young men wound up their lungis and washed, using no more than a few metal pots of water. They might have been oblivious to general filth and squalor, but Indians' morning cleansing was a religious rite. Cleanliness came next to godliness, but most Indians consider baths disgusting and you would struggle to find a tub in an average home in India.

At home, Indian mothers blanched as English mums dumped their entire brood into shallow water before bedtime, allowing their children to wallow in their own dirt. In the morning they would be bundled straight out of bed and into their clothes, then sent to school with little more than a wet flannel across the face. By contrast, Indian kids woke up to thunderous showers, or baths using a mug dunked into a huge bucket. The grand finale involved filling the bucket to the top and tipping the entire load over your head, yelling as the cascade tumbled mostly over the side of the tub. Ed took one look at the bucket in my cousin's bathroom in Delhi. 'What do you do with that?'

Ed's flight to Sydney departed mid-afternoon, after which Passepartout and I went to visit an old friend. She was seated at her desk, her head bent over a prayer book in her lap. We crept up, slid into the opposite seats and waited until she had finished her page. She closed the book and looked up.

'Oh my God, you are here again!' Anusha Thawani laughed and slapped her forehead, though I detected an undertone of fear pricking her voice. It was only 3 pm, so she had no excuse for abuse and seemed to be in a perky mood.

'Here, take some forms, fill them in and give me.'

Nitin, the filmmaker, had provided useful information and there was indeed a new train travelling directly from Delhi to Khajuraho that Anusha tried to reserve. But as he had predicted, it was fully booked due to the dance festival and we would have to travel there via Jhansi. After Khajuraho, Orchha and Jhansi, our plan was to swing west to Ahmedabad and snake across Gujarat to Dwarka, the westernmost tip of the railways. Anusha booked us onto the Bhopal Shatabdi from Jhansi back to Delhi so that we could experience the fastest train on the network. Anusha was a good sport. Our lack of knowledge gave her the chance to feed us titbits of information that gave the journey a good shake-up. She handed over a new stack of tickets and waved us away.

'We're coming back again, you know,' I called over my shoulder.

'Oh God,' she wailed, fanning her dupatta across her face.

Ten years ago, Passepartout had lived briefly in New Delhi and he was now itching to visit his old house in Rajendra Nagar. A long, dusty auto ride was unappealing, as was the prospect of sitting in traffic for two hours. Even though it was not a member of the Indian Railways, the Delhi Metro provided the perfect mode of transport and, more importantly, meant that one more train could be ticked off the list. In terms of position, Central Secretariat seemed to be the equivalent of Oxford Circus and a sensible place to start. The metro was also one of the few bits of Delhi that truly functioned. Most of central Delhi was under tarpaulin or behind barriers in preparation for the Commonwealth Games. If preparation meant scratching bellies and strolling between inert cement mixers, swinging a child's bucket and spade, then they were doing a fine job.

An orderly line of people floated down the escalator, which had a sign politely reminding passengers that, in addition to not sticking feet and fingers into the mechanics, shoes must be worn at all times. The station gleamed. Its neatness had rubbed off on passengers who had formed a real queue, one behind the other, waiting to buy tickets. Only tickets were not used on the metro. Having collected all our stubs to date, in a growing pile of colours and perforated edges, we had to make do with the Ludo token that popped out of a machine and was then swallowed at the turnstile.

Security was high, bags were searched and scanned and cameras forbidden. We scoured the platforms, crouching low on the hunt for discarded sweet wrappers and gum, to no avail. A space-age machine slid up to the platform and I braced myself for the big push. It never came. Waiting passengers stepped to one side as the doors opened and they allowed others to descend before boarding. After the group had moved in, I spotted a row of arrows painted on the floor that directed passengers into an orderly queue. With a little bit of guidance, passengers were willing to abide by rules that made their own lives easier. Either that or I was still asleep on the Duronto Express and would wake to find it all a dream.

Before the doors slid shut again, we stepped into train 27 along with a pigeon who hopped in for a ride. Now here was a glimmer of India Shining. Inside was wide and spacious, signs were digitised and, above all, the carriages were air-conditioned. A yawning gentleman sat in a seat by the doorway, his topi at a jaunty angle, below a sign saying 'Ladies-Only'. Another gentleman standing by the doors kept his balance by inserting one finger into a hole for the air conditioning, but the compartment was otherwise empty. Ten minutes into the ride, the train reached Rajendra Nagar and we jumped off, greeted with a hug of humidity on the platform.

Passepartout barely recognised his old apartment, but received a thorough drenching from an old washerwoman who flung the soapy contents of her tub over a top-floor balcony just as he strode past. He pretended not to notice, though his shirt was stuck to his skin, while I squatted behind a parked car and cried tears of silent laughter. I missed Ed.

Just as train 28, the Sampark Kranti Express to Jhansi, creaked and began to move, I panicked and pushed my nose to the window. Passepartout had got off to find water and was nowhere to be seen. A grandfatherly gentleman with soft, red cheeks and leaky eyes was staring at me, and had been since we boarded. Pretending not to notice, I watched him go through a laborious process of checking his pockets for his glasses, opening the case, polishing the lenses with a handkerchief, putting away the box and pushing his glasses onto his nose. Once he had finished, he stared at me properly, then beamed, his toothless mouth flopping into a loveable smile.

'Where is your friend?' he asked.

Confused, I looked around. He had boarded after Passepartout got off and our bags were hidden away, so how he knew there should be two of us was odd, but quite exciting. I hoped he was a soothsayer. At that moment Passepartout burst in, after jogging to catch up with the train. He sat down, out of breath, and grinned, clutching two bottles of water.

'Aha!' The man raised a finger in the air. 'I knew I recognised you,' he lisped, 'you were sleeping in the cupboard on the train from Pune.' He laughed and slapped his thigh. 'I might be getting old, but I'm not senile yet.'

The journey to Jhansi flew by and an auto ride from the station brought us to the town of Orchha, a set of sandy crossroads where the only sound came from the bells of the Hanuman temple ringing in the distance. Once home to the Bundela kings, the palace in the centre of the town looked like a lonely version of the City Palace in Udaipur. Its cream walls were stained with black as though it had endured a great fire, with nobody but vultures as survivors: they slouched on the tips of domes, gathered on turrets, or squatted on balconies like feathered gargoyles, fending off visitors. Beyond the walls, an emerald forest carpeted the land for miles with tips of turrets poking up in between the treetops, the remnants of broken shrines, bouncing back the last of the evening sunshine.

Down the main street, stall owners had settled cross-legged before pyramids of powders, as though an industrial chemistry experiment was about to take place. A puff of sky-blue powder shot up like a mushroom cloud and ripples of laughter broke the stillness as a group of Rin-soap-coloured teenagers appeared from around the corner, reaching out to smear handfuls of turquoise over each other's hair, faces and necks. A sheet of yellow spray came flying out from behind a wall as two girls darted across the street, splashed like rainbows with white teeth.

And so began the festival of Holi. Despite its Hindu origins, Holi is deemed one of the more secular festivals in India and is a celebration of spring. Its raucous and relaxed nature appeals to every faith, class and caste and it is impossible not to be sucked into the tornado of colour and noise. Over a banana lassi, we watched as scores of teenagers ran through the streets flinging colours in the air, heralding the change of season when new shoots grew, buds burst open and winter was forgotten. Despite our quirks, Passepartout and I had ironed out our differences and now seemed as good a time as any to forget the old, wave goodbye to the cold and welcome in the new.

9 | Sunburn and Spasms

A skinny figure crept against the wall, darting from shadow to shadow, then peered over the balcony. He ducked and slowly peeked through the bars.

'Fack!' he cursed, jumping back into the middle of the terrace, where he took a packet of Davidoff cigarettes from his pocket, pulled out a Gold Flake and parked it on the edge of his lips. Thinning his eyes, he blew a smoke ring into the air, then edged back over to the balcony and looked down again. The boy was wearing a baggy T-shirt and drainpipe jeans that hung off his ballerina-sized waist. It was as though he had shrunk in the wash and his clothes no longer fitted.

'What are you doing?' Passepartout asked.

'Fishing,' came the stony reply. His racoon eyes followed a movement below the balcony.

'Oh, I didn't realise you could fish near here, where do you go?'

'No,' he smirked, *'fishing.'* He made a reeling-in motion as two European girls in vest tops walked by below. I looked down to where the main street was quietening for the evening. Hurricane lamps and bald bulbs dangling from wire lit up stalls curtained with beads and stacked with pottery, lamps and statues of Hanuman. A girl with bleached hair coiled at the nape of her neck was turning over an oil lamp, her shoulders shining in the light. Her friend paid for a necklace and put it on, allowing the pendant to slip into her cleavage. The boy's eyes gleamed. Both girls walked into our hotel and he leapt back again.

'Ah fack!' he cursed, tottering around in a circle and rummaging in his pocket for his phone.

'What's the matter?' I frowned.

'I've double-booked a date tonight.'

He looked no more than 16. Passepartout spat a mouthful of beer back into the bottle.

'So, which one is first?' he asked.

'The bald one,' the boy grinned, referring to the girl with cropped brown hair and the motherly bosom. 'European girls are easy, they sleep with one guy one night and then another guy the next night. I love being here, I have a different one every night – but I didn't know those two were friends. I'm doing the other one later.'

Ricky Joshi was 22 and lived in Khajuraho, but his 'business' brought him to Orchha. He claimed his father was a retired cardiothoracic surgeon and his mother an ex-law professor, who now ran a shop in Khajuraho. Ricky was pally with the owner of our hotel, who allowed him to lurk on the terrace at night, supplying potent charas to grateful guests, a couple of whom were flopping about in the shadows.

'So what do you do for a living, then?' Passepartout put down his bottle and dragged his chair closer to listen.

'This and that… everyone knows me in Khajuraho. You just have to say "Ricky Joshi" and anyone will tell you where you can find me. So, Indian girl,' he winked, 'what are you doing here?' He pointed his cigarette at Passepartout, who was laughing behind his laptop. 'You two a couple or what?'

'No.'

He briefly leered at me, then ignored me and turned to Passepartout.

'Indian girls are a nightmare.'

'Why?'

'They just want you to say you love them. You have to say that shit to them or they won't get into bed with you. They're a pain in the ass.'

I looked up over my book. 'Maybe that's because once you're done, you bolt to the next blonde you can find.'

He took this as a compliment, bobbing his head and lighting another cigarette. 'So how long are you staying here for?'

'We're leaving tomorrow for the Khajuraho dance festival.'

'It finished last week.'

'What?'

'Yeah, they moved it.'

Suddenly the little town drowned in blackness as a power cut hit. Dotted along the street were halos of light from candles in doorways and stoves browning late-night rotis. A cloud sailed by overhead, revealing a milky moon that spilt a patch of light across the terrace, as the resident Roadside Romeo began a story about his night with two Cathay Pacific air hostesses. I took the opportunity to bid goodnight to Mr Joshi, while Passepartout amused himself for a little longer.

No trains ran between Orchha and Khajuraho, forcing us to take a shared taxi. It was apparently owned by Ricky, who was skulking under a nearby tree watching two girls with rucksacks climb out of an auto. The long car journey made me realise that my growing clinginess to the comforts of train travel was pulling me towards professional laziness. It had also allowed me to develop an affinity for poking my nose into strangers' affairs, a habit less sustainable in taxis and buses. An Indian train ticket was a permit to trespass on the intimacies of other people's lives and certain improprieties became instantly acceptable: tearing strips of chapatti from a man I had known for five minutes; sticking my fingers into the masala potato his wife had lovingly packed that afternoon; lying in bed watching a dishevelled stranger mutter and twitch in his sleep; eavesdropping on boyfriend troubles and mother-in-law disputes; or joining a wedding party, clapping and singing along as their gifts of glass bangles slipped over my elbows. Finally, my destination would tap at the window, rudely interrupting and heralding a curtain call on the show. Cramped, thirsty, carsick and bored, we arrived in Khajuraho after three hours of pining for open doorways, tea and a couple of bent paperbacks.

Khajuraho was a town where time ambled along. Cows strolled by swinging their loose neck skin and shop owners squatted on pavements, watching the sun rise, then watching it set. Its previous residents were markedly busier. The Chandela Dynasty of Rajput kings, who rose to power ruling Central India during the early tenth century, had established their cultural capital here and commissioned the carving of the temples. According to local historians, there were originally 85, but abandonment and ruin meant that only 22 had survived. Over time, dense jungle had crept around the sandstone structures, gently cradling them out of sight from marauding Mughals who had rampaged through numerous other clusters of Hindu and Jain temples. But in 1838, T.S. Burt, a British army officer, came upon the ruins, and so began their restoration.

Ricky was right: the classical dance festival, which took place against the backdrop of the western temples, had been brought forward by a week and there was neither a kohl-rimmed eye nor a bell-covered ankle in sight. Preened gardens lined with hedges and rose trees criss-crossed around the temples, which, in the fading light, took on the colour of toasted almonds. Each structure sat on an elevated platform with a tiered tower shrinking towards the tip, capped with a round carving, like a stone Tam o'Shanter. Wrapped around each wall and carved into the stone were rows after rows of leggy figures, wearing nothing but jewellery, weaponry and expressions of indifference. Unlike the delicate faces at Ellora, these figures had square heads, heavy jaws and wide-set eyes, but swayed softly, tilting their hips in unison, in a rippling wave of seduction. Not only were the Chandelas gifted craftsmen, they also had boundless optimism for the potential of coitus: each line of erotic figures was engaged in a variety of sexual acrobatics that would have made the most hardcore porn star feel like a prude.

An elderly guard wearing a moth-eaten beret beckoned us around a wall and waved his stick at a row of carvings that featured a particularly fruity group who, during their ambitious exploits, had enlisted the help of a horse and were repaying the animal in kind. The guard waggled his eyebrows and coughed a phlegmy laugh. Most of the carvings looked like the results of copious amounts of alcohol and an ill-advised game of naked Twister. Not one orifice was left unfilled.

Four local studs wearing eye-wateringly tight trousers and tank tops were hovering in front of a spicy subject who was bent over, clutching her ankles, while her mate held her in place with one fingertip on her back. Two of the group linked pinkie fingers and giggled like girls, while the other two took photos of the carvings on their phones. It was the provincial alternative to hovering after school by the top shelf at a newsagent. Sex was such a taboo in India and the temples were an anomaly in a culture that condemned sexual expression and eroticism, and yet centuries ago, their ancestors had heartily embraced their sexuality – and that of their pets.

A peach haze had emerged from behind the treetops and an oversized moon drifted upwards as we left the grounds and made our way across the road. A cycle rickshaw driver spotted us and swung his rickshaw round, zigzagging towards us to give us a lift. Templed out, we slid into the back and watched guiltily as his legs pumped up and down like pistons, his backside never touching the seat. A kid on a motorbike soon drew up and slowed down to chat.

'Hello... from?'

'England.'

'Oh, you seen the temples?'

He switched off the engine and pushed himself along with his sandaled feet, so as to move at our pace.

'Yes,' I replied, then a thought popped into my head. 'Do you know Ricky Joshi?'

'Yah, I know Ricky.'

'How?'

'He's that guy who cheats tourists all the time.'

'Really? Why, what does he do?'

The boy grinned and shook his head. 'I'm not telling.'

'Why not?'

'Because he does the same things I do. It would give away my secrets.'

The driver reached out to slap the boy away, catching the side of his head as we arrived back at the Usha Bundela hotel, where Passepartout was dismayed to discover he had head-to-toe sunburn, the colour of Alaskan salmon.

The following afternoon, I came down to the forecourt of the hotel where an old Maruti van was waiting to take us to Jhansi station. My heart sank; it often did when faced with long-distance car or bus journeys in India. A lack of seatbelts and drivers sitting sideways with one foot tucked under them, determined to under- and overtake every vehicle from bulging buses to solitary cyclists, gave cause for a series of mild heart attacks. It did not help that spaced out along the highways were the ominous remnants of burnt-out trucks and buses nose down in ditches. It was safest to try to fall asleep at the beginning of the journey and hope that if I ever woke up, it would be at the destination and not in intensive care.

Dry afternoon heat twinned with Passepartout's moaning about his sunburn had the desired soporific effect and I woke up to find that a combination of sweat and saliva had glued my face to the seats. Peeling my cheek off the plastic, I peered through the window, elated to see the pink station with its red Tudoresque trimming. Train number 29, the Bhopal Shatabdi Express, was due to depart just before 6 pm, so there was just enough time for a cup of tea and a samosa, which I munched in the station corridor, in front of a huge painting of Lakshmi Bai, the Rani of Jhansi. She was one of the leading figures to revolt against East India Company rule, in what the British called the Indian Rebellion of 1857 and Indians called the First War of Independence. She was depicted on the back of a mighty white steed, wielding a sword and carrying a shield, with her young son tied firmly to her back in a shawl. The Rani died defending her kingdom, allegedly taking a bullet from a British soldier.

'Shatabdi' meaning 'centenary' was a fleet of super-fast trains introduced in 1988 to commemorate 100 years since Nehru's birth. The carriages were smart, fitted with soft, fabric-covered chairs that faced one direction, and were divided into only two classes, both of which were air-conditioned. The Bhopal Shatabdi was currently the fastest train on the Indian Railways, averaging a speed of 93 kmph and reaching 160 kmph. At around 8:30 pm it drew into Agra Cantonment and through the window a familiar train with gold trimming gleamed from across the tracks. The Indian Maharaja-Deccan Odyssey was in the middle of its Taj Mahal daytrip and guests behind the blacked-out blinds would now be dining on roast lamb shanks and puddings drizzled with raspberry coulis. I looked down at my foil containers of chicken and dal and wondered how Benoy the butler was faring. The Bhopal Shatabdi arrived in Delhi at 10:30 pm prompt – and at precisely that moment I realised that I had finally fallen victim to Delhi Belly.

All plans to spend the following day digging up bits of Old Delhi were rapidly shelved in favour of holing myself up in a mid-range Paharganj hotel and writhing around in bursts of agony. The Swarna Jayanti Rajdhani to Ahmedabad was due to depart just before 8 pm and arrive around 10 am the following morning. Fourteen hours on an overnight train was a terrifying prospect, but a connecting train was already reserved through to Veraval and I was in no mood, or physical state, to go crawling to Anusha. There was no option but to munch handfuls of Imodium in preparation for the ordeal.

The general consensus among travellers was that the green and purple capsule was more of a hindrance than a help. It did not have the immediate corking effects that the desperate were looking for, and once the severity of the situation had passed it then kicked into action. It was the medicinal equivalent of a tube light. The delayed response rendered the user unable to ease out anything more satisfying than a couple of pebbles and a disappointing fart or two, and left them lumbering around for a week with the distended belly of a child with kwashiorkor.

Once train number 30 had begun to move, I clambered up to my berth hugging a large bottle of water to my chest, curled into a foetal position and prayed for the Sandman to hop aboard and put me out of my misery. My stomach felt like a ball of dough being kneaded by spiked knuckle dusters. They had so far been so loyal to me, but now I was frightened to breathe out lest my stomach muscles should betray my trust. Floating in and out of sleep and unable to ignore the spasms any longer, I slid sadly down the end of the bunk and made my way carefully to the toilet. The harsh light made my eyes shrink and the only sound was a low *clackety-clack, clackety-clack*. Flicking round the lever, I tiptoed into the wet, dimly lit toilet. It was 3:40 am. For the umpteenth time that day, I squatted on my haunches and an overwhelming sense of resignation swept over me at the same time as a muscular spasm struck the lower half of my body. This must be what childbirth felt like. The train chose that point to approach a bend in the tracks as I approached a new milestone in my life. Clutching the wonky tap ahead of me with both hands, I closed my eyes against my knees and wondered what the fuck I was doing in this country. It was 4 am and I was shitting in zigzags. Drained of both fluids and the will to live, I stumbled pathetically back to bed and prayed for the morning to arrive at the soonest possible opportunity.

Passepartout and his sunburn had spent their first night together sulking in a cold bath, and he had now adopted a cowboy swagger to prevent his inflamed skin from rubbing against his trousers, although the desired effect was less James Dean and more piles sufferer. The surface of his skin had come to resemble patches of tissue paper, which had now started to flake off around the seats like an early spring flurry of snow. We drew into Ahmedabad and sped straight to Hotel Serena, where I collapsed under the shower, then lay in a ball on the bed, watching newsflashes about Swamiji Nithyananda. The self-proclaimed holy man had been 'nabbed' in a sex-tape scandal with an unidentified Tamil actress, causing his ashram to be attacked by 'miffed' followers. The 'absconding' swami claimed that she was taking care of him while he was sick; judging by the gloriously repeated footage, it was clear that the actress had an extremely attentive bedside manner.

Passepartout spent the day loafing about the city, photographing the eerie step wells at Dada Hari Vav, a handful of monkeys and one defecating dog, before meeting me for dinner at the Green House on Mirzapur Road. It was an airy, cheerful spot under a pavilion concealed from the pavement by a jungle of cheese plants in terracotta pots. Inside was lined with polished white wooden tables lit with plump candles, and a reassuring quota of tourists floated around, which meant that there would be bland food on the menu. Anything but yoghurt was probably a bad idea, but the khichdi looked too good to ignore. When it arrived my stomach somersaulted in resistance. Passepartout dunked his onion uttapam into a bowl of sambar and shook his head.

'I know exactly how you feel. When I was sick my stomach was literally contorting itself. And it took ages before I felt like I could eat anything either.'

He munched thoughtfully, tearing a strip off the tomato uttapam.

'I remember the first day, the spasms were so bad. If I'm honest, it will probably get worse.'

I watched the butter dribbling down the dome of rice before me. Raising my eyelids up to him was exhausting, but I did not need to see his expression to hear the smugness melting into his voice.

'Look, I feel like shit already, I don't need you sitting here and telling me how terrible it's going to be. I'm fully aware of that.'

He fixed me with an even look.

'You don't have to be a bitch, all right? I get that you're sick, but if you're going to be like this we can get the bill and leave.'

After a half-hearted poke at the bowl, we paid up and left. Passepartout strode on ahead to the hotel while I wobbled behind like Bambi, pausing briefly to vomit quietly into an open concrete bin full of cats.

Train 31, the overnight Somnath Express to Veraval in Gujarat, was scheduled for a 10 pm departure, but before we flagged down an auto, Passepartout stopped to buy himself a watch. Grave warnings of theft on the railways had prompted us to relieve ourselves of watches and jewellery in Chennai, but it all felt a little unnecessary. Our farewell party, filled with forecasts of doom and foreboding, smacked of the Indian tendency to exaggerate the dangers of anywhere that lay outside their own immediate surroundings, which were, of course, perfect in every way. We had promised not to take the train through Bihar, where as recently as seven years ago kidnapping had been the most lucrative industry. In turn, I was promised that dacoits would sneak on board at night and apply oil to my wrists to remove my grandma's gold bangles from my arm. But I liked carrying a little part of her with me, and if anyone had the gall to try to twist the diamond stud out of my nose, I would happily give it to them, along with the bangles, as a commendation for bravery.

We were both watch-less and our movements were, more than ever, reliant on punctuality. Trains were rarely delayed and using phones to tell the time was risky in case the batteries died, while asking a passerby was as reliable as using a sun dial. Ahmedabad's backstreets sold a bizarre range of goods from boxed underwear, advertised by tanned Americans wearing banana hammocks, to frilly dresses and shoes for toddlers, and fake jewellery. Pleased as punch with his new faux Rolex, Passepartout swanned off to hail an auto. This smelt like a recipe for disaster. Roving magpies were unlikely to believe that a Norwegian carrying two Nikons and a MacBook Pro would be wearing a 300-rupee piece of junk from Ramanlal Sheth Marg. However, contrary to horror stories, Passepartout would later leave his credit cards, money and passport in the toilet of a train to Varanasi, only to have them returned by a fellow passenger who then refused a finder's fee.

A sandy, sharp-eared dog picked her way through a pile of wicker baskets covering the platform and sniffed at each one in turn, licking gingerly at a wet patch. Overhead the sign read 9221, signalling our train to Veraval. She cowered as we neared, her ears flattening as we heaved ourselves up the steps and into the compartment. Pulling my feet into a cross-legged position, I dug out my redundant logbook and thumbed through the stacks of ticket stubs, hotel receipts, menus and business cards, as a colourful image of the journey formed an unfinished jigsaw in my head. Certain names made me smile, others made me sad, but overall I was touched by the number of people who had offered help, advice, food – and even a bed for the night. My body was now fixed in a perpetual state of rocking from side to side and I barely noticed the occasional cockroach or mucky floors. The compartment was my safe house and it was beginning to feel like home.

Threading deeper through Gujarat brought a new dynamic to our undertaking. With the exception of Jaipur, I had, until now, never ventured north of Mumbai. Gujarat was home to the last sanctuary for Asiatic lions and the island of Diu, a Portuguese colony relatively unknown to westerners infatuated with Goa. But above all, reaching Dwarka was the highest priority. Along with Rameshwaram, Badrinath and Puri, it was one of the four *dhams*, or abodes of the Gods, regarded as the holiest places of pilgrimage. Dwarka was revered as the home of Lord Krishna. By the time the Somnath Express pulled into Veraval the next morning, it was barely 6 am and Passepartout's new watch had already stopped working.

The skies were yet to lighten in the fog, which clung to my sleeves and hair in a layer of sparkles. Passengers vanished quickly through the murkiness, leaving nothing but rows of empty carriages that soon merged eerily into the darkness, like a ghost train. Unsure which way to go, we stared up and down the platform, when a nose suddenly appeared in the doorway of the next carriage. It was followed by a sandy body that gauged the situation carefully before hopping out of the door and onto the platform. It was the dog from Ahmedabad. She began to trot confidently towards the exit and seeing as she knew where she was going, we followed her and came out at the front of Veraval station.

Within minutes the sky whitened and shutters began to snap upwards on shop fronts. There was a two-hour wait before the passenger train to Talana, which connected the mainland to Diu, so we looked around for a good coffee spot. Across the road was a handpainted sign for Somtirth Guest House and we ventured up the stairs to where a man in bright blue pyjamas and a matching T-shirt was sitting at a desk. He looked up and smiled with an endearing overbite.

'Come-come, sit-sit.' He gestured to the couch in his reception, which was little more than the tiled hallway of his home, with a few posters of the Somnath temple on the walls and a couple of faded cushions. Exhausted, we decided to give the temple a miss. The room rate was less than the normal price we paid for breakfasts, so I asked if we could have a room for a few hours to nap and shower. He brought out two frothing glasses of coffee.

'I am Vijay. There is plenty of time for the train. You're very welcome to stay here.'

Vijay disappeared, then returned with a bunch of keys. Wrestling with bolts and padlocks, he opened up one of the rooms so I could clean my teeth and shower, after which he sat with us both, perched a pair of well-thumbed glasses onto his nose and pulled out a map of Gujarat.

'Diu is a very nice place. Very calm, quiet. But you will see many people...' He pointed a thumb into his mouth and rolled his eyes back into his head.

Gujarat was a dry state, but Diu was a Union Territory and alcohol was tax free. The little island was used by Gujaratis – much the same as the English use Ibiza – to go and get hammered.

With a blunt pencil, Vijay made a shortlist of the best spots in Diu and tore the page out of a child's exercise book, handing it over. As I counted out the payment for the room and the coffees, he held up his palm and screwed his eyes shut.

'No, ma'am, this is being my pleasure. No need.'

Reaching Diu was awkward, but this made the journey all the more fun as it involved two more passenger trains: one from Veraval to Talana, then another from Talana to Una – the second of which we only discovered while on the first. Wedged in between a farmer with magnificent tufts of white hair winding out of his shirt and a woman with earlobes that swung low by her chin, we began another sign-language conversation with our companions. As train 32 paused at Talana, a bow-legged man boarded with a set of old scales over one shoulder and a basket of sapotas balanced against his hip, small round fruit that tasted faintly of caramel. The farmer bought a paper bagful and passed them around the compartment, smiling with a set of teeth that looked as though he had cleaned them with beetroot. Licking juice from my wrist, I muttered that we were going to Diu, prompting the compartment to wave and point across the track at a train that was about to move. Grabbing our bags, a couple of teenagers on mobile phones helped us off the train and I stumbled across the rocks, trying to reach the ladder to the doorway. My wet fingers slid from the railing and halfway up the ladder and I felt the weight of my rucksack tipping backwards, taking me with it. I lost my footing and one handhold and began flailing like an upturned beetle, when two pairs of hands shoved my bag from below, boosting me up through the doorway, where I fell onto my knees as train number 33 began to move.

10 | Oh My Dog!

An empty packet of Parle-G biscuits blew across the ground and came to rest by my bag as our auto driver saluted, yanked the ripcord and put-putted his way up the street. We looked around. Shutters were down, padlocks in place and the dusty streets deserted. The biscuit packet lifted briefly on the breeze and came to rest in the middle of the street. Its creepy picture of the little girl with a missing finger was the only other face around. We had stumbled on a technicolour ghost town, or at the very least the set of a Rodgers and Hammerstein musical, where the whole town would suddenly fling open the bright orange shutters and leap through the pink doorways in chorus. But for now there was no sign of human activity. It was late afternoon and the sun blazed down from a low, china-blue sky, chalk-marked with wisps of cloud, as we set off on a hunt for signs of life.

Since the early sixteenth century, after their occupation of Goa, the Portuguese had been eyeing the tiny island of Diu, which they saw as key to controlling the northeastern Arabian Sea. In 1535, after several unsuccessful attempts to find a foothold, they spotted a way in. Bahadur Shah, ruler of the Gujarat Sultanate, was embroiled in a battle against the Mughal emperor Humayun, so the Portuguese waged an alliance with Shah and were given Diu as a reward for their support. However, it became a violent struggle to rid the island of its Mediterranean settlers and for over 400 years Diu remained under their control, until December 1961, when the Indian government reclaimed it along with its sister island, Daman, both of which are now governed by Delhi as a Union Territory. Though the majority of Portuguese had left, one legacy remained, which explained the seemingly lifeless town: the siesta.

Salty wind followed us down the streets, past low-roofed houses painted like sugared almonds. Although their walls were faded and stained with patches of decay, their original pastels perked up the crumbling façades, suggesting that the town was once a jolly place to live in. Now it looked in need of a good wash.

Diu was originally home to a number of Catholic churches, but as the island's Christian community had dwindled, they had reduced to three: St Paul's, where mass was celebrated every day; St Francis of Assisi, now partly used as a hospital; and St Thomas's, a small museum displaying wooden relics. It was at this third and final house of God that we chose to seek sanctuary. Built into the back of the church was a handful of rooms run by George, a gentle Goan who now lived on one floor of the conversion with his two children and his wife, who was standing at the corner of the church, waving us over.

Our room had the deliberately distressed look of a Shoreditch boutique hotel, except that the peeling paint and crumbling walls were wonderfully authentic. A tiled blue floor with a Donald Duck shower curtain across the windows made the room resemble a bathroom with two beds in the middle. The actual bathroom was hung with a sign requesting that used toilet paper be put in a bin. It was the ultimate in shabby chic.

A beam of evening sunshine swept through the doorway like a sniper ray and I basked in the warmth for a few minutes, wondering how Passepartout was coping in such close proximity to a beacon of religion. Perhaps it would have the effect of Kryptonite. Or maybe it would have the reverse effect. I glanced across to the other bed where he was dozing and half hoped to see the beginnings of the stigmata.

Balmy air wrapped around my shoulders as I stepped over a couple of cats and crossed the yard, which was now strung with fairy lights and a selection of my damp vests and pants. George's wife had cooked calamari pasta and fried meaty rockfish, attracting the attention of two more cats. The female, and more cunning of the two, was sitting in Passepartout's lap when George approached holding a bottle of rum.

'Can I sit with you?'

'Of course.'

George was a soft-spoken man with receding hair and three gold hoops in one ear. He had wide-set eyes and gleaming, reddish-brown skin pulled tight across his high cheekbones, which made him appear to be smiling all the time. Since the early 1960s, George and his family had had a rough ride. After a trip to visit relatives in Goa, they had returned to find the government had seized their home with all their papers inside. To earn a little money they began to invite foreigners from the beach to come and party on the disused church grounds, where they hosted barbecues. With the church authorities' permission, they opened a small restaurant.

George unscrewed the bottle. 'It was very successful, but then the local Catholics got jealous and took it away from us.'

At the mention of the 'c'-word, my heart sank. Passepartout sat up. My heart shrivelled.

'Catholic priests, man!' he snorted, lighting up a cigarette.

'This was probably around 1992,' George said. 'At that time this property belonged to the local community, so I went back to the church and asked them if I could start running guest rooms.' He gestured to the rooftop. 'We began inviting people to sit on the roof to watch sunsets. The priest said he was going to help me renew the licence and instead went to the police and made sure it wasn't renewed.'

Passepartout was shaking his head.

George glanced up at the sky as a shooting star sliced through the cluster of white lights. He nodded towards the rooftop.

'Let's go up, it's a lovely night.'

A cat's cradle of washing lines criss-crossed the terrace, draped with old duvets that provided shade to a couple of charpoys. As the highest point in Diu, the rooftop offered a panoramic view of the town, its lights flickering under an aura of skin-tingling romance. A maximum of 45 people could sleep on the roof for the sum of ₹100 each, often finding themselves alongside George, who came up in summer. We perched on a charpoy and were soon joined by Mikkel, a German in a kurta pyjama who had lived in Goa since the 1980s and regularly visited George.

'No thumping trance in this Portuguese town, huh?' He bit his bottom lip, pounding the air with his fist.

This was what made Diu a speck of gold dust. Peacocks sailed from one treetop to another, warm waters lapped against unpolluted shores, the air was clean and the only booming beats came from a wedding across the road. George sipped his rum and smiled. 'Sweet family, they invited us all – they'll be there all night.'

As recently as three years ago, the family home was closed again and George's family was forced to spend seven months in Goa living off their savings. They eventually won the case and received a staying order, but George was still fighting for compensation from the government. He took a long drink and looked at the floor. His financial battles were far from over.

Passepartout watched him closely.

'At least you're doing something useful with a church.'

George nodded, a grateful curve at the corner of his mouth.

'They're hypocrites. And I would know, I used to be a Sunday-school teacher.'

George looked up. 'Really?'

'They claim to want to help everyone and yet most of the world's wealth is owned by the Catholic Church!'

I turned away to watch the lights of the liners blinking on the ocean. Despite the bhangra beats from across the road and the enticing whoops and claps, my bathroom-cum-bedroom beckoned.

Auto drivers and other informants with a hidden agenda had sworn blind that Una was the only train station that could connect the mainland to Diu and vice versa. This was another lie. It was also possible to take a passenger train from a stop at Delwada. It was an 8 km journey from Diu, so after three days of peace we piled our bags into the back of an open auto rickshaw and made our way to the station to catch a passenger train to Sasan Gir, Junagadh, the next pin in the map. On the approach to the bridge connecting Diu to the mainland, it appeared that a bundle of clothes had been dumped on the side of the road. Sniggering, the driver slowed down. It was a bundle of clothes, but someone was still wearing them – and was now paying the price for a heavy weekend on the booze.

By the time I bought tickets, Passepartout had vanished. There was only one platform and as I scanned it, a circle of heavily embroidered, dyed cotton began to close in on me. A tribal troop of Rabari women wearing necklaces and earrings akin to wedding jewellery had flocked to investigate and were now clamping tattooed hands across their mouths. Beautiful grid-like work, considered to contain magical symbolism, emblazoned their arms, necks and giggling faces. Where their braless breasts sagged low, their hard chests resembled chessboards. By tradition the Rabaris were camel herders, but had begun to move towards the big cities to seek employment as labourers. Meanwhile, Passepartout had been returned by a tiny man and his family, who had taken him to look at turtles in their garden. Train 34 arrived and I shuffled up the steps among the women, feeling terribly underdressed. By the time it departed they had got tired of me and gone back to gossiping, their earlobes swinging wildly, so I took out a notepad and tried to look busy.

Hemant, a 30-year-old from Bharuch, was sitting opposite me reading a copy of *Angels and Demons*, following the words with a plastic ruler and a lazy eye. He pretended not to be watching me making notes, but I could see his mouth open and close as he looked for the right moment to begin a series of questions that he eventually unloaded like a round of machine-gunfire. 'Is the UK giving free education? How is employment? Is there crime in London? What is the government doing to stop it? Are men having relations with men? Are there places where they are going for this?' I picked my way slowly through each one, explaining state schools, benefit fraud, knife crime and Clapham Common, when the train halted for a moment and Passepartout jumped down to find a packet of Lay's and some water. Hemant crossed his arms and, with his good eye, followed Passepartout out of the door.

'Husband is from?'

'Norway.'

'You are having issues?'

'Sometimes.'

'Tell again?'

'Sometimes, but that happens when you're with someone all day, every day.'

'How many?'

'How many what?'

'Issues. Boys?'

He meant children.

'Oh. No, sorry, no issues.'

'Why?'

'I'm too young.'

'What is your age?'

'28.'

'Running 28?'

'Sorry?'

'Means, you are completing 28 or running 28?'

'I'll be 29 next birthday.'

'Then you are old. By now you must be having issues or trouble will come.'

Passepartout returned carrying three palm-sized packets of Jal Ganga water that smelt like plasticine. Moments later the train pulled into Sasan Gir and I thanked Hemant for his advice. It was now much easier to let the assumption slide that Passepartout, my barren womb and I were a family than go through the torturous process of allaying suspicions of harlotry.

Gir National Park turned out to be a disappointment. We had joined a group of backpackers and at 5 am a jeep arrived to drive us into the sanctuary. Not only were the windows blacked out, but they did not open, prompting fury from those with cameras and demands for a reimbursement. Serbian threats encouraged the guide to take heed and he eventually produced an open-top jeep, which then ran out of petrol and broke down in the middle of the park. Fortunately we had seen one lethargic lion by this point. He was slimmer faced and smaller than his African cousins and wore his mane in a shorter, more bedraggled fashion. He had arched his tail, sprayed a jet of scent on a tree, then strolled off into the bushes. Shortly after the sighting, the jeep coughed then rolled to a standstill in a rut, where we sat waiting for help to arrive. Only in India, among innumerable potential hazards, would a park guide encourage everyone to get out and stretch their legs, pee and have a cigarette.

From Gir, 90 minutes on train 35 – the Dhasa-Veraval passenger train – took us back to Veraval Junction, from where we could connect to Rajkot, and from Rajkot to Dwarka. A steady blast of humid air steamed straight up my nostrils as I rolled about in exhaustion, sticking to the seat like velcro. We stopped for an early dinner of *mackeroni cheej back* that had more sugar in it than a treacle tart, before boarding the Somnath Express for the second time.

Pushing the door into the dimly lit carriage, we were met with a sharp slap of cold air. As much as I had grown to adore passenger trains for their warmth and the distinct lack of boundaries, it was a momentary relief to be back in the restrained, cooler confines of the second-tier carriage. Our only other companion was listening to an iPod and nodded politely before shifting up to the window and continuing to work on a spreadsheet. Shortly before midnight train 36 arrived into Rajkot, where we spent the night sleeping soundly in motionless beds before the long morning journey to Dwarka.

It was now mid-March and two months of cooked food, twinned with soaring temperatures, had led to pangs of longing for the cold crunchiness of an M&S salad bowl. Before boarding the Saurashtra Mail, the nearest available option was at a wooden cart just outside the station, where a pyramid of apples gleamed like polished cricket balls. Once train 37 had begun to thunder into its five-hour journey to Dwarka, I moved into the doorway with a bottle of Aquafina and sat down to rinse my apples. Drumbeats and bell ringing came from the adjoining carriage, where pilgrims to Lord Krishna's home were singing and clapping their way through the afternoon, tapping their thighs with the backs of their hands. The stretch to Dwarka was desolate and felt detached from the rest of the country. It had the pleasing serenity that foreign eyes searched for in Indian village life, but its calm belied ugly truths. Agricultural mechanisation and the government's handing over of much of the land to industrialists had stripped many farmers of their livelihood. Production costs far exceeded revenue from produce, causing a decline in profits and a reported increase in farmer suicides, though Gujarat's chief minister vehemently denied this was the case.

Both apples devoured, I returned to our compartment, where Passepartout was reading *Shantaram* and copying down a section spoken by Didier. I leant over his arm to read it:

'In the face of all that is so wrong with the world, the very worst thing you can do is survive. And yet you must survive. It is this dilemma that makes us believe and cling to the lie that we have a soul, and that there is a God who cares about its fate. And now you have it.'

I went back to my book.

Legend has it that Dwarka was once the kingdom of Lord Krishna, submerged in the ocean after the epic Mahabharata war. Archaeologists believe that Dwarka emerged and then disappeared under water on a further seven occasions, but the town's main interest was now the Dwarkadhish temple, which sits on the banks of the Gomati river. Around the corner from the limestone structure a carnival of pilgrims bopped along the street, pushing a wooden cart fixed with three megaphones. Revellers wore marigold cravats and pumped both arms in the air, as shop owners and residents leant out of doors and windows to join in the merriment. Kids jiggled on fathers' shoulders and families danced their way towards the water's edge, carrying paper boats filled with flowers and flames to immerse beside shoes that were now bobbing on the water, lapped off the steps by the rising tide.

The temple entrance was clogged with noise makers, so I slipped in and out of the cool shadows, then drifted towards the seafront, picking up a little friend along the way. Ajay was no more than 10 years old and was dressed like Huckleberry Finn. He left the basket of garlands he was selling with a friend and tagged along behind Passepartout, fascinated by his camera. Ajay and I sat on the edge of a sandy hill, where friends and lovers had gathered to watch the sunset, and scrolled through photos. He turned to ask if he could join Passepartout, who was now paddling in the water. As the setting sunlight reached his honey-coloured eyes, they glowed with delight and he handed back the camera, hopped down the rocks and ran to the edge of the waves, where he stood with one hand on his hip, his legs bowed with rickets, chatting to Passepartout.

Even if we were devoid of one, Dwarka had a soul. It lived within the drumbeats, the ripples of laughter and the waves that chased young women, grabbing at the hems of their saris. While much of India made way for shopping malls and coffee shops, bulldozing history and turning its culture to rubble, Dwarka was a pocket of peace. Whether or not there was a God who cared about its fate, its people did.

Dwarka was not the end of the railway line. Highly questionable map-reading skills meant that I had failed to notice that the end was, in fact, one stop away in Okha. Passepartout had tried his best to point out my mistake but train 38, the Okha-Puri Express, was already booked back to Ahmedabad, where we had one final errand before catching the Ranakpur Express to Jodhpur.

The watch seller put down his paper and jumped off his stool as we approached.

'Niiiice watch, sir, goooood watch, sir. Rolex?' he asked, dangling a couple in the light, pleased with their shininess.

Passepartout slipped off the broken watch and handed it over.

'No. I bought this from you about a week ago and it's not working.'

'Noooo problem, sir.' He took it and without bothering to look for the fault, laid it back in the glass case for some other sucker to buy. He then allowed Passepartout to choose another, shook his head happily and waved us off.

Time was ticking by. In terms of train journeys, we had almost reached the halfway mark. But it was mid-March, half our time was up and we were nowhere near Udhampur, the northernmost tip of the railways. As a result, Jodhpur was allotted an unjust 24 hours. We dumped bags at a dormitory near the station and walked into the blue-walled city of jhari bedspreads and masala markets, on a primal hunt for meat. After Gujarat's vegetarian cuisine, our carnivorous cravings had taken over and we devoured a biryani filled with hunks of soft mutton draped in ribbons of fried onion, as the Umaid Bhawan Palace shimmered in the distance. Mid-afternoon heat soon took its toll and we came back to the dormitory for a post-biryani nap.

An Indian man with a satin-smooth head knelt on his bed, frowning over a map of the railways. He spread it out, holding the bottom corner down with one knee, then squinted through his John Lennon glasses. At the foot of his bed lay a younger version of Neil from *The Young Ones*, wearing mid-calf shorts, a Che Guevara T-shirt and a pair of high-top Converse that hung over the edge of the bed. His face was hidden by a curtain of unwashed hair.

'Not sure whether to get the train to Delhi and then head down to Kerala…,' the Indian man pondered with a South African lilt, '…it looks like a really long journey.'

He turned the map on its side and followed the route with his finger. A hand swiped idly at the curtain of hair and a sun-deprived face appeared from behind.

'Kerala's pretty boring, everyone does it,' Neil offered.

'But I've never been and I've only got a week left. I might just spend a couple of nights on a houseboat and just chill for a bit with some good seafood.'

Memories of the fried prawns on our houseboat came flooding back, so I interrupted.

'Sorry to eavesdrop, but we took the Kerala Express from Delhi to Kottayam and then a houseboat through Alleppey. It's one of the most beautiful parts we've seen so far, plus the 48-hour journey cuts right through the centre of the country, so you get to see plenty that way.'

'Wow, that's long. What class were you travelling in? I'm Anil by the way.'

'Monisha. AC two-tier. At this time of year it's too hot not to travel at least in three-tier for such a long journey.'

Neil picked at a spot on his chin. 'I only ever travel in general class.'

'Well, it would be pretty uncomfortable for 48 hours.'

'I don't mind that. That way you actually get to see real India.'

'Real India?'

Neil sat up and rearranged his hair so that even less of his face was visible.

'Yeah, you don't get to see what real India is like if you travel up in the air-conditioned classes. You can't sit and talk to real people or understand how they live.'

'Because the Indians in third, second and first tiers aren't real people?'

'They're not the ones who define India. It's the poor who make this country what it is.'

Anil's forehead creased in thought and he was watching Neil closely as he went on. The spot was now bleeding.

'Westerners get a false impression of India when they travel in higher classes, you don't learn anything about this country by sitting with those people.'

Neil was a walking advert for the poverty tourist board. While it was true that the majority of Indians could not afford to travel in higher classes and that those lower down were more representative of the way in which the population lived, it was foolish to think that nothing could be learnt from within those air-conditioned walls. Neil had rolled off the bed and onto his own, and I dug out a wilting copy of *The 3 Mistakes of My Life*, thanks to a leaking bottle of Biotique Green Apple shampoo. Anil was packing his bag and had broken out into a panic. He had lost the anti-bacterial cover for his toothbrush and was tearing the room apart looking for the small plastic cap.

Later that evening I found him sitting on the terrace with a real Indian lassi, and made sure that he bought tickets to Kottayam in third tier.

The Jaisalmer Express had seats available in only one class and was our first overnight journey in sleeper. It was also the 40th train – the halfway mark! At midnight we boarded in the darkness, barely able to make out bundles of bags from sleeping bodies. Passepartout crawled into the bottom berth and I took the middle, pushing my smaller rucksack up to the open window and balling up my fleece as a pillow. A hand dangled from the upper berth, catching my hair, and a pair of wide-awake eyes watched me from across the aisle. That night, horns blared through the open windows and the wheels clattered louder than ever. At 3 am the train ground to a halt. Shivering, I slid out of my space to go to the toilet, where someone was smoking. Fog was collecting in the doorway, but the area was empty. It turned out to be dust sweeping in from the desert through the open windows. I glanced out and saw that we had arrived at Pokhran. In 1998, Prime Minister Atal Bihari Vajpayee, leader of the 'nonviolent' Hindu nationalist Bharatiya Janata Party (BJP), had conducted five underground nuclear tests at Pokhran, with rightwing Hindus then pushing for a temple to mark the spot. I zipped up my fleece and crawled back into my sheets.

Travelling by camel was in conflict with our specified mode of transport, but avoiding Jaisalmer's main attraction would have been churlish for the sake of petty logistics. And so, after spending a night at the Jaisalmer Fort, we found ourselves atop a jaded quartet of blinking camels, along with Steve and Ayelet, a dry-humoured Irish couple we had met at the dorm in Jodhpur. Ayelet was a sculptor with a jagged fringe, mischievous eyes and a pin-sized stud in her freckled nose that wrinkled when she laughed, which was often, and mostly at Steve. He had spread on sun cream as thick as cottage cheese and was sporting a cerise headscarf tied like Lawrence of Arabia. As the sun blazed angrily, our guide, Ali, trudged ahead and we began to bob and lurch into the heart of the Thar desert to spend the night on the dunes.

Ali was of an indefinable age. He had the build and suppleness of a teenager, performing all manner of tasks on his haunches, and attributed his more colourful English vocabulary to repeated listening of the Black Eyed Peas. But his hands were calloused and worn and he handled his camels like a veteran. His eyes flicked around as though he had been taught to be suspicious of everyone he met, but his pout frequently gave way to laughter that sounded like a combination of an asthma attack and a braying donkey.

We had stopped for lunch under a tree and were watching a herd of goats playing up a group of women running after them with sticks, when Ali looked up from where he was kneading dough.

'You want goat?'

'A goat?'

'We can get goat for dinner.'

'How will you cook it?'

'With port.'

'Port?'

'Yes, port!'

'You've got port to cook us goat?'

Goat in port sounded a little fancy considering our plates had just been cleaned with dirt and the tea stirred with sticks. Ali spat out the twig he was chewing and jumped up in exasperation.

'Oh my dog!' he shouted, stumbling across to where two other guides were brewing tea and chopping cauliflower. He picked up the steel pot from the fire and waved it over his head.

'PORT!'

'Oh, you mean POT!'

'Yes, cook it in port! Tonight's gonna be a good, good night!' he sang, waving the pot around.

'Oh my dog? Don't you mean "Oh my God?"' I asked.

'Yes, yes, GOD!' Ali yelled, hee-hawing with laughter.

'I would normally say "Oh *your* God".' Passepartout chipped in.

'It's just a turn of phrase,' I replied.

'Yes, a phrase that has absolutely no relation to reality. It's been bent into a literary device that we all use now, like "heavenly" or "paradise".'

Ayelet flashed me a cheeky grin.

After a Rajasthani thali, a nap under the trees and another cup of sandy tea, we restacked the camels with quilts and bedding and set off across the parched expanse, passing little more than rocks, a dried cow's skull and a scattering of depressed-looking trees. Our camels, from the outset, had adopted an air of endearing ignorance, but plodded into the thorny branches with suspiciously precise direction, causing the needles to slash across our cheeks, adding insult to already injured, sunburnt skin. Just as my throat had become so dry that I could barely croak up enough saliva to form words of complaint, we arrived at the dunes. A shack was waiting, which looked from afar like a haystack thatched with blankets. Santa had already visited, leaving a hessian sack of Kingfishers and Pepsi bottles covered in rapidly melting ice. Passepartout and Steve took a couple of beers and clambered onto the top of a dune to watch the beetles embroidering the sand with their tracks. 'I used to be a Sunday-school teacher…' drifted down as they walked away.

I crept inside the shack and dug a hole that I sat in for the next hour, venturing out briefly to watch the sun come down over the creamy curves of sand. Apparently the Thar desert was equipped with 24-hour room service and the unsuspecting goat had arrived just after we did, and was now tethered to a pole, enjoying what was to be its last supper. The meal was soon hacked out in an undigested mound as the headless goat twitched its last and ended up in the 'port'.

That night Ali and the guides squatted around the fire using two hands to stir the goat curry, as though manoeuvring a canoe. The sand had dampened with cold and the air had turned sharp and icy. Clutching bowls of curry with near-gangrenous fingertips, I was thankful that it was so steeped with chillies, as the slightest increase in body temperature, even if it made my nose run into the bowl, was an improvement. Using the roti to warm my palms, I began to nudge the bits of meat to one side. It was marginally less stretchy than bubble gum and even in the dark, I could sense that it was grey. Sporadic tufts of hair found their way into my mouth, which I quietly spat out and then disposed of with hard but discreet throws into the darkness, flinging the fatty lumps across the sand. As I licked my fingers, Ali began to scream. He ran around in a circle, pointing at the shack, claiming that he had seen a snake track curling its way across the sand. His discovery triggered yelling and pot banging, generating enough drama for the other two musketeers to join him in running around, waving flames through the darkness. This was, presumably, included in the trek's cost as after-dinner entertainment.

Nevertheless, I opted to climb up onto a charpoy for the night. I pulled my socks over my knees, pulled my hat down over my ears and lay on my back watching shooting stars burst and fade like a delicate display of God's own fireworks. I turned over and instantly regretted throwing the bits of goat as far as I had. Wild dogs were now sniffing around the charpoys, snuffling at lumps of hairy gristle. Meanwhile, Steve and Passepartout made their way through the remaining beers, which had begun to lend themselves to a well-lubricated lash-out against the evidence for intelligent design.

'I mean, it's ridiculous! The human eye is one of the most flawed examples of design.'

Passepartout was working through his usual repertoire. Having heard this so often, I knew what was coming next and giggled as I muttered to myself: *if anything it shows a rather unintelligent designer.*

He cracked open the last bottle of beer and took a sip. 'If anything it shows a rather *unintelligent* designer.'

I started to laugh so hard that I had to stuff my sleeve into my mouth, while Ayelet pulled her duvet up to her chin and turned over. A cut healing itself satisfied my feeling that the human body was far from unintelligent, but I knew better than to join the conversation and cause desert warfare, so I drew my knees up to my chest and prayed that the dogs would eat me, or at the very least chew off my ears. In the morning, I awoke to find snake tracks trailing beneath the charpoy like unravelled wool.

Only two trains ran from Jaisalmer to Bikaner. After the sleepless journey from Jodhpur, we opted against the night train and chose the 11:10 am that arrived at 4:40 pm in Lalgarh Junction, a short ride from Bikaner. Only five others were on board: the ticket inspector and four members of the Indian Air Force, who boarded at Phalodi airbase. As we picked up speed, blood-red dust soared through the windows. Grappling at the shutter, we yanked it down. This was why everyone else travelled at night. It was the lesser of two evils. Slow-roasting for five hours at high temperatures, turning over once, we awoke fully cooked as train 41 pulled into Lalgarh.

11 | The Venus Flytrap of Insanity

During our time on the Indian Maharaja, we had covered Udaipur, Jaipur and Sawai Madhopur, so we were now free to climb north Rajasthan and continue into Punjab. If all went to plan, we would reach Udhampur within the week.

Originating in Barmer, a small town in west Rajasthan famed for carved wooden furniture, the express train we boarded at Bikaner (number 43) was bound for Kalka, the main junction for passengers joining the Himalayan Queen to Shimla. The well-loved toy train was high on our list of priorities, but Chandigarh, the 'City Beautiful', had piqued our interest for its status as not only India's first planned city, but also its cleanest. In a country where chaos and stink form the basis of daily existence, planning and cleanliness were two notions that had very much fallen off my radar and become something of a lost hope. Post-partition Nehru had commissioned the development of Chandigarh to reflect new India, proclaiming it 'unfettered by the traditions of the past ... an expression of the nation's faith in the future'. Such a statement made it impossible to bypass this anomaly. Besides, we had heard that there was a garden made from recycled rubbish and broken bangles that Passepartout was itching to see.

Bikaner was half a day's journey from Barmer, so there was a fair chance that whoever had boarded at the train's origin had either adopted our berths as their own or used them to store excess luggage. Arriving at the compartment we were dismayed to find that a combination of the two had taken place. Dismayed, but inwardly thrilled. Over the last couple of weeks I had grown to enjoy a fleeting sense of Schadenfreude when someone else had taken my seat and I was compelled to ask them to move. Elderly or injured passengers and families with children were the exception, and I was happy to make allowances. But for the most part, culprits were young and able-bodied – their only afflictions being a combination of selective hearing and an inability to make eye contact. This game became all the more enjoyable when they refused to move until a ticket inspector arrived and threw them out.

The seeds of this ruthless new behaviour had been incubated during my time at university, after many Sunday evenings spent squashed into the luggage racks between Birmingham New Street and Leeds. The London Underground had provided some degree of nurturing, but now, finding themselves in a truly hospitable environment, the seeds had sprouted into a Venus Flytrap of insanity. Two and a half hours cramped on a Virgin Voyager was one thing, but 48 hours without a seat was not to be sniffed at. It was only a matter of time before I started diving headfirst through moving doorways to bag one.

In the interim, standing around and waiting for people to move was torture. In addition to the 75-litre Lowe Alpines on our backs, we had succumbed to wearing our smaller rucksacks on our chests, like Spanish exchange students who often block the entrance to the tube at Piccadilly Circus. We stood there, bodies sweating like luncheon meat in picnic sandwiches, wondering how and where to offload. An elderly gentleman with round cheeks and a beaky nose hopped up. He looked like a big, smiley bird. He unchained his suitcase from under our seats and, dragging it across the floor, suggested that, seeing as he had already used my berth, we could do a mutual swap.

Easy.

Unexpected.

And a bit disappointing.

Barely five minutes had passed when a flash of white trousers appeared and the inspector plucked the tickets from my hand. Scrolling down his clipboard, grimacing at the withering passes, he peered through his glasses and demanded to know why we were in the wrong seats. The gentleman closed his eyes and nodded.

'It is all right, between us we have reached a mutual agreement and we are happy. Thank you.'

No longer required to assert any kind of authority, the inspector flicked a pen across our tickets with visible disappointment and carried on to the next compartment. Hoisting myself up the side of the berth, I marked my territory by placing the bag of bedding in the middle before settling down with my book. My iPod was now a redundant artefact buried at the bottom of my bag, along with limp jasmine flowers and the odd five-rupee coin. Aside from being thoroughly bored of my music, it hindered my eavesdropping. Passepartout slotted away the rucksacks and settled down with his laptop to trawl through his photographs. While pretending to read, the gentleman glanced continually at the computer screen until his curiosity gave way.

'Was this taken in Deshnok?' he asked, finally.

Passepartout, who was only too pleased to offer a private viewing, nattered with the man, who sat with his hands pressed between his thighs, swinging his crossed feet.

That morning, after a stack of roadside aloo parathas, we had taken train 42, the Link Express, from Lalgarh to Deshnok, Rajasthan's answer to Hamelin. Among the many variations on the story, legend has it that Karni Mata, a fourteenth-century mystic believed to be an incarnation of the Hindu goddess Durga, had requested Yama, the Lord of Death, to restore life to one of her clansmen. Yama was unable to grant her wish, as the clansman had already been reincarnated, so Karni Mata declared that from then on, all her tribesmen would be reincarnated as rats until they could be born back into their clan. Queues into Karni Mata's temple bulged with pilgrims armed with ladoos and French tourists wearing plastic bags over their feet, eyeing the hordes of brown rats that flitted around the floors, lining up to drink milk from steel dishes or dozing in corners. Their friendly, beady-eyed faces came as a surprise. These were not the black, yellow-gnashered fellows that slunk about at night, slipping in and out of drains. As we walked around, coconut barfi sticking to our toes, it was evident that the holy rats would never be reborn as humans. This was moksha: the end of the cycle and the ultimate goal. A dwelling where hand-fed sugar delights were an hourly occurrence was akin to paradise.

In the courtyard children crouched in corners, showering the rats with goodies while they darted around, dodging lumps of sugar, scurrying into cracks in the walls. A wire mesh stretched overhead, protecting the temple's tenants from low-circling hawks scouring the ground for treats. Keeping our own eyes peeled, we stepped around the clumps of marigolds, puddles of warm milk and jalebis scattered like broken bangles, searching for a white rat. It was considered good luck, auspicious even, if a white rat ran over a visitor's foot. That these overweight murines were able to move at all was remarkable. A few lay flat on their backs, paws splayed out to the sides. Their cause of death was most likely coronary failure or early-onset diabetes.

The photograph that the gentleman was pointing to was, in fact, not of the rats, but of a baby pigeon whose face was just visible from underneath a protective mother; the rat in the corner had simply given away the location. Back in the mid-1990s a roadside advert had asked why we never see baby pigeons; after discovering this one in the temple, the answer was clear. Baby pigeons are one of the few young animals to make onlookers recoil in horror. The bird had the jaundiced hue of a Tesco's corn-fed chicken, few feathers and an oversized beak. It is the only creature that looks old in its youth. However, to prove they existed Passepartout had snapped away, much to the annoyance of the mother, who flapped her wings and nipped at the other pigeons who had ventured over to investigate the tamasha.

'My name is Khanna,' the gentleman offered, 'and you are?'

'Monisha,' I replied, putting down my book.

'What are you doing going to Chandigarh?'

Khanna listened open-mouthed as I explained the journey.

'My, but this is wonderful!' he said, throwing both arms up with operatic flamboyance.

'And this makes you Passepartout,' he added, rhyming it with 'spout'.

He was the first person to make the immediate connection and I tried subtly to make a note.

'It's *Professor* Khanna,' he stressed.

I glanced up guiltily. Professor Khanna was a retired military man from Jodhpur and a mechanical engineer, who was taking a group of 22 university students on an industrial excursion to Chandigarh. He saw me look around for them and laughed, waggling a finger beneath my nose.

'They are down in sleeper class where they need to learn to be tough,' he said, flexing his biceps. He frowned a little. 'You mustn't write anything bad about India, many journalists do this and it's not good. There is much that is very good. Don't take photographs of villagers and snake charmers and all that sort of nonsense, that isn't the only part of what makes India. Photograph the malls and their wonderful new buildings. Have you seen them? They're incredible.'

The fixation with impressing developing infrastructure on visitors to the country was beginning to grate, but it was all part of the 'forward-thinking' strategy that had engulfed the middle and upper classes. If I had wanted to see shopping malls and multiplex cinemas I would have caught the 20-minute overland train to Westfield at Shepherd's Bush, not embarked on a 40,000 km journey around the country. After his cursory warning, the professor bounced back into spirit and asked Passepartout to run a slideshow of the luxury train we had travelled on across Rajasthan.

'Ah yes, the Palace on Wheels!' he exclaimed, pointing at the screen.

'No, that's actually the Indian Maharaja-Deccan Odyssey,' I corrected. 'It was launched towards the end of last year but it covers a similar route, taking in Ajanta and Ellora as well.'

'But this is fantastic, I didn't even know that all these trains existed. Now this is the sort of thing that Indians should be proud of and people should be talking about. How was the food?'

'Excellent. Catered for by the Taj Group.'

'And was it Indian or continental? Some of these tourists find it difficult to handle the rich food.' He wrapped his arms around his stomach and rocked back and forth in mock agony. 'And then they live on curd and bananas for the rest of the time.'

Outside the window the sky was beginning to darken along the horizon, and with the Thar desert fading from view, entertainment was now focused on the inside of the carriage.

'Have you been to Punjab before?' Khanna asked.

'No, first time, I've always wanted to see the Golden Temple and I've heard about a stall in Amritsar that does the best jalebis in Punjab.'

'Ah yes,' he said, raising a finger, 'the queue goes all the way around the shop. But you must eat them then and there when they're hot-hot. And don't forget the Amritsari fish and tandoori chicken.' He paused and leant forward. 'You aren't vegetarian or anything, are you?'

Amused at the idea of Passepartout living on dal and chana, I shook my head. I was also desperate for non-vegetarian food. With the exception of the biryani in Jodhpur, we had mainly lived off aloo parathas and packets of stale banana chips. Passepartout was also looking forward to bottles of Kingfisher, his only comfort after particularly gruelling days, though he had recently taken to carrying a small bottle of vodka in the pocket of his rucksack that he brought out before bed.

'Oh-ho! Well, Punjabis love their meat and their rotis,' Khanna said, gnashing his teeth. 'Big strong Sikh warriors they are, lots of meat, lots of whisky, big tough men.'

All this talk of rotis, meat and jalebis was making us miserable. It was 7 pm and we had had nil-by-mouth since around midday at the temple, swigging two warm 7Ups and a bottle of water. Dinner would not arrive for another two hours at least and I was beginning to get nervous as Passepartout was starting to scrunch his toes, a sign of restlessness, which normally stemmed from hunger. In the last hour the train had barely stopped for more than a few minutes at each desolate station, so hopping out for a packet of Magix cashew biscuits was not on the cards. Suratgarh was the next station and a growing crowd was jostling to get off, so there was a high possibility that this was a bigger, food-stacked stop. A thud brought the train to a halt, but we stayed put and allowed the shoving on both sides of the carriage door to pass. Passepartout pushed back the torn curtain, cupped both hands against the window and peered into the murkiness. Every few metres crooked street lamps cast down spotlights that did little more than to light up the base of the lamppost, making it impossible to gauge the extent of activity on the platform.

A commotion was brewing in the doorway. A squat man in a tight red T-shirt was trying to balance a foil plate on his palm, his chubby fingers spread out. He was using his other hand to lift a bony boy up the steps by the arm and in through the door. The boy twirled around beneath his father's grip like a Christmas tree decoration, clutching a golden-fried kachori to his chest. As both sandaled feet came to rest on the floor, he dropped it. The dumpling landed with a soft thud, leaving a sorry mound of ground dal and gram flour on the floor, which his father kicked to one side, spreading the mess all around the entrance to the toilets, and simultaneously donated a sharp whack to the back of his son's head. At least there was food available.

Passepartout bolted for the door as I went back to reading *Two States*, the latest bestseller from Chetan Bhagat. The blurb was traditional fodder for Indian love stories. Boy likes girl, girl likes boy and they fall in love against their parents' wishes. But Bhagat is somewhat of a tearaway, adored by twentysomethings and loathed by their parents. In this tale, boy likes girl, girl likes boy and they have sex when they should be attending lectures. Boy is Punjabi, girl is Tamilian and they know their families will never approve the match, because money-hungry, classless Punjus cannot stand black-faced Southerners who eat curd rice with their hands. Bhagat's previous three books were good fun and I wanted to see what all the fuss was about. So far, *Two States* was not rating highly. It all seemed rather a perfunctory conclusion for the reasons behind the Great Indian North–South Divide – not to mention generalising – but perhaps India's internal racism was more straightforward than I had realised.

Passepartout had been gone a while, so I went through the usual motions of asking three different people what time the train was departing. By this stage in our travels I had learnt not to ask a question that could be answered with 'yes', as that tended to be the response and was invariably wrong. Nor did I rely on one person. Two people would always offer conflicting advice, and if the third produced an answer that neared either of the other two, then that was the answer I accepted. Indians also hate to be the bearer of bad tidings. So if a journey takes over an hour they will squint, bring their fingertips together and declare no more than 20 minutes.

Looking around for someone reliable, I noticed that the professor had vanished. He was either on the platform – in which case we were safe – or he was in sleeper class, checking on his students. Two elderly gentlemen in dhotis and white kurtas were sitting in the adjoining compartment, each with one knee drawn up to his chin. Both wore gold watches as well as glasses with thick black frames, normally spotted on media trendies in Hoxton Square, and each had grown the nails of their little fingers to an unacceptable length. They would have to do. Their discussion involved loud and animated Punjabi, which appeared to be an argument until both sniggered and clutched each other's hands. Smiling gingerly, I waited for what looked and sounded like a lull in the conversation, tapped the gentleman closest to me on the knee and asked what time we would be leaving. He tipped his head to one side, placed his Freddy Krueger finger into an ear and shook it vigorously before answering: 'Five minutes.' He withdrew his finger and examined the contents before delving back in for a second round. On cue his friend piped up: 'No-no, 10–15 minutes.' The first shook his head in disagreement, but they soon ignored me and went back to their conversation.

None the wiser, and lacking the third-party assurance, I decided that, as Passepartout had been gone for almost 15 minutes, we should soon be on the move. Humming drifted up the carriage and the professor reappeared, content that his brood was behaving. He slumped in his seat, then pointed at the empty seat opposite me, fanning out his fingers like a kathak dancer, which loosely translated as 'Now where is your friend?'

A couple of jerks announced that we were on the move, but before I had time even to consider a heart attack, Passepartout pushed open the door, out of breath, clutching a paper bag shaded with two oil patches. As we moved away from the platform, the ear picker caught my eye and shot me a smug look. Passepartout sat down heavily, tearing the bag open in desperation, causing one of his two kachoris to leap out like a billiard ball and roll into the aisle. He leant forward, grabbed the runaway and wiped it on his T-shirt, offering me the other one. I declined. We had reached a sorry state of affairs if we were willing to eat food off the floor of a train.

Thankfully, dinner arrived early and I climbed into my berth and placed a copy of *Outlook* underneath the various foil containers. The train clanked violently, causing the carriages to tilt awkwardly to one side. Rhythmically my dal and vegetable spilt alternate puddles all over my berth, until I gave up and handed down the whole stack to Passepartout, who was only too pleased to wipe up the remains while engrossed in an article about Naxalites.

Far too tired for anything cerebral, I set to work making up my bed, perching on the edge of the berth below and trying not to slip off as the train continued to lurch. We were due to arrive in Chandigarh at around 5 am, so 10 pm seemed a reasonable time to call it a night. Through the curtains I could hear Passepartout and the professor discussing Henry VIII and the dissolution of the monasteries. Wanting neither to indulge Passepartout and his vehemence against the Church nor to be reminded of my poor performance at A-level history, I pulled the sheet up to my ears, plumped my fleece under my head and tried to ignore the pair of feelers waving through the air-conditioning vent. Less than a fortnight into our journeys I had established a rule not to look at anything in India too closely. If you did, you would never eat any food, drink any water, use the toilet, breathe the air from the air conditioner or cover yourself in blankets. Abiding by my own rules, I shut my eyes.

An ascending chime woke me with a start. I fumbled around to switch off the alarm on my phone and panicked. It was 4:50 am and we were due into Chandigarh in 10 minutes. Sliding down the berth I shook Passepartout, who was deeply asleep despite always complaining in the morning about how badly he had slept. Darkness filled the rest of the carriage, twinned with rumbling snores and the steady da-dum ... da-dum ... da-dum of the train. No phlegm clearing. No clanging chai wallah. No bright lights in your face. Something was wrong.

Fishing around for my flip-flops, I picked my way down the carriage and found one gentleman sitting up in the dark, checking his phone.

'What is the next station?' I asked.

'Chandigarh,' he replied.

'Rajpura Junction,' came another voice, 'train is delayed by two hours.'

No third party was available, so with a leap of faith I crept back to share the good news with Passepartout and crawled back under the covers to enjoy an extra two hours of sleep. Contented snores from the professor made me wonder whether he and the rest of the passengers had some sort of inbuilt sensor that had alerted them to the delay.

I awoke to the sound of singing and put the pillow on my head. But the singing was lovely: deep and melodious, harmonised by a nasal 'carfeeee, carfeeee, chai-carfeeee' coming up the aisle. It was 7 am and the scene was in full swing. Passepartout had cleared away his bed and was sitting up, clutching a coffee and a book. His eyes were two tiny creases in folds of puffy skin and he had a look of bemusement on his face. The professor was singing with his eyes closed. He leant back against the wall, waving his chubby forearms: a Punjabi Pavarotti caught up in his own morning reverie.

As the train drew to a halt in Chandigarh, the morning sun was already warming the air and the platform activities were well underway. Coffee huts rattled up their shutters, steam rising from slim glasses. Porters swooped down on those with smart luggage, barefooted kids were washed under drinking-water taps and the professor was standing in the middle of a group of students chattering like mynahs. When I was at school, Indian teachers, no matter how appalling, demanded by default a fearful respect from pupils as their God-given right. But on observation of the throng of young adults around their guru, it was clear that the aura of respect and admiration that hung around this gentle professor was well earned. He turned and saw us.

'Miss Monisha and Passepartout, you take care and I will call you when I am in London.'

Waving back, we watched as the professor and his stream of followers made their way down the platform and out of sight.

12 | Toy Trains and Afternoon Tea

'Bastards. The Koh-i-Noor was not *presented* to Queen Victoria, it was stolen by her. Along with all the other loot they plundered.'

An Indian lady, with an accent from deepest Harrow, smouldered in front of a glass cabinet in the Jewel House at the Tower of London. A few months before leaving England, I had made a visit to examine the object of the heist, whose return Prime Minister David Cameron was soon categorically to refuse during a state visit to India. Shaking her head, the woman turned to me. 'My foot was it a gift,' she muttered, while the queue of onlookers bunched in front of the Queen Mother's crown, where the Koh-i-Noor sat winking in provocation. In 1846 the British had emerged victorious after the First Anglo-Sikh War and drew up the Treaty of Lahore, inserting a 186-carat footnote, which gave them possession of not only key Sikh territories, but also the largest diamond in the world.

After a comfortable stay, the British were not averse to taking more than just the complimentary toiletries: their imperial kleptomania extended to robes, duvets and anything else that was not nailed down. As Cameron later explained, returning the diamond to India would start a trend: the British Museum – a monument to plunder – would soon be empty. However, considering the nomadic diamond had passed as the spoils of war through the hands and pockets of maharajas, Mughal emperors and shahs, the Koh-i-Noor was at least now safe and sound and available for the world to gape at. Had she stayed in India, it was more than likely that she would now be sitting on the ring fingers of at least 20 Delhiite Punjabis.

Griping over the return of the Koh-i-Noor boiled down to little more than Indians being difficult for the sake of it: an elbow in British ribs, lest the actions of their forefathers be forgotten. Remnants of British presence were firmly entrenched in Indian life, embraced when convenient and sniffed at sporadically – over cucumber sandwiches at the Gymkhana club. Along our planned route, one Indian town had earned a pin in the map for its staunchness in remaining as English as weak tea and football hooliganism. Shimla was a ridge along which the British Raj had built its official summer capital, a Little England from which to escape India. Not only was the hill station still a favourite of Joanna Lumley types reminiscing over summers in 'Shimler', but reaching the town involved taking a toy train from nearby Kalka: built in 1903, the train still ran on 2 foot 6 inch narrow-gauge track and passed through 102 tunnels and over 864 bridges – a well-loved slice of British leftovers.

The Himalayan Queen Express to Kalka was due to depart from Chandigarh at 10:35 am, but was delayed by almost an hour, which meant that we would now miss the toy train's final departure of the day. However, I had now learnt that in India there was always an alternative option. It could cost one greased palm, require a shifty uncle, or take double the time and a dozen phone calls, but there were no dead ends. Rather than squatting on the platform in a panic, a more fruitful way to pass the time was with an omelette sandwich, an *Archie* comic and a couple of coffees in the station café. It was barely bigger than a walk-in wardrobe and housed two tables and a fridge that wheezed and trembled in the corner. Passepartout was already seated at one table, clutching his thermos in one hand and a bottle of Nescafé in the other. In an attempt to have black coffee, he was trying to explain the concept of boiling water to the waiter, who was gazing at him with an expression that hesitated between fascination and compassion for the mentally subnormal. He listened without a word, his head cocked to one side, eventually picking up the thermos and strolling into the kitchen. He reappeared less than one minute later and made a figure of eight with his head. Passepartout unscrewed the lid and stuck his finger in, his face flickering with resignation.

A Sikh gentleman at the other table was wiping up the last of his curd and I asked him to write down the Hindi phrase for 'boiling water'. He wrote *ubalta pani* in Hindi on the back of a receipt for a Hot Millions meat burger, which I then scribbled into English and pushed across the table to Passepartout.

'Learn this if you want to have black coffee for the rest of the trip. It has the equivalent power of "Open Sesame".'

An eruption of activity outside the door indicated that the train had arrived earlier than expected. Fighting through the tsunami of limbs and luggage, we boarded the chair-car train, number 44, arriving half an hour later in Kalka. At the top end of the station, a row of carriages, like a string of garden sheds painted vanilla and peppermint green, was lined up on a platform: the toy train was still waiting for delayed passengers to arrive. Thrilled not to have to suffer a bus or taxi ride, we sought out the ticket inspector, who was obscured by a mob of fellow latecomers looking to worm their way on board. Although the train was heavily pregnant with passengers, carriage C was entirely empty. But much to the stragglers' chagrin, it had already been reserved for a delayed tour group.

As the minutes crawled by, the inspector endured varying degrees of harassment: parents dispatched offspring to tug at his sleeves; boyfriends used big-toothed girlfriends as bait; and one couple simply climbed on board, stacked their bags and began to unfold leathery puris. The inspector poked his head through the window.

'Pleeeeezgeddown!'

Tucking his clipboard under one arm, he climbed into the carriage and a trio of schoolboys followed him in, leaping onto the seats and waving at their friends who were hovering on the platform, swinging bags strapped across their foreheads. They soon followed. I was beginning to love all of this and moved around the group to get a better view of the show.

'Getttt ... owt!' The inspector swiped at the couple, then clipped the ear of a boy whose parents appeared to have combed his hair through with ghee. Tying up bags and with a half-hearted hunt for chappals under the seats, the couple sauntered off the train. It was almost 40 minutes since the scheduled time of departure to Shimla and faces were now poking out of the windows and doors, hands slapping the sides of the carriages as though geeing up a racehorse. For a train climbing 96 km at an average speed of 19 kmph, the journey would prove a task for the restless.

Over the din, a swarm of baseball caps and straw hats arrived and the inspector almost fainted with delight. He sprang like a ballerina across the platform and met the group with bows, directing them towards the carriage with pirouettes of encouragement.

'Please-please-come-sit-sit ... heh-heh ... please-please ... heh-heh ...'
He fell over himself as the delayed Australians clambered aboard, with all
the grace of ogres climbing into a dollhouse. The carriage rocked and sank
beneath the motion. Once the group was seated, arms hanging from the
windows like slabs of boiled pork, I turned to the inspector. He examined
his list and shook his head. He had too much integrity to fall prey to a pair
of Disney eyes. Pointing silently to the station exit, he flicked his index
finger to the left. To the bus stop it was.

For the price of a Kit Kat we were soon on board a bus farting black clouds
up the hill towards Shimla, and now it was my turn to sulk. As much as I
loathed car journeys in India, bus trips unearthed one particular childhood
trauma. During the Madras days, I used to catch the school bus, part of a
fleet of death traps owned by a conglomerate of vegetable sellers in Besant
Nagar. Each contained one row of sponge seats that ran around the inside
of the bus, which was fitted with the suspension of a trampoline. My friend
David, when not retrieving his balls from his stomach, was employed to
hold the door closed during journeys. One afternoon, on the way home,
the back of the bus had dropped from beneath me, my knees flying back
over my head, as metal slammed into the ground, sending up sparks and
scraping the tarmac like a furrowed field. Hauling my nose up to the
window, I saw the rear wheel rolling into the path of a Maruti 1000.

Hesitating, I stood watching the other passengers climb aboard. The
bus sounded like something from *Chitty Chitty Bang Bang* but its wheels
seemed secure, so I climbed on reluctantly and shuffled up to a window.
A woman with a wicker basket, two carrier bags and a box tied in twine
tumbled into the seat next to me, filling the immediate surroundings with
the stench of marigolds and burnt camphor. She smelt like a temple. Her
hair had been scraped back with such enthusiasm that her powdered
cheeks stretched into a do-it-yourself facelift, while her sock-covered toes
gripped a pair of chappals like a North Indian geisha. Passepartout sat a
couple of rows behind reading a copy of *80 Questions to Understand India*
with his earphones wedged in. Not long after the bus departed, it rolled
into a traffic jam. Less than three minutes had passed when the men began
to stand up in their seats, sigh and climb down for a better look. They
smoked with one knee up on the walls, held hands or skidded down the
slopes to pee in the trees.

My neighbour dug between the packets of peanut candy at the top of her basket and brought out a lacquered fan that she used to waft the warm body odour of the man in front straight across my face. Fighting back an already growing sense of carsickness, I craned my neck out of the window when a 'poooooooooooooooooonk' rang out from above, accompanied by a 'clack-clack, clack-clack, clack-clack'. From between the gangly tree trunks the train emerged and snaked its way past, a long cheer accompanying the clatter, before vanishing together into a tunnel. Once the train had passed, cyclists remounted their saddles and wobbled off before the lorries had even restarted their engines.

For the next two hours, the train popped in and out of the hillside until it picked up speed and rattled ahead, leaving us to crawl up the remainder of the hill alone. Passepartout leant forward and pulled out his earphones.

'Do you know why cows are holy?'

I could sense that this was going to be some kind of trick question to prove my lack of knowledge and, therefore, unworthiness of calling myself a Hindu. What the heck, it had to be more fun than staring out of a window.

'I'm pretty sure that it's because if a mother dies, the only way a baby can be fed is with cows' milk. And because cows can be used to pull carts and their dung provides fuel. An animal of all-round benefits, so you don't harm it.'

'Did you know that as recently as the eighteenth century, cows were eaten by Hindus?'

'No, I did not.'

'Yeah, well they were.'

'You know that there is no set text that defines every Hindu's philosophy? Pluralism is a concept embraced naturally by this country, and apparently not by you.'

'It's called cherry-picking. Just like how Christians will follow a book that condones cutting pregnant women's bellies open, ripping their unborn babies out and bashing their heads on rocks. They just ignore those bits.'

During the last half hour of the journey, the curves tightened until the bus began to spiral up the hillside, struggling past a crushed Fiat and a burnt-out Ambassador, slipping back then lurching forward over rocks and ditches. I had thrown up my stash of anti-emetics back in Ahmedabad, so there was nothing for it but to slump out of the window. High altitude brought a new cleanliness to the air and I closed my eyes. Suddenly I felt a hand on my wrist. The geisha was pressing her fingers against my skin. With the other hand she fished out a ball of peanut candy for me to suck and gestured for me to shut my eyes and breathe. She was applying acupressure to my wrist to alleviate my nausea – and it worked.

Towards the peak, scarves, shawls and balaclavas began to emerge from bags. The geisha snapped on a pair of earmuffs as the bus gave one last growl, shuddered and then stopped – all its wheels intact. We had arrived in Shimla.

A driveway flanked by pine trees reaching out to touch each other's tips curled up and around the corner, and down it came one golden and four black retrievers, sneezing in excitement. Thunder, Sambo, Rambo, Cinders and Tara, the golden girl, gambolled around their owner, Kanwar Ratanjit Singh of Kapurthala, whom we had come to visit. The Kanwar was the owner of Chapslee House, a bastion of Victorian architecture, partially hidden by clay pots of nasturtiums and dog daisies and creepers knitting their way across the brickwork. Dressed in sports gear, with a fine crop of silver hair, the Kanwar wound his way through the tangle of tongues and tails and welcomed us across the lawn. He owned a moustache that must have been combed and set around a pair of heated rollers at bedtime. Extending both arms, he led us along a patchwork of paving stones to the main entrance, where the dogs hovered in dismay, knowing the house was off limits to their muddy paws.

The Kanwar was the grandson of Raja Charanjit Singh of Kapurthala, whose nephew, Maharaja Jagatjit Singh, had ruled the Kapurthala principality from 1896 to 1950. In 1938 the Raja had bought the house for ₹66,000 to use as his summer residence: it had been built in 1830 by a Briton, Dr Blake, then rented by Lord Auckland, the governor general of the East India Company. Auckland had lived next door in Auckland House but used Chapslee as the Secretaries Lodge, where the British declared their first ill-fated war on Afghanistan in 1842, both issuing and signing the Simla Manifesto within its mud walls. Chapslee was now partly used as a hotel, managed by the Kanwar.

Adjusting the pleats of a pair of eighteenth-century velvet curtains, which came from the Doge's Palace in Venice, the Kanwar led us into a hallway that resembled a hunting lodge. Gazelle and deer antlers spiralled out from the walls like giant coat hooks, between an arsenal of swords, daggers and axes fixed to the wallpaper, which, over time, had absorbed moisture from the walls and begun to ripple and crease like used wrapping paper. Gold silk cushions shone like caramel on matching sofas and the smell of old velvet and mahogany hung in the air. Upstairs, the bedsteads gleamed, inkwells sat on desks and lace-edged duvets were tucked into place. At the back of the house was a library available for guests. I was in awe of the Kanwar's home. It looked frozen in time and I was scared to tread my Adidas across his carpets. I knelt down to examine the cases of books that the Kanwar had numbered by hand, including *A History of Amersham*, while he rubbed a bridge table with his arm until it shone. He glanced up.

'I had to do that as they had begun to go wandering.'

Skidding across the cedar-wood floors, we followed the Kanwar into the dining room, which was hung with an eighteenth-century tapestry from Bruges, next to which stood an Italian candelabra, sprouting more branches than a Christmas tree, and a glass case containing a collection of at least 100 silver spoons, including one that his grandfather had brought back from George VI's coronation. Running his finger around the rim of a jardinière from Multan, then inspecting the tip, he looked up.

'All brought back during my grandfather's travels.'

I looked down at the rugs. 'Where are these dhurries from?' I asked.

His moustache twitched at the ends.

'It is a major insult to call them that. These two are Persian and Afghan carpets and they are each about 125 years old. Dhurries are made from cotton, these are wool. But not silk. Silk is normally used for hangings.'

He trailed off as a white-gloved orderly arrived carrying a gold tray, on which lay a folded piece of paper notifying the Kanwar of the arrival of hotel guests. He opened up the chit, then waved it in the air.

'What time are they coming? How are they coming? Where are they coming from?' He put the note in his pocket and waved off the boy, who reversed around an eighteenth-century piano, then fled.

Showing us into the conservatory, the Kanwar gestured to where a spread of pakoras, cake and home-baked cheese straws lay next to a floral tea cosy. It reminded me of post-Christmas shopping at Fortnum & Mason.

'When my grandfather died, what was left of the estate became a major financial burden for me. It was very difficult to maintain and I needed to generate some income. Funnily enough, it was one of your Britishers who gave me the inspiration to open this place as a hotel in 1976. The Duke of Bedford wrote a book called *The Book of Snobs*, where he described the ridicule he faced from the rest of the nobility when he opened Woburn

Abbey to the public, even building a funfair on the grounds. But he stuck it out and look what happened.'

The Kanwar lifted the tea cosy and filled a delicate cup that barely withstood my grip.

'He became the pioneer of the stately home industry. It was a turning point in Britain – and for me. It gave me some gumption and showed me what to do. But I am very selective about who stays.'

Summers in Shimla were still de rigueur and the original Mall Road was dotted with hotels that catered to families on ice-cream-and-pizza holidays and streams of students shopping for mufflers. However, British visitors still felt the pull towards the Kanwar and his home.

'We are the kind of thing that Europeans look forward to – food in particular.' He paused to mop drops of tea quivering on his moustache. 'Good asparagus and anchovies. I once had a theatre owner from Bath who said that ours was the best bread and butter pudding she had ever had. Apple crumble too.'

A waiter slid a fresh plate of cheese straws onto the table, swept a napkin across my crumb-covered knees and disappeared without a sound.

'Today nobody wants European cuisine. My food was very famous, but one must move with the times. My grandfather served very traditional food and that's what I serve too. I specialise in various forms of mutton, particularly pulao. Grandfather's table was known as the best in northern India, so I do like to keep up that tradition. My family legacy and tradition are more important than what I do personally.'

My index finger was now stuck in the cup handle and I politely declined a refill in silent panic as he held the lid of the teapot in place and drew another perfect arc into his own cup. As he did so, I noticed a pair of pearl and ruby rings that would have looked more at home on a Tudor than the athlete in a tracksuit. He allowed one side of his mouth to release the first smile of the afternoon.

'I am very sorry to say my rings are of no value at all, they're worn for good luck. I was told that I would never retain any money, and it's very true, mind you, that I never could. Whatever came in just went. Then a family friend told me that if I wear a pearl, I will retain at least some of the money, and it worked.' He turned over his hand and squinted at the ruby, which gleamed like a summer cherry. 'This one is so that no harm comes to me. I don't mean to sound superstitious, as I'm not, but at the same time I can be.'

In England, Chapslee House would have been fixed with a blue plaque, the rooms cordoned off with an assault course of ropes and hung with signs urging visitors not to touch the displays. Instead, the Kanwar took pride in living among the luxury collection of his family's holiday souvenirs, welcoming guests into a rare preservation of grandeur.

As we got up to leave, he stopped in front of a photograph of Lord Minto, the Indian Viceroy, with his wife. He chuckled. 'People ask why I keep the pictures and there are two reasons: one is for the frames, which are lovely; and the second is for the size of her waist. It's tiny.'

Overfed and watered, we began to thank the Kanwar for giving up his morning as he gestured towards the dining room.

'Come, my boys have prepared lunch.'

The following morning we traced the Mall downhill and arrived in the middle of Stratford town centre, outside Anne Hathaway's cottage. At least it might have been, were it not for the Nokia and Godrej adverts nailed to the gables. Clinging to their colonial remnants, Shimla's wonky hotels, shops and restaurants thrived behind the mock Tudor façades, while honeymooners and families dawdled around the streets, haggling over handicrafts or basking in the sun on benches. But from afar the stepped hillside of lower Shimla looked little different from a Rio favela. Not an inch of land was visible through the patchwork quilt of corrugated iron roofs and stacked buildings jostling for space. This was the Croydon to Chapslee's Kensington.

Having already bought our train tickets at the tourist office, we ambled down towards the station for the 10:30 am departure to Kalka. Train number 45 was already on the platform, wobbling around as passengers climbed on board. As we began to move, I poked my head out of the window and suffered a vicious bout of train envy as a red-velvet-seated train pulled into the station. The Shivalik Deluxe Express, a living room on wheels, left Kalka at around 5:30 am and was the organised traveller's dream. Fitted with reversible cushioned seats, wall-to-wall carpeting and offering breakfast, the train made ours feel like the easyJet equivalent.

I soon settled as the train began to clatter its way down the hillside. Red flowers laced the trees like fairy lights and sunshine poured in between the branches, warming the tops of my arms and cheeks as I leant out to get a view of the Himalayan peaks.

'Ma'am, you will become dark.'

Across from me sat Karthik, an engineering student from Delhi who had spent a long weekend in Shimla with his classmates.

'Ma'am, the sun is not good for you, already you are little dark in colour.'

I pulled my arm in to shut him up, but he liked to talk.

'Ma'am, are you seeing all these numbers on the tunnels? Every single one is numbered. Previously there were being 103, but now only 102 are used.'

On the approach to another tunnel, he slid up to my side, flinching when he touched my thigh, and pointed out of the window.

'See, there was one British engineer named Barog.'

'What was his first name?'

'Barog.'

'But he must have had a first name.'

'Barog only.'

'Go on.'

Karthik had a strange concept of emphasis. His voice rose towards the middle of a sentence where he would pause for effect, in the hope of keeping his listener guessing.

'His role was to... dig the longest tunnel. From one end he started digging, and then... from the other end he also started digging. But the two sides did not meet.' He flicked his wrist as though changing a light bulb. 'Then your government fined him... one rupee for wasting their money.'

'So what happened? Did he build the rest of the tunnel?'

'*Chee*, poor chap. Killed himself.'

One variation of the tale claimed that the body of Colonel Barog was buried in front of the tunnel, but between the government and the railway authorities nothing had been done to preserve his grave and it was anyone's guess as to where the poor man lay.

Karthik pointed out the window.

'See these cuttings in the rock? When it is monsoon there are... many waterfalls coming down. It's *rer-ly beaudiful*. Truly I tell you, this is one of the most *beaudiful* places.'

He held out a packet that had covered his palms with oil. It appeared to contain fried bread covered in batter, then deep-fried again. I shook my head and he balled it up and flipped it out of the window.

Soon the novelty of the rickety train was beginning to wear off, when it came to a halt. A group of hormonal males hopped out and began stretching for the benefit of a carriage of giggly girls, while others strolled off for a handful of pakoras, showing little concern that we might suddenly leave. Passepartout also got out and was treading towards a stone wall displaying a sign in white paint:

THE ALLAH OF ISLAM IS THE SAME
AS THE GOD OF CHRISTIANS AND THE ISHWAR OF HINDUS

He took a photograph, then picked his way back across the tracks. 'Yup, they're all bullshit.'

Everything was running like clockwork. The toy train had returned to Kalka, leaving us plenty of time to take train 46, the Kalka-Barmer Chandigarh Express back to Chandigarh. Tomorrow the Rock Garden was first on the agenda. While Chandigarh was being redesigned and divided into neat sectors, a young man named Nek Chand, now 86 years old, had collected the refuse and filled a secret space with sculptures made from broken bangles, pottery and recycled waste. After lunch we would head to Amritsar, then continue on the Tata Jammu Express up to Jammu, with one last push to Udhampur, the end of the railway line. At this rate we would be back on track and ready to tackle the second half of the country within the appointed timeframe. To celebrate, we found a bar in Sector 26.

A table of twentysomethings was taking advantage of Happy Hour and watching the highlights of an IPL cricket match over a basket of chicken lollipops and a selection of cocktails that were more like props from a 1980s music video. Planting an orchard into a collins glass, amid an array of paper umbrellas, the barman was transfixed by the television. Another had been wiping the same glass for five minutes, his eyes glued to the overhead screen. A waiter holding a basket of garlic bread, poised to end up on the floor, twisted his neck round at the noise, while a cleaner mopped the same patch of wooden floor, his mouth wide open. The source of the distraction was the Little Master. Passepartout glanced up at the screen and I attempted an abridged explanation of cricket.

'Who is that?' he asked.

'Ah, that's Sachin Tendulkar. He's just incredible.'

His eyes flicked back and forth, following the loop of the ball from the crease into the crowds and the eruption of cheers.

'That's the one they worship like a god.'

So close. Cricket had seemed a safe topic of conversation and yet I had failed to see the hole in the fence.

'What's wrong with you? Can't you see the sport for what it is? Or admire the artistry of natural talent?'

'It's the whole "us versus them" concept again.'

'But it has nothing to do with religion! Indians don't cheer for him because he's Hindu, or Harbhajan Singh because he's Sikh, or Zaheer Khan because he's Muslim. They support them for being successful Indians who are good at a sport they love. When will you ever stop this?'

'When you learn to think. You just listen to what your parents have told you since you were a child and follow blindly.'

'You know absolutely nothing about two people you have never met or, for that matter, what I think.'

He went silent, then said carefully, 'I know what imaginary friends are.'

Before I could react he grabbed his bag, flung his chair back and stormed out of the bar, leaving me with the bill and a waiter who hovered gingerly near the table. He wobbled his head.

'Peanuts, ma'am?'

Outside, Passepartout was nowhere to be seen. It was almost midnight and the cluster of autos had disappeared from under the trees. Our hotel was only two blocks away, but walking along the edge of the unlit road would soon have me smeared across the bumper of one of the many lorries that wailed by, demon masks hung up in warning. A cycle rickshaw appeared in the car park, its carrier stacked with plastic containers of water. The driver was going home for the night, but I begged him to drop me off. He moved them up so I could squeeze in and struggled to pedal, hauling his body from one side to the other. Refusing to accept money, he accompanied me to the hotel, making sure the gate was unlocked.

Upstairs the room was empty, but within 10 minutes Passepartout was hammering at the door. I let him in and he threw his bag down.

'Why are you such an angry person?' I asked.

'I'm passionate. You're not passionate about anything, are you?'

'I am about things that actually matter on a daily basis. Ultimately, you can't prove that there is no God and I can't prove that there is. There's a lot more in life to worry about, so why waste so much time arguing?'

'You're an intelligent person, I'm trying to get you to use your brain and THINK!'

'I do and I'm quite happy with my conclusion. Just because it's not the same as yours doesn't mean you can shit on someone else's beliefs.'

'You have the arrogance to call yourself a Hindu and yet you know NOTHING about the religion!'

'Or rather, *you* know nothing about Hindu culture. There is no one right or wrong.'

'Your dad gave you a picture of Superman.'

'What?'

'Neither of them is real.'

'Do you know why I carry that picture?'

'Because you think it has special powers.'

'No, I don't. I don't know anything about Shirdi Sai Baba. And frankly, I have no interest. But my dad gave me that photo right before I left home, and when I see it, all I remember is that he hopes that I'm safe. He could have given me a pencil or a piece of paper and it would mean the same. And that goes for the tiny Ganesha my mum gave me.'

'That's my point! They are all as worthless as each other. Why do you have to waste money buying trinkets and photos of fake people?!'

'You're just jealous.'

He snorted. 'Of what?'

'Jealous of my family, because they care.'

'Fuck off, bitch.'

I froze.

He was sitting with his back to me, facing the wall. I leant forward on my bed.

'Say that again.'

'No.'

'Go on, say it to my face.'

He turned to look at me over his shoulder, then stood up. He walked around to my bed, put one knee on the side and leant in, bringing his face inches from mine.

'Fuck off, bitch.'

'Get out.' I leapt up, pointing at the door. 'Go on, get out.' I walked over to the door and reached for the handle, but an arm swiped me out of the way. I jumped onto the bed with both hands on my hips. My ears burned and I was annoyed that my fingers were trembling. He climbed onto the bed and a pair of thin, watery blue eyes met mine. He said nothing, but stared at me until I hopped off the bed and disappeared into the bathroom, slamming the door behind me. I sat down on the toilet and the lid slid to one side, knocking me awkwardly against the wall.

I could hear crying, crying that swelled into sobs, sobs that echoed in the pipes running up the middle of the building – bleating, bellowing sobs that I realised were coming from my chest. A cockroach ran up the wall and onto my shoulder. I could see its feelers waving out of the corner of my eye. Another scurried out of the plughole and across my foot. In India there was always an alternative option. It was time to leave.

13 | City of Gins

Barfi was not my first choice for breakfast – a bacon sarnie was – but at 8:30 on a Sunday morning there was little else on offer. A Sikh family of six stared at me sitting alone at the table in the sweet shop, nursing a steel tumbler of tea and a lump of almond barfi, pretending that this had always been my plan. Half an hour earlier I had crept around the room stuffing T-shirts and books into my rucksack in an attempt to sneak out as Passepartout slept. He woke just as I pulled on the straps and he tried to slam the door behind me, but it was too late. I was already gone. As I skittered past reception, I caught sight of a photograph of Shirdi Sai Baba on the wall, his palm raised in farewell.

My rucksack was still heavy, but the weight on my shoulders had gone. There were now two options. Go back to Chennai, torch my rucksack, slide back into skinny jeans and treat the remainder of the time as a holiday, or finish the journey on my own. I assessed the rail pass withering on the table. It looked exhausted. A tea stain from a jolt on the Mangalore Express had blurred the ink on the first two pages, a TTE in Pune had ripped off the right corner and the back was covered in dried dal from Dwarka. Like its owner, it was in need of some tender, loving care.

As a single girl travelling alone, it was madness to consider finishing the trip. Propping the map up against the booth opposite, I stepped back to look at the route. A purple blob marked Chennai and a line of marker pen trimmed the bottom edge of the country down to Kanyakumari, then clung

to the western coast all the way up to Ahmedabad. It looped underneath
Gujarat, then wiggled across Rajasthan up to the small yellow patch that
was Punjab, where it suddenly stopped. The distance of three thumbprints
would have taken me to Udhampur.

I felt like I was playing a live game of Snakes and Ladders. Just as
the goal was in sight, a roll of the dice had taken me to the penultimate
square, where a snake awaited to take me back to base. A pink line
divided the map – the North–South Corridor Highway – worming its
way from Udhampur, past Delhi, Hyderabad and Bangalore, ending in
Kanyakumari. It was in this downward direction that I was about to slide
in defeat. It was fitting that the original version of Snakes and Ladders
was an Indian game called Moksha Patam, designed to emphasise the
role of karma in the journey of life. Perhaps I had once been a mosquito,
or a Congress party official, and was now paying my dues. But worrying
about past and future lives was a waste of the present. Another roll of
the dice and I would get back on the board. And with a few well-placed
ladders, I could pull myself up again. Feeling better, I finished up my tea
and marched off to Sector 17 to nose around the bookshops and buy
myself a DVD of 3 *Idiots* with subtitles.

The bravado lasted for less than two hours before I bit into a piece of fried
chicken and burst into tears. People were staring. Even more than usual.

Amritsar and the Golden Temple were so close, but then, so was Delhi.
Here was another option. If I took a detour to Delhi, I could stroll about
Lodhi Gardens, breathe for a few days and take stock of the situation,
instead of wandering around strapped between two rucksacks, weeping
intermittently like a hormonal suicide bomber. Pulling myself together
long enough to hail an auto, I returned to Chandigarh station and decided
to roll the dice and leave it to fate, seeing as it was so keen to take control
of my plans. Within the next two hours trains were due to both Ambala –
from where I could connect to Amritsar – and Delhi. An express train to
Ambala drew into the station first and I scoured the carriages as it flashed
past. Bodies jammed in the doorways stayed where they were as waiting
passengers piled forward and contorted themselves around the protrusions
of elbows and knees. Feeling a bit down was one thing, but a death wish
was yet to embrace me. Stepping back, I allowed the train to move on
and squatted on the platform with a bag of *murukkus* and a three-legged

cat. Scouring the departure board, I could see that the Kalka–New Delhi Shatabdi was not too far away.

As the train pulled in, a force of determination swept over me. Like a woman possessed, I launched myself through an open door, banging my shin against the steps. Even if I had to pull a 'Passepartout' and sit on the laundry bags, or hide in the toilet, I was going to get to Delhi tonight. Wiping the blood from my leg with the edge of my scarf, I glanced around and went to push open the glass door.

It slid back.

Dark cushioned seats, wide enough for both me and my bags, beckoned me in. This was the executive class. Newspapers were tucked into the seat backs and tell-tale furrows from a vacuum cleaner ran along the carpet. LCD TV screens were due to be fitted to the backs of the seats, but the plan was shelved after an overhead satellite dish fell off due to high speed.

Most seats were taken, but the train was soon to depart and a few empty spaces remained, so I sank into the nearest. Backrests, footrests and reading lights were a novelty. I stretched my toes into the carpet and stared ahead, enjoying the new-car smell of the upholstery, slightly marred by the medicinal tang of magic markers. Across the top of the seats, a pair of dark eyes met mine and a head of brown curls tilted to one side with a slight frown. The woman looked away, then a few seconds later looked back again. She seemed so familiar, as did the man to her right, but there was no way that they could be on a train in the middle of Chandigarh… or could they? While train 47 began to creep away from the platform, I leapt from my seat and pushed down the aisle as the pair pointed at me and jumped up from their seats.

Lynn and Chris Palmer were the parents of my best friend Jane, who lived in Cambridge. Lynn had the shiny eyes of a naughty schoolgirl and a toothy grin. She gave warm hugs, baked delicious quiche and always curled up on couches with her feet tucked underneath her. Chris was surrounded by a wild fuzz of grey hair, which often caused him to be mistaken for an eccentric Cambridge professor. This was his intention, as this presumed status gave him privileged licence to walk across the grass at King's College. The Palmers were on an impromptu holiday with a group of friends, had just finished a week-long trip to Amritsar and Chandigarh and were to fly out of Delhi the next day. They seized me, giving me a joint hug and a mouthful of Chris's ponytail. I had forgotten the power of a hug: the warmth of their hands and breath prompted a prickle of tears that I blinked back in annoyance as they both beamed at me, looking like two halves of Jane.

'What the bloody hell are you doing here?' Chris exclaimed. 'Janey mentioned you were in India, but she had no idea where.'

'This is our daughter's best friend!' Lynn announced to the group around the table, kissing my cheek.

I knelt on the carpet and debriefed them on the previous night's events as Samsonite carry-ons were wheeled past.

'Oh, what a load of bollocks. Can't he talk about nice things like books and telly?' Lynn asked.

'I should jolly well tell him to bugger off.' Chris added.

'Well, I sort of did, or rather, I decided to bugger off.'

'And a bloody good job too.' Lynn giggled.

'Good girl, now I suggest you sod off and have some proper fun.' Chris squeezed my shoulder and I made my way back to my seat.

Just at the moment when I desperately wanted to see either my parents or Jane, fate had handed me the nearest available combination of the two. Geographically I was no closer to getting back on track, but inside I felt that I had got my foot on the first rungs of the ladder.

My seat was now occupied by a gentleman wearing a navy turban, a pinstriped shirt and tan shoes peering out from under stiff cords. He was dressed head to toe in Jermyn Street splendour. His white beard was clipped under his chin and his moustache swooped out to the sides with the tiniest of curves at the ends. He moved across to the next seat.

'Don't worry, this is my seat, but now that we've left, I doubt anyone else is coming,' he said.

I thanked him and sat down, waving back at Lynn.

'Friends of yours?'

'Yes, I can't believe they're on the same train. I wasn't even supposed to be on it.'

'Life has a way of doing that ...' – I knew he was looking at my tear stains – 'when we need it most,' he added.

He glanced across at my logbook, where I was adding the Shatabdi to the list.

'It's nice to see people keeping notes and writing diaries, it's all lost now with emails and computers. May I see?'

He ran his finger down the list. 'I remember travelling by train in the 1950s with my father. That was the golden age of train travel. Dinner would arrive at the coupé with our names on the plates. Certainly trains are now faster, cleaner and more purpose built, but that old glory has gone now. You must be having a wonderful time?'

Now was probably the worst time to ask me that question, but I knew once the storm had passed, that I would mean what I said next. 'I've loved it.'

'I hope you have not been travelling in executive class the whole way?'

'Certainly not, this is the first time and it wasn't even planned that way.'

The ticket inspector arrived and I panicked. I handed him my pass, hoping he could find me a seat anywhere on the train. Thumbing through his lists, he looked up.

'There is only one seat left on this train and it's at the other end of this carriage. But don't worry, ma'am, stay here, and when the passenger boards at the next station I will ask if he will take the other seat.' He scribbled on my pass and handed it back, moving on to the next carriage.

The gentleman laughed. 'Is that some kind of golden ticket? You're very lucky, even in executive class I had to book this three weeks ago to guarantee a seat.'

Foraging around the floor, he produced a carrier bag of magazines including *Newsweek* and *Business Week* and pulled out a copy of *The Economist*.

'I don't value Indian newspapers and magazines. Their articles are poorly researched and badly written, filled with mistakes.' He started to flick through it, then closed the magazine.

'May I ask you something? I hope you won't take this personally.'

After questions from other passengers that had ranged from how much money my brother earned to why I did not bleach my face and how I could allow my womb to remain so empty, it was safe to assume that the gentleman would adopt a more delicate approach.

'Sure.'

'What is Britain like now in terms of integration? Do you ever feel like you're treated like an outsider?'

'No. Never. Maybe living in London is different as it's so cosmopolitan, but I grew up all over England and I can't remember ever feeling anything but British.'

'Were you never subjected to any kind of discrimination?'

'Maybe called a chocolate bar once or twice in the playground, but my school and university friends were everything from English, Indian and

Malaysian to Iranian, Belgian and Kenyan, and then on top of that they were Jewish, Catholic, Buddhist and Bora Muslim.'

'It's very reassuring to hear you say this. I'm so pleased that Britain has progressed.'

'I know my father faced battles in his career when they moved to England in the 1970s, but now he's held in the same regard as his contemporaries.'

'But you have never felt like a foreigner?'

'To be honest, the only place where I feel like a foreigner is in India.'

He sat up. 'Really? Why?'

'Here, Indians make it a point immediately to draw attention to the fact that I'm an NRI. I had never even heard the term "non-resident Indian" until I came for a cousin's wedding a few years ago.'

'In what way?'

'Well, they constantly call me "angrez" or "you firangs". They seem to think that Indians who live abroad don't understand anything about the motherland. It's almost as though because we "rejected" our homeland, we surrendered the right to have an opinion about India, or to come back and teach them anything they might not know.'

'Give me an example.'

'When I had just left university, I did a work experience stint at a magazine in Delhi. Initially they gave me copy to proofread, but as soon as I started to pick out archaisms and anything else that was incorrect, they looked put out. They ignored my changes and gradually stopped giving me work. I'd just sit there at my computer eating cheese sandwiches until they didn't even talk to me any more.'

'Good grief.'

Outside the window the sky had darkened and the fields were already far behind. High-rise flats, graffiti and Uninor billboards began to whip past the window. We were approaching Delhi. The gentleman flipped open a beautiful holder and handed me his card. It was white with a gold embossed stamp of the four lions, the national emblem, beneath which was written in italics:

*Ambassador of India**

His Excellency reached across to a blank corner of my logbook and wrote in the names of two more trains that I should include on the trip. He wrapped the ribbon around the book and handed it back.

'Enjoy the rest of your journeys, you have many left.'

---

* Name withheld for confidentiality.

Delhi's sensory assault normally struck as soon as I stepped out of the carriage, but this time it was barely noticeable. Instead, it welcomed me back in its muggy embrace. I allowed lungfuls of heat, laughter and dried fish to flood my insides. I knew now what I had to do.

But there was only one person who could help me do it.

Her desk was empty.

Looking up from a stack of papers, her colleague flicked her chin towards a door to the right and I wandered over to where a white coat was hunched over a desk covered in files. Feeling braver now, I rapped against the glass and waved as she turned.

'Oh my God, again you're coming!' Anusha squashed her temples between her palms.

'I told you I'd be back.'

'Where's your friend?'

'Er, he wanted to go to Haridwar and Varanasi, so we're travelling separately at the moment.'

Anusha said nothing, but shot me the same look my mum used when I told brazen lies about my after-school activities. She yawned like a walrus and gestured for me to sit down at her desk, chucking a handful of forms at me.

'Where are you going now? Make sure you are going safely if you are alone.'

'Well, this is where I need your help. I want to go to Amritsar and then up to Jammu.'

'Jammu?!'

'Yup.'

'Why Jammu? God…"

'I need to get to Udhampur.'

'But the line finishes at Udhampur.'

'Precisely.'

'God… anyway I will give you seats on the morning Shatabdi to Amritsar. You will be there after lunch. But you come back to Delhi and I will give you tickets for the train to Jammu.'

'You're actually *asking* me to come back?'

She flicked her ponytail and laughed. 'There is a good Rajdhani from Delhi to Jammu and I will feel happy if you take that. There are only four stops.'

'Deal.'

Anusha handed me the ticket to Amritsar, scribbling the details into her logbook and then, remembering it was missing, fixed her scowl back into place. I stuffed my tickets into my bag and waved.

'Be careful,' she warned.

A colleague in London had put me in touch with a friend of his who lived in Delhi. Dan was a television reporter for a well-known American network. That night we arranged to meet in a bar in Sundar Nagar. A steamroller of a man sat at the bar with a buzz cut and beard, his shirt sleeves rolled up and a whisky in one hand. If he stretched too hard his pecs would have split his shirt in two.

'Hey, I thought there were two of you?'

I dumped my Fab India clutch bag on the bartop. 'How much time have you got?'

'Man, this sounds good. What are you drinking?' Dan slapped a stool. 'Hop on up.'

Over a healthy dose of Bombay Sapphire, I jogged him through the previous two months, skimming over the intricacies. He rested his chin on his fist.

'Come on, tell me the good bits.'

I recounted the Sai Baba debate in Madurai and his face lit up.

'There are a lot of intelligent people who have relevant things to say on these subjects, but others are just so incredibly boring. I mean, jeez, I'm Jewish, but barely. Who cares?'

He ordered a pizza with rocket and Parma ham and swirled the dregs of his whisky, raising one finger to the barman. Pointing at my empty glass, he raised an eyebrow. I wrinkled my nose and he swiped his hand.

'Ah c'monnnnnn, God knows you need it.'

Six whiskies and two pizzas later, Dan had recharged his journalistic charms enough to twist out the details of my journey, which, loosened by six gins, was not such a hard task. I relayed the IPL conversation and he roared and slapped the bartop.

'Oh my God, that is hilarious!' He put his head down on the bar and wiped tears with the edge of his palm. 'Tell me more, I can't get enough of this!'

I started to laugh and he rocked back on his stool, swinging around in a circle and hooting with laughter.

'So you're a cricket fan?' he asked.

'Hell, yes.'

'India or England?'

'England. I'll support India if they play anyone else, but if there's a face-off, it's always England.'

'Wow, controversial.'

'Well, I grew up in Edgbaston and supported Warwickshire at school, so it would have been weird to then start rooting for the other side at international level. Besides, I was born in England, bred in England and don't see why I would suddenly start cheering for another country.'

'Fair play. You know Kapil Dev lives just around the corner?'

'Really?'

'Yup, I can show you his place. But first I need a cigarette.'

We walked outside and across the square to where a tobacco wallah was dozing in his hut.

Dan raised one finger again and a single cigarette was pulled out of a packet and handed over.

'I didn't know you could buy single cigarettes!'

He sparked up and squinted through the cloud of smoke.

'You can do anything you want in India.'

Just around the corner was a fenced green with swings and slides surrounded by a series of sprawling houses set back from the road. Dan stopped in front of a gated home flanked by two pillars and guarded by two chowkidars – one asleep inside the gate, and one asleep outside the gate.

'How do you know this is his house?'

Dan pointed to behind the chowkidar's hut, which obscured a backlit plaque that said, quite simply:

K. DEV

For a few moments we watched the two security guards sleeping, one with his chin on his chest, the other with his head rolling back over the rim of the chair. His arms dangled to the sides and a blanket slipped off his knees. Having had our fill, we began to walk down the road as a pack of pye-dogs followed, bored with their usual nightly jaunt and up for a fight. Dan waved them off and stamped after them. They scampered backwards, growling from a safe distance.

'Wow,' I began, 'he must have the shittest security in all of Delhi.'

'I know, right?'

We walked on in silence. Crickets and the occasional bark broke the stillness and our footsteps crunched over the rocks and uneven tarmac. I could not stand it any more.

'I bet I could climb over that gate without either of them waking up.'

'Give you five hundred rupees if you do.'

'Done.'

Filled with a renewed sense of purpose, we raced back around the corner, tailed by the pye-dogs who could sense something was afoot. Both chowkidars were still asleep. Dan hid beneath the shadows of a gulmohar tree next to a car, holding my handbag, already bent double in anticipation.

'Fuck, my wife would kill me if she saw this...' he groaned.

I crept forward, kicking my Havaianas to one side, and hitched my skirt above my knees, gauging the potential for footholds. It looked relatively easy. Pulling myself up, I fixed my toes between the wrought-iron swirls and worked my way up the bars, reaching the top in under a minute. I edged across to the pillar and then squatted on the top, waving at Dan as a neighbouring chowkidar came over to ask what was going on. Dan chucked my handbag behind the car, pointed at me, then made drinking gestures. The chowkidar nodded in acknowledgement. They shook hands, clapped each other on the back and he walked off. Just as I was about to climb down, the guard inside the driveway woke up.

I froze and looked at Dan, whose eyes had become a pair of saucers. He backed further into the shadows and I sat like Rodin's *The Thinker*, propped up on my elbow. Stretching both arms out in front of him, the guard leant forward and cleared a volume of phlegm from his lungs. He bent forward to pick up the blanket, then stood up. Shuffling across the driveway, he stopped below me as the gins began to fill my bladder with fear. One glance upwards and he would have seen me trembling above his head. Looking around, he caught sight of the other Sleeping Beauty, snoring against the hut. Vindicated, he sat back down, pulled the blanket across his knees and scratched the back of his neck. I had almost stopped breathing and my legs had fallen victim to an army of mosquitoes thriving off my paralysis.

Within a few moments a croaking came from below.

'Crggghhh.'

'Crgggggggghhhhhhhh.'

'Crggggggggggggghhhhhhhhhhh.'

Convinced that he was finally asleep again, I waved a foot around the gate, looking for a hold, and inched my way down, just as the curtains in the bedroom began to twitch and a light came on. Jumping down the last metre or two, with a stripe of grime bisecting my front, I grabbed my flip-flops and we fled around the corner, collapsing on the ground with relief. Dan pulled a wad of notes from his breast pocket and peeled off a 500-rupee note.

'You earned it. Though I'd have paid a fuck load more to see you get caught.'

Sunshine blazed around the rim of the curtains, desperate to push its way into my room. It was 6 am and the Shatabdi to Amritsar was due to depart at 7:20 am. Sweeping back the curtains, I looked down across the gardens. Walkers were powering past in salwar kameez and trainers, girls bounded by in baggy T-shirts, their ponytails flying from side to side, and the koels were cooing in approval. With a cup of tea slicked with skin, I sat down to check my emails before leaving for Amritsar.

One jumped out.

An invitation.

Dear Monisha

Please find below your train ticket.

Hope this is in order.

Best regards.

The Golden Chariot

Attached was an itinerary.

Bangalore–Mysore–Hasan–Hampi–Gadag–Goa–Bangalore

(Check-in time is at 12:00 pm at Leela Palace.)

That settled it. Chennai, skinny jeans and burning my rucksack could wait. Services had been temporarily suspended, but now all lines were up and running as normal.

14 | Monty Python at the Wagah Border

Over the previous two months, while Passepartout had been playing mute, ranting or simply ignoring me, I had still enjoyed the pleasures of fine company. Jhumpa Lahiri had stayed up with me one night when I could not sleep, Paul Theroux had grumbled to me from Trichy to Chennai and Amartya Sen had detailed the Hindutva movement and India's history of heterodoxy. Books had been my saviours, but I was now carrying a library on my back. A Kindle would have been kinder to my spine, but these books were now my friends and they had shaped the curves of my journey. Arundhati Roy had beckoned me to Kerala, Suketu Mehta to Mumbai and Kiran Desai was soon to entice me to Darjeeling. Swapping books with fellow travellers and rummaging through bargain basements to find a well-chewed copy of a classic was a joy that no Kindle could match. On a train to Hyderabad I had opened a copy of *Maximum City* to find a handwritten note:

> *To the one I love*
> *14ᵗʰ Feb '05*
> *Lexxy*
> *PS: Enjoy...'*

Whether the book had been traded in because it had not been enjoyed or because Lexxy's love was not reciprocated added an extra layer of intrigue. How far had the book travelled? Why had its owner underlined those sections? What were they eating when they spilt food across those pages?

While waiting for the Amritsar Swarna Shatabdi, I went in search of a new friend to come along for the ride. Towards the end of the platform, a yawning youth manned a hut strung with comics and magazines. He stood with one hand wrapped around his back, clutching his opposite elbow, and with his free hand rearranged the rows of magazines like a game of Solitaire. Scouring the covers, I realised that they were mostly in Hindi. Chetan Bhagat's books were the only English choice, but I had finished them all. I stood on my tiptoes to peer inside the hut, hoping at least to spot a faded Agatha Christie or two.

'Ma'am, *Two States* very nice.'

'Thank you, but I've read them all,' I said, waving my hands at the stack.

Still holding his elbow, he passed me another book and flicked the cover in approval. It featured a shiny man biting the lacy underwear of a woman who had lost key items of clothing on her way to a polo match. I passed it back.

'Can I come inside and have a look?'

He shook his head.

Even if it was in refusal, I had come round to the Indian way of not taking 'no' for an answer. I got on my hands and knees, crawled under the hatch at the side and began to thumb the dusty towers against the wall. Aside from a range of get-rich-quick manuals penned by Americans wearing veneers, the English selection was an homage to manic depression: *Why Men Lie and Women Cry, By the River Piedra I Sat Down and Wept, Veronika Decides to Die* and *The Inheritance of Loss.* Having finished crying in Chandigarh I was pretty certain I did not want to die, so Kiran Desai was now my new travel buddy. I held it up to the boy.

'How much?'

He broke into a smile. '500.'

I turned it over to where the original price read Rs 495 and a chunk of pages fell out. I looked at him and he grinned sheepishly.

'200.'

Handing over ₹200, I flicked through the pages whose lines arced and occasionally trailed off the edges. It was a photocopied version and I hoped that Kiran would forgive me. A hardback edition sat on my bookshelf at home, so I tempered my guilt with the belief that the legitimate purchase cancelled out the fraudulent.

Not long after leaving Delhi, the train rolled without stopping through a station called Subzi Mandi. A bank of mud, ankle deep with plastic and paper, stretched from the tracks up to the roadside, where two men squatted next to each other engrossed in conversation. A few metres away another pair was squatting side by side, sharing a joke. A circle of women had also gathered with their saris wound up past their knees and were resting on their haunches, chatting and fending off a group of piglets scampering around their feet.

'Ablutions,' my neighbour explained over the top of his newspaper, seeing my nose and palms pressed against the glass. He was right: this patch of land was the communal shithouse where the local residents came to make their morning offerings. Instead of getting together at the pub after work, they displayed an admirable grasp on time management and had turned a necessity into a social gathering: a pit stop for exchanging gossip and news. Counting sheep in the Derbyshire Dales was my favourite 'timepass' as a child, but in the absence of spring lambs I began to count the buttocks winking in the sunshine, a salute to the posh passengers munching on their cornflakes and hot milk. As the train crawled by, I counted 87 people dotted along the carpet of rubbish, which brimmed with piglets foraging through the poo. It gave a whole new meaning to my 'log' book, in which I made a note, along with a reminder not to eat Indian bacon.

The early-morning start began to take its toll and with my faecal fascination now over, I dozed off against the window, waking as my neighbour shook my shoulder.

'Excuse me, ma'am, we are coming to Amritsar.'

I thanked him, cringing at the line of drool that had wound its way down my chin.

'Ma'am, be careful, if you sleep people will take your things.'

In 48 train journeys, neither Passepartout nor I had suffered theft of any kind. We had observed fellow passengers securing briefcases and suitcases with what appeared to be bicycle chains, and equally observed their horror as we stored rucksacks under the seats with little more than a half-hearted kick and a leap of faith.

'To where you are going?' he asked.

'The Golden Temple and probably the Wagah border ceremony if I have time.'

'Oh, that is very funny.'

'What is?'

'Wagah border. It is like your Monty Python man.'

I knew little about the ceremony and had absolutely no idea what he was talking about, but I smiled anyway and shook my head.

'John Cleese,' he said.

'Yes, John Cleese was part of Monty Python,' I replied, in the tone of a primary-school teacher.

He said nothing, but looked at me strangely. As the train drew to a halt he whipped out a comb from his breast pocket, scraped his side parting back into place and smiled at me, a piece of cornflakes stuck in his teeth. He picked up his briefcase and made his way off the train as I stretched and hunted about for my flip-flops.

Amritsar, like other holy cities in India, danced to a different beat. On the surface it resembled any big city: buses belched grime and grease; dogs hobbled and scratched; steam rose from karahis hissing on the pavement; cows lived off a diet of Aamir Khan posters; rubbish reeked; and women with umbrellas picked their way between potholes, dodging cyclists and sunlight amid the clanging, yelling, pushing and selling. But beneath that layer the city throbbed with the thrill and excitement that came with pilgrimage. The word alone was enough to incite the kind of delirium that 'road trip!' brought to American college students.

On the approach to the Golden Temple, a carnival thronging with turbans was moving and shaking its way through the streets while men handed out handkerchiefs for visitors to cover their heads, and drums beat out a welcome between trumpets and horns. Exchanging my bag and shoes for a small token, I waded through the footbath, adding more muck to my feet, and descended the stairs to the enclosure.

Rising from the middle of a lake of water was the gurdwara, gleaming like a treasure chest recovered from the seabed. Its gold-plated walls and turrets fired back flashes of sunlight that skipped across the ripples in the water, which was said to contain amrit, or immortal nectar. The lake looked inviting until I noticed algae floating on the surface like a layer of lime marmalade. Sikh men, stripped to the waist, bathed at its edges or sat cross-legged with their friends and families, basking in the aura radiating from their holy shrine. Despite the hundreds of men, women and children of all faiths circling the lake, no more than a murmur was audible beneath the music playing through loudspeakers. Overhead the sun was at the peak of its rage, searing my neck and arms as heat bounced back and forth between the whitewashed walls of the compound. I tried to tail the crowd around the lake, scalding the soles of my feet, but gave up within minutes as hunger and heat exhaustion got the better of me.

Stepping into the passages between the walls, I moved into the shadows and pressed myself to the stone, cold against my palms and cheeks, until the smell of food and the din of ravenous pilgrims drew me towards the langar. Here, free vegetarian food was served daily to both Sikhs and non-Sikhs to ensure that equality was maintained, in keeping with Sikh philosophy. Diners of all colours, ages, shapes and sizes sat shoulder to shoulder on the floor as voluntary servers ladled out dal and flipped steaming chapattis onto metal plates. An average of 100,000 people were fed here every day. Daunted by the clamour of crowds, I lingered for a few moments behind a pillar, watching friends and families, then went to collect my bag as an overwhelming sense of loneliness kicked me in the stomach.

An elderly gentleman with a beard that reached his waist took my token and handed over my backpack. As I pulled on the straps, he gestured to his mouth with bunched fingers. Shoulders sagging, red-faced and with an upper lip running like a tap, I shook my head.

'No, I'll eat later, I'm not hungry now,' I lied.

He raised a palm and reached down to behind the bench separating us, then stood up holding a metal jug and bowl. He began to pour rajma into the bowl and it splattered over the sides as he produced a foil packet and started to unroll a pair of rotis. It was his own lunch.

'Come.'

The gentleman gestured for me to climb over the bench and I shook my head.

'Oh, no, thank you, that's your lunch.'

Ignoring me, he began to clear a patch of bags from the floor, then laid down a sheet of newspaper. He put down the food and waved me over. I stepped over the bench and took off my bag as he turned the table fan towards me.

'You must eat,' he said, sending a colleague down to bring up some water.

I bit into a roti and started to cry.

Meanwhile, visitors had bunched on the staircase waiting to hand in crates, suitcases, packets and boxes. As they filed past, they stared at me sitting cross-legged on the obituaries pages amid a mountain of backpacks. As the gentleman went back to bag duty, another man in a grey safari suit came upstairs.

'I'm Daljinder,' he said, wading through the bags and boxes, placing a steel bowl of water on the ground.

'And he's Lali,' he said, pointing to the first gentleman.

Daljinder and Lali were both volunteers who manned the 'leggez house'. He sat on the edge of the bench.

'You are Punjabi?'

'No, I'm from London. My mum's family is from Hyderabad and my dad's from Chennai.'

'But Indian only?'

'Yes.'

'You are studying?'

'No, I'm a journalist, but I'm riding the railways for a few months.'

'Oh! Where are you going to next?'

'I'm heading south to join the Golden Chariot.'

'I have a niece in London, you may know her.' He scrolled through his phone. 'You must call her when you go home,' he said, showing me a number that I typed into my phone.

'So you have seen the temple then?' he asked.

'Yes. It's really beautiful. But what I like most is that everyone is welcomed in.'

'This is Sikh culture. You can be president or pauper and it is the same.'

'How often do you volunteer?'

'I am retired now so I come here most days.' He refilled the water bowl. 'Now from here where are you going?'

'To the Wagah border.'

'You finish your food and I will take you to find a proper taxi.'

Once I had finished my rajma and rotis and stopped sweating and crying, Daljinder led me to the front of the temple where he put me in a taxi to the Wagah border, calling to check that I had arrived and again that night to make sure I had returned safely to Amritsar.

Wagah is a village that since Partition has lain half in India and half in Pakistan. It sits on the Radcliffe Line, the border between the two countries, where tourists now gather every evening before sunset to watch a 45-minute flag-lowering ceremony that culminates with the slamming of the border gates. It is like the Berlin Wall of the East.

A roar ripped through the air as I squeezed between video cameras, elbows and banners and hauled myself onto a wall to watch the ceremony that was already underway. On the Indian side of the gates an army of mothers with children danced on the road to 'Jai Ho', waving arms and blow-dried curls, while packs of men wearing flags as capes pounded fists, their cheeks puffed out by whistles. Western tourists sat along the front rows, knees together, clapping along. On the other side of the gates the Pakistani crowd appeared to be partaking in a memorial service. Not a face flinched. Green flags wilted like dead leaves. As a furious chorus of 'Hindustan Zindabad!' came to an end, the revellers collapsed in their seats and the Pakistani crowd erupted. It was their turn.

Just below me an Indian man began to thump his chest and chant: 'Hindustan Zindabad! Hindustan Zindabad! Hindustan Zindabad!'

From the back of the crowd he ploughed his way forward, shoving children out of the way, then swam through bodies to get to the front. To my left a man wearing an ill-fitting toupée shook his head.

'Stupid bloody idiot.'

Grappling at his chest, the man began to tear off his shirt when a guard, a Terminator in white knee socks, strode over and pushed the man back by his face. He pulled out a baton and began to swipe at the crowd, shoving anyone within reach. As a riot broke out, the Indian Border Security Force began their parade. Each wore headgear that fanned out and shook as they strutted around like a set of cockerels. One by one they began to speed up and down the lane towards the gate, pausing to kick their polished heels above their heads with such vigour that they could have kicked holes into their own foreheads. The Pakistanis began to do the same.

I thought back to the man on the train to Amritsar. Monty Python was an accurate description. This was the Indian version of the Ministry of Silly Walks. Both sets of guards stomped back and forth, yanking each other's arms in symbolic handshaking, before eventually lowering the flags to a cacophony of Pakistani and Indian patriotism. As the sun finally set on the spectacle, the gates were clanged shut and the crowds drifted off, leaving a trail in their wake of popcorn, empty bottles, ice-cream tubs and teacups, amid the atmosphere of a cricket match that had ended in a draw.

'GET OUT OF MY TRAIN!'

I spat a mouthful of samosa into my hand and looked up.

'What? Why?'

'My train is full! Get out!'

The ticket inspector threw my pass into the seat beside me and pointed to the door. A couple in matching polo shirts stared at me over their tea. I had decided to leave Amritsar after a late lunch and caught the afternoon Shatabdi, number 49, back to Delhi. My train pass covered the fare, but there had been no time to reserve a seat.

'Next station is Beas. You get out there!'

'But there are empty seats everywhere.'

'You get out of this carriage and go now to the backside!'

I stood up. 'Fine, I'll go, there's no need to fly off the handle.'

He snatched my tea from my hand and banged it down on the table, spilling the contents onto the paper plate of ketchup and the half-eaten samosa.

'Can I at least take my samosa with me?'

He looked like he was about to hit me with his clipboard. Swelling with rage, he pulled open the door and gave me a shove between the shoulder blades.

'Go!'

I ambled down the aisles as the train began to mock me, snaking its way along the tracks and threatening to launch me into a variety of different laps, before I found a row of empty seats and sat down. Beas was less than 20 minutes away. It was my fault for not making a reservation, but few passengers had boarded at Amritsar and there were seats available.

Glancing over my shoulder, I settled back into the chair and opened up *The Inheritance of Loss*, wiping the tea-stained pages with my sleeve. I ordered a replacement cup as the chai wallah came past, took a sip and went back to the story.

'... Jemubhai, his face apuff with anger, grabbed at his wife.

She slipped from his grasp and his anger flew...'

'You go to the backside!'

The door burst open behind me and the inspector appeared again. He stood over me, his lips curling up like two overcooked frankfurters.

'Get up!'

'Oh for fuc...'

I threw my book down on the seat, gathered my things and stood up.

'Where would you like me to sit? In the toilet? Or on the laundry bags?'

'Go to the backside!'

'Where is the backside?! I don't know what you mean!'

'Are you an idiot? GO TO C5 OR C6 AND SIT THERE!'

'That's all you had to say.'

Trudging through a further four carriages, I found another row of seats in coach C6 just as the train pulled into Beas. Few passengers boarded so I stayed put, but slouched low in my seat until Ludhiana, where I was hauled out again and made to sit with the laundry bags. They were quite comfy and I dozed off on them until we reached Ambala, where another inspector found me a window seat.

My neighbour was wedged into his chair with both arms splayed out to the sides. His stomach pushed against his tray table and one of his knees was already occupying my leg area, while the other massaged the thigh of a small man trying in vain to twist himself away. Once he had prised himself up and into the aisle, I slithered around him and into my seat, pressing myself to the wall. He fell back into the space and his upper arm came to rest against my left ear as I prayed that this was the last round of musical chairs – and that I would not need to use the toilet until Delhi.

After a good sleep, scrambled eggs and a flick through the party pages that always featured Z-list 'PYTs' (pretty young things), who only ever had first names and wore black tops, I took an auto to New Delhi station.

Anusha visibly braced herself.

'Oh, you're here again.' She patted a form on the table. 'Write down train number 2425…'

'Ah. I'm not going to Jammu now.'

She kneaded her face into a series of scowls before stopping on a particularly good one.

'Oh God… where are you going now?'

'Chennai.'

'It's the other direction!'

'I know, but I need to offload a stack of books in Chennai before I move on to Bangalore.'

She sighed and scoured her screen, shaking her head. Without looking up she asked:

'So, where is your friend now?'

'I'm not sure, I think he's still in Varanasi.'

The truth was that I had no idea if Passepartout was still in the country. For all I knew, he could have packed up, left Chandigarh and flown back to London. Anusha took off her glasses and put them on the table, a smirk growing.

'Oh, all right, I don't know where he is. We fought and I ran off.'

'Ha! I knew!' Anusha waggled her finger in victory. 'I knew when you came.'

I allowed her a few minutes to gloat, then I slapped the table.

'Hurry up!' I shouted.

She tapped a few numbers into her computer.

'Okay, there is one Chennai Rajdhani train that is fast.'

'How fast?'

'Twenty-eight hours.'

'Oh my God.'

'Everything else is 30, 38 hours. Take this, it's comfortable and food is good.'

'Okay, then I need to get to Bangalore the following morning.'

'Nothing is available.'

I looked at the Golden Chariot's itinerary. If I missed boarding at Bangalore, I could join it the following day at Mysore. 'How about Mysore?'

She scoured the screen. 'Mysore Express is there.'

Anusha printed out the tickets and watched me wedge them into my logbook.

'Be careful.'

I leant across her files and kissed her on the cheek.

The Chennai Rajdhani Express departed from Delhi Hazrat Nizamuddin station at 4 pm, so there was just enough time left to buy a packet of banana chips and a couple of packets of Hide and Seek Bourbons. Curious about the glass jars of cookies that seemed to have sat in most vendors' stands since the beginning of time, I requested one and watched the vendor wipe his fingers on his shirt, then bury his hand into the jar, pawing the load before bringing out a dusty disc. It was like chewing on a brick. A puppy lay under a bench licking at his prolapsed rectum, so I crushed the biscuit with a fist, poured water over the mess and left him to work through the mulch, as two girls watched in amusement.

Crossing the footbridge, I arrived at the bottom of the stairs and found carriage A3 directly opposite, affixed with a list stating that I was sharing a compartment with Rohit Malhotra, Adil Chopra and Sanjeev Acharya. Trying to look as casual as possible, though nauseous at the prospect of spending 28 hours with three strange men, I swanned into the compartment and nodded curtly at the three who were already sitting cross-legged and chatting in Hindi. I barricaded myself behind my logbook as the train began to move.

Train number 50 was about to cover 2176 km in just over 28 hours. A ticket in this compartment cost the equivalent of £38 – less than the price of an 80-minute journey from London Euston to Birmingham New Street – and included three meals.

'Ma'am, where are you travelling to?'

I lowered the book. 'To Chennai,' I replied to the gentleman wearing glasses, a collared shirt and suit trousers.

'Are you having family there?'

'Yes, but I'm just travelling through to then take a train to Mysore where I'm due to board another train...' I trailed off, realising how ridiculous this must have sounded, and briefly explained the journey.

'We saw you writing and we were discussing among ourselves what you were doing,' the second man said.

The three turned out to be friends who were travelling to a wedding in Vijayawada. The first gentleman, Rohit, was an accountant and the second, Adil, the director of a Delhi-based business. Their friend Sanjeev stayed curled up against the seat back, barefooted, muttering occasionally in Hindi.

'So where all have you been?' Rohit asked, thumbing through my notes.

'I started in Chennai, then went down to Kanyakumari and up along the western coast to Gujarat, then Rajasthan and Punjab. But I want to get up to Udhampur and across to Ledo, as they're the northern and easternmost tips of the railways.'

Both men pointed immediately at Sanjeev, who was now eating a packet of butter.

'He is from Ledo.'

'If you would like to visit you should tell us and we will organise the stay for you,' Rohit offered.

'Really?'

'Of course,' said Adil, 'it would be a pleasure. Sanjeev works for the Lok Sabha. He can arrange this with a good friend of ours who is in Tinsukia. From there he will take care of you and get you to Ledo.'

They handed over their business cards and I added them to the growing stack. A lady sitting across the aisle eyed me, tossing a pinch of soan cake into her mouth.

Dinner soon arrived and Adil spread out a sheet of newspaper under my containers. All three sat cross-legged, sleeves rolled up, licking fingers and swapping food. It was like eating with my family.

'You haven't eaten much?' Rohit scolded, looking at my tray then stopping the vendor as he passed the door. 'Bring some more vegetable for her, please.'

'Yes, sar.'

'No!' I protested.

'By European standards I am sure that your weight is acceptable, but by Indian standards you are very underweight,' Adil declared, tipping a container full of vegetables onto my tray. It really was like eating with my family.

Although big cities were growing more aware that devouring rice and deep-fried food did little to bless the waistline, the pale Victorian look was still considered preferable to the tanned and toned bodies of India's labourers, a look hankered after on the other side of the world by subscribers to *Men's Health* and *Glamour*.

The train screeched to a halt, slopping dal across the seats. After a few minutes I got up and went to investigate. Nobody else seemed to notice, or care, that the train had made an unscheduled stop. Pulling down the latches, I heaved open the door and leant out. Through the darkness I could hear voices further down the track. Suddenly nervous that I was about to encourage dacoits aboard, I slammed the door and turned to a gentleman rinsing his mouth in the sink.

'I thought this train only stopped at Jhansi before Bhopal.'

'Yah, officially.'

'So why have we stopped?'

'Someone has pulled the chain.'

'How do you know?'

He clicked his teeth with scorn. 'I travel this route many times. It is unusual for a Rajdhani train, but sometimes these fellows who live in between stations will pull the chain. Train stops, they jump out and go home.'

'You're kidding.'

'So many people there are, who knows who pulled what.'

After a lie-in, I slid down the berth to find that my companions had saved an omelette sandwich and tea for me. Adil was flicking through the paper, reading a story about cohabitation and shaking his head. In 2005 diehard

Hindus had accused a Tamil actress named Khushboo of criminal behaviour for declaring in a magazine interview that no educated man would expect his bride to be a virgin. A recent ruling by the Indian Supreme Court had resulted in her favour, pointing out that even the deity Krishna had lived unmarried with his lover Radha.

Adil frowned. 'I think this will work against women.'

'Why?' I asked.

'Cohabitation will give men an easy get-out clause. If they are living together then they have nothing binding. It will make it easy to leave a relationship, or men will start having casual relationships before they eventually get married.'

'But most young people have relationships before marriage, they just hide it.'

'How do you feel about living together?'

'I have no problem with it. If you're going to spend the rest of your life with someone you need to know what it's going to be like. You don't buy a car without test driving it.'

'But what if they leave?'

'If they leave, then they were probably always going to. Isn't it better for them to leave before they get married than spend a lifetime in an unhappy marriage?'

'I see your point,' Rohit interrupted, 'but I think that ultimately children will suffer if they are a product of those relationships.'

I took the paper from Adil and read the article. Most pertinent was that religion had played a positive role in the outcome of the court case. Rather than clamping down, citing archaic tradition, the case showed that even Hinduism was open to evolution.

I looked up. Around me bags were packed and bedding stacked.

'We are getting off in Vijayawada,' Adil announced.

'Oh.' I was disappointed by the desertion.

'You must let us know when you would like to go to Ledo,' Rohit said.

'I will, I promise, that is so kind of you.'

'It's our pleasure, enjoy Chennai and Mysore and please be in touch.'

The train drew into Vijayawada and the compartment emptied. Looking around the bare berths, I wrapped the blankets around myself and sat by the window to finish my photocopied book, whose page numbers had begun to jump back and forth at the crux of the story.

'All train talk.'

The woman across the compartment was shaking her head at me.

'Sorry?'

'All train talk, lip service if you will.' She waved her hand towards the platform. 'They won't do anything. Simply timepass chat. Nothing you will hear from them again.'

I nodded and began to feel foolish. Pulling my blanket over my knees, I smoothed the pages out and hoped desperately that she was wrong.

15 | Silk Sheets and a Wad of Human Hair

On the rare occasions when you find yourself alone in India, it is never for very long. Like a heat-seeking missile, someone will appear by your side. While this can be interpreted as no more than a simple act of friendliness, the truth is that you are considered a walking opportunity. Less than a minute will pass before an attempt will be made to peddle wares, ask for money or pens, offer a ride in a rickshaw, extract seemingly banal information or exchange contact details. Even if you are stranded in the desert, rest assured a boy will appear over the dunes selling bottles of water.

Boarding coach S4, I looked around at the empty compartment. No chained briefcases. No games of rummy. No babies rocking in makeshift cribs fashioned from saris. No important phone calls. No smell of fried potato and puris.

Nothing.

Nobody.

I flipped on the fan, which did little more than flick clumps of hairy dust at the floor. At the start of the journey travelling in sleeper class at night ranked low on my wish list, but after the dust storms in Rajasthan I was now unfazed by anything that came through the barred windows: rain, wind, horns, roasted nuts in twists of newspaper or upturned palms. I sat down and looked around. Had I boarded the wrong train? The Kaveri Express departed from Chennai Central at 9:30 pm and was due to arrive in Mysore Junction at 8 am, leaving me plenty of time to find the

Golden Chariot before its passengers surfaced from under their duvets. It was 9 pm.

Within minutes, passengers and their families began to stream in and out of the doors like an army of lemmings and I was joined in my compartment by Shiv. With his matching T-shirt and shorts, runny nose and right hand thrust into a bag of Lay's, he resembled an overgrown 5-year-old with a moustache. Pulling off his backpack, he drew his feet up onto the seat and offered his half-eaten bag of crisps.

'You are from Chennai?' he asked.

This was more like it.

'I live in England. Where are you from?'

'I live in Mysore only but I come home to Chennai every weekend. My canteen food is terrible. I need home cooking.'

'Are you a student?'

'I studied engineering in Mysore, but now I am working.'

'What do you do?'

'IT engineering. I live in accommodation with many others.'

'Why don't you learn to cook?'

He looked at me in disbelief. 'Not possible.'

At university, budding Jamie Olivers were few and far between among the boys I knew, but even the most culinarily challenged could manage beans on toast or a bowl of sweating pasta.

'So when you get married your wife will take care of the cooking?'

'There is that possibility, but many girls are very independent now. We will have to look for one who is willing.' He reached for my logbook. 'You are studying?'

'No, I'm a journalist.'

'I would love to write. Really... doing something creative would be great.'

'Why don't you, then?'

'I have to send money to my parents.'

Heating a tin of beans might have been within their remit, but none of my contemporaries would have stretched that far.

'What do they do?' I asked.

'Father is bus conductor, mother is with poor health. I must help them pay for my younger brother's schooling.'

'That's very good of you.'

'Why? That is what we do. Parents take care when we are young, we take care when they are old. That is life.' He pointed at me. 'I tell you one thing, you take my email address and we will be in contact. I will send you my poems.'

Shiv propped up his head with his backpack and closed his eyes as train 51 began to thunder through the outskirts of Chennai.

A burgundy train trimmed with gold stood at the furthest platform at Mysore Junction, waiting patiently for her residents to rise. The Golden Chariot, launched in early 2008, was a lesser-known member of the royal family, normally found in and around Rajasthan. She carries her guests through the Golden Triangle of the South, departing from Bangalore every Monday afternoon and travelling across Karnataka through Mysore, Kabini, Shravanabelagola, Belur, Hampi and Badami, ending in Goa before returning to Bangalore the following Monday morning. The seven-day tour largely comprises temples, archaeological wonders and World Heritage Sites, most of which are difficult to reach by regular trains without hiring taxis or suffering local buses to make connections between each destination.

After a hot shower and a rummage through the gels, foams, sprays and lotions lined up in the bathroom, my tan was now swirling down the drain. I lay swaddled in a towel with my feet in slippers, allowing the air conditioning to slip over my newly moisturised limbs – now two shades paler. Sleeper class was all well and good, but silk throws on twin beds and a plasma screen with a DVD player made for a welcome interlude. Voices drifted down the corridor, so I got dressed and made my way to breakfast, arriving in darned Ali Baba pants and a vest beaten to death on rocks, hoping a pair of pearl earrings would add polish to the getup.

Unlike her younger brother the Indian Maharaja, the Golden Chariot looked tired: upholstery was balding in a way that no combover could conceal and smudges dotted the crockery and linen. The staff still beamed and bowed, however, fawning around the many Indian families with children who filled the booths wearing Bata sandals and baseball caps. Scouring the dining car for an empty spot, I joined an Australian gentleman and helped myself to his toast.

'Did I miss much in Bangalore?' I asked.

'Not really,' he replied, buttering what was left of it, 'just a lot of pro-India PR. You know, the usual, "look at our shops and malls and gorgeous hotels" and then some guff about how the Garden City has now become India's Silicon Valley. A bloody shame if you ask me, was once such a tranquil spot.'

Patrick was at least 70, with thinning hair that curled beneath his ears and a tan like a terracotta pot.

'Are you travelling alone?' I asked.

'No, I'm not alone. I'm by myself.' He speared a piece of watermelon. 'Since my wife died I've only ever gone on holiday by myself. Best way to see the world. Went on horseback across Mongolia last year and every other year I go back to the same spot in Ko Phi Phi. They know me so well now they save my favourite room for me. They've become like family.'

'Don't you sometimes wish you had someone you could reminisce over those times with?'

'I'm telling *you* about it now, aren't I? Trust me, the only way to get under the skin of a new place is by being free to come and go as you please.'

Like the Indian Maharaja, the Golden Chariot played the role of a cruise ship on wheels, setting sail at night while guests rocked between the covers and docking at a new destination before they had the chance to stretch, take tea and wonder why their room was upside down. That afternoon a group of 30 boarded a coach to the Rajiv Gandhi National Park in Nagarhole, to spend one night at the park's lodges. Once the old hunting grounds of Mysore's maharajas, the park was built on the banks of the Kabini river where wild elephants curled their trunks around their young, sambar flinched in the trees and a number of big cats lurked in between bushes, none of whom felt compelled to confirm their elusive presence. As the sun sank on the lake, unrolling a tongue of gold that lapped at the edges, we returned to the main lodge, tailed by a number of langurs who sat on the walls, idling like a group of teenagers. They waited for the platters of pastries to be abandoned before bouncing in to help themselves, much to the distress of the staff, who tried to deter Hanuman's army while maintaining a façade of unflappable geniality in front of the guests.

Patrick took his tumbler of tea and went to examine a bunch of mini bananas that hung from the roof for guests to pluck, when I was approached by James Shakespeare, an 80-year-old beanpole wearing a sweater vest and Argyle socks pulled up to his knees.

'Now, where have you come from then?' he asked, inspecting a banana the size of his thumb.

Unsure if he was addressing me or the banana, I replied, 'London.'

'Here to trace your roots?'

'Something like that.'

'I'm awfully deaf in one ear, you must shout.'

'I'm travelling around India by train for a few months.'

'I beg your pardon?'

'TRAIN, travelling around India by TRAIN.'

He peered up at the sky. 'Yes, it does look as if it might, but those nice people have left some brollies here for us.'

He handed me a golf umbrella and began to fiddle with the handle. It flicked open, poking him in the stomach, and he jumped back and beamed. 'Born in Shimler m'self, have you been?'

'Yes, I took the toy train up there two weeks ago.'

'Funny old place now, quite a mishmash. Old hill train still running, you know, used to ride it when I was a lad. You really should try to visit if you can.'

'I will.'

'Visited Darjeeling?'

'No, I haven't been yet, but it's on my list.'

James was now facing the other way but leaning precariously towards me, waggling his ear. 'Bloody long journey, if I were you I would skip it and just do the short loop round to Ghum. You see enough and you won't want to kill yourself before you reach the bottom.'

Back in Mysore the following afternoon, I had time to kill after lunch and went for a walk around the station. Shankar had informed me that Mysore Junction housed some of the best retiring rooms in India: like the trains themselves, retiring rooms varied from immaculate to downright inhumane. They were offered on a first-come-first-served basis unless passengers were looking for lodgings at Mumbai Central Station, where Western Railways was soon to launch an inquiry into five officials who were alleged to have lived illegally for several years in the station's rooms, while claiming a monthly housing allowance.

At the top of a staircase was a carved wooden frame engraved with flowers and creepers that contained eight lights and a switch, labelled:

PLEASE PRESS THE SWITCH TO KNOW THE
AVAILABILITY OF THE ROOMS
RED LIGHT INDICATES THAT THE ROOMS ARE OCCUPIED

I pressed the switch and the whole row glowed red. Disappointed but curious, I wandered into the pillared hallway, whose marble floors had been polished to a sheen. Slipping inside an open door, I found a beautiful old bedroom flooded with sunshine and fitted with arched windows. Curtains twisted in the breeze and two colonial-style wooden beds stood against the wall. The sound of scrubbing and gushing water came from the en-suite bathroom, so I poked my head around and spied a bent back slapping a rag at the floor. An array of toiletries lined the sink – a vast improvement on the dried dregs of soap nibbled by rats in Delhi.

From across the platforms Patrick waved to tell me that the coach had arrived to take us to Mysore Palace, so I abandoned sniffing around toilets and joined the group. On board I took out my logbook and began to count up the trains as the guide swayed in the aisle, fellating his microphone.

'We are now passing the University of Mysore which is comparable to the Oxford University in London...'

The Golden Chariot was train number 52. If I hopped off in Goa before it looped back to Bangalore, I could climb the Konkan coast to Mumbai. Within a couple of days I would be back on track and heading to Udhampur.

'There are 600 plus steps to the top of the hill, so if you're feeling tough then you can wear some socks and climb, otherwise there are palanquins available.'

Murmurs of relief buzzed around the group just as a man sidled up to the guide and whispered in her ear. She clicked her fingers in the air.

'Aaaaactually... the palanquin bearers are on strike today, so there are no palanquins to take you to the top.'

Half the group got back on the coach.

Shravanabelagola, which seemed to elicit more intrigue from the group for its name than for its importance as a site of Jain pilgrimage, was a township in the Hassan district in Karnataka. Translated loosely as 'the white pond of the ascetic', it was home to a multiplicity of temples, monuments and shrines scattered between two hills named Chandragiri and Vindyagiri, attracting hundreds of meditating monks and tourists. Six hundred steps up the Vindyagiri hill led to the Gomateshwara, a 17.5-metre-high statue of one of Emperor Rishabhadeva's sons, who had renounced his kingdom to pursue meditation, living in forests until he achieved enlightenment. Carved out of a single piece of granite in AD 981, it towers above the township as a symbol of salvation and enlightenment to the Jain community. *The Times of India* readers had voted it at the top of the seven wonders of India.

Digging around for my iPod, I took a deep breath, located the *Rocky* soundtrack and began to power up the 600 steps, determined to count each one, but collapsed halfway to nurse a cramp in my calf. Most of the Indian families bounded ahead. There was something about pilgrimages that triggered determination, drive and a superhuman power to reach a goal, even if the goal was simply to touch the feet of a smiling monolith. Squatting on a step, I looked down onto the view. In the foreground Chandragiri pushed through the rubble and boulders, sprouting tufts of green, while an otherwise pancake-flat expanse reached to the haze on the horizon. A patchwork of palm trees and lakes blanketed the landscape, the tips of temples and pillars peeking out from in between. Next to me stood a man wearing an orange cloak, striped scarves, a stack of beads and peacock feathers sprouting from his turban, with the outline of a swan chalked onto his cheek. He looked me up and down, smirked and lit a beedi.

At the top of the hill, visitors milled at the feet of the naked statue, said to be the tallest monolith in the world, although the Sphinx vied for the same title. Vines snaked between the Gomateshwara's thighs and curled around his upper arms like wedding bracelets, indicating his time spent in the forests. His ears hung like the Buddha and his face bore an air of contentment. While I lingered, watching the priests wash the toes with milk, a second priest beckoned me forward and pressed his thumb from the bridge of my nose up into my parting. Patrick wandered over.

'Quite something, eh?' He eyed the overzealous swipe of kumkum on my forehead.

'Are you Hindu?' he asked, stressing the second syllable, as we made our way down the steps, springing like gazelles on the slabs of hot rock.

'I am, but I'm not religious.'

'Why's that?'

'I'd rather put theory into practice instead of getting bogged down with ritual.'

'It has a real lure, doesn't it?'

'Ritual?'

'No, I meant India. Westerners are very taken by its exoticism. And understandably, it's a very beautiful country.' He thrust his arms up at the expanse ahead. 'I mean, it's so easy to fall in love with this.' He paused and grinned at me. 'Very clever people, you lot.'

'In what way?'

'Like Brazilians to coffee and the Arabs to oil, Indians have an abundance of spirituality to sell to the West.' He squinted back up the stairs. 'I don't believe in God myself, but I still admire the workmanship that goes into what they believe in. There's a lot to be said for the hard work and diligence that comes with that religious mindset.'

At the bottom of the steps (615, 616 or maybe 617?) a vendor was hacking the tops off fresh coconuts. He popped a straw in the top of two and handed them over as Patrick and I drained them, scooped out the flesh and climbed back onto the coach.

Over the next three days the train ploughed through the heart of the old Vijayanagara Empire, unloading us to pick through the city of broken boulders in Hampi and clamber through the temple caves at Badami. It arrived on Easter Sunday at the Goan Basilica of Bom Jesus, to sneak a peek at St Francis Xavier – at least what was left of him. On a rare display of the body for veneration, a Portuguese woman had bitten off his big toe, now displayed in a reliquary in the basilica, while one of his hands resides in Rome and a forearm in Macau.

On the last night on board, I lay in bed watching a newsflash about a bomb blast in Kakapora near Srinagar that had damaged the only railway track in Kashmir. Since late 2008 the service had run between Qazigund and Baramulla in an attempt to strengthen ties between the occupied territories and India. It had been added to our train list, albeit within brackets, beneath a hovering question mark. I drew a pencil line through the listing, switched off the television and lay listening to the hum of the air conditioner.

I was now ready to get back on the real railways.

Peering out of the window at Vasco da Gama station, I kicked off my flip-flops and put my feet up on the ripped vinyl.

Home again.

The Vasco da Gama Kulem passenger train was due into Madgaon just before 2 pm, leaving enough time for me to join any number of overnight services up to Mumbai. Munching on a handful of banana chips, I flipped to the back page of my logbook where a list of trains caught my eye:

1. Ooty toy train (do after mudslide, otherwise scary)
2. Fairy Queen – she might not be running but check anyway
3. Gorakhpur to Nautanwa
4. Goa to Londa, MOST BEAUTIFUL

I recognised the scrawls from our first meeting with Shankar at his Wembley office. The list was a handful of trains that he had run off the top of his head as unmissable routes. As the train jerked and began to move, number four stared at me. I grabbed my bags. It was criminal to come so close and miss the most beautiful route. Two boys sniggered as I struggled with my things, one leaning across to take a photo of me as I tumbled down the steps and onto the platform to await the Goa Express to Londa.

'Come, sit with us only!' Pramod sucked his teeth. 'Why do you want to sit here? There are many seats that side, come!' He cocked his head to one side, his bouffant flapping at the front. 'You are really mad, I tell you.'

Pramod was a recent engineering graduate who had just started work at a bank in Pune. He and his colleagues had taken the Easter weekend off to come down to Goa and – he put a thumb to his lips – get 'high'. The aftermath of their 'wodka-fest' hung about his T-shirt and he grinned.

'I need to change my shirt before I go home or I'll get such a hiding from my mother.'

He tugged at my rucksack and I gave in. On his way to the toilet he had seen me sitting in the doorway watching women thrash laundry in the river, and refused to let me stay put.

Eleven of Pramod's colleagues sat squashed into one compartment, elbows resting on each other's knees and shoulders, chatting, reading and teasing one another. Not wanting to impose, I perched on the edge of the side berth opposite a girl wearing a nose-ring the size of a five-pence piece. Her eyes sloped upwards with tails of liner running parallel with her eyebrows. She looked like a Kishangarh painting.

'What are you reading?' I asked.

She held up the red cover with both hands. '*Two States*. Have you read it?'

I nodded.

'Like it?'

'It was fun, but a bit over the top. People can't be that bad.'

She slapped my leg. 'My God, that is *just* how they are.'

'Really?'

'Yah-yah. To-tally. My mother is from Chennai and she studied in Delhi. Same problem she had there. Ex-act what you find, you find in these pages. Hillll-arious.'

Pramod's friends began to flip through my logbook, pushing each other's heads away like puppies at feeding time. He reached for my Moleskine notebook, scribbled in it and slid it back in one smooth motion. I turned away and flipped to the page where he had written in swooping curls:

'Don't get personally
if they are laufaing.
They are enjoing.'

I smiled. 'Don't worry, I don't mind. In fact I'm going back to the doorway for a while.' I picked up my camera as Pramod shook his head and fingered my scarf.

Heaving open the door, I squatted down as train number 53 hugged the curves of the hills. Streams of water spilt down crevices, appearing from a distance like silver wire weaving through the rocks. The express train clanked along the rocky terrain, then skimmed across the bridges as olive-green bodies of water shifted quietly below, while the breeze turned to gusts that wrestled with my hair. Palms flanked the banks like bending windmills, parting to reveal whitewashed villas and workers in vests.

A yell broke the reverie and two policemen appeared behind me. One shouted in Hindi while the other banged the door shut. Once they had clumped through to the next compartment, I feigned ignorance and handed my coffee cup to a little girl with two plaits and a paunch who was waiting for the toilet. Pulling the door open again, I looped both arms around the handrails and breathed deeply as the sun began to swirl behind a film of cloud, a grey-blue ball looking for a place to reappear. A sharp bend brought the police marching back and the girl thrust back my coffee, not wishing to be implicated. They spat more Hindi at me, pointed their sticks and growled, until Pramod claimed responsibility for my behaviour and the door was slammed for good.

'Come and sit down,' he pleaded. 'Just a few moments ago, someone fell out of the train.'

On the approach to Londa, an ominous glow fired the clay-covered ground. It was a tiny station and it cleared as fast as it had filled. Soon there was nobody but a cloud of mosquitoes fighting for my attention. In my haste to make it to Londa, I had made one fatal error: I had not checked the return train timings. Towards the end of the platform, a sweeper was clearing paper plates from a doorway and I asked him when the next train returned to Goa. He held up two fingers.

'In two hours?'

He shook his head and flipped his hand forward.

'Two o'clock?!'

It was now just before 7 pm and I had almost seven hours to wait alone. The sweeper gestured for me to follow him as he led me to a waiting room, whose only other occupants were a cockroach and a pair of gekkos transfixed by a naked light bulb. Desperate for the toilet, I nudged open the door with a toe as the stench of mothballs and urine wriggled up my nose. Crouching in the dark, moisture dripping onto my back, I hurried out and found the seat with the fewest paan stains, where I sat, hugging my rucksack to my chest.

What a fuck-up.

I fished out my book and began to read, but being alone does not last long. A figure appeared in the doorway. He watched me for a minute or two while I pretended not to notice. He crept in and stood with his back to me, facing the platform.

'You are alone.'

It was more an observation than a question.

'I'm waiting for a train.'

He nodded. 'Where are you going?'

'To meet my husband.'

'Oh. Why is he not here?'

'He works in Mumbai.'

'He is allowing you to be here alone?'

'I'm going straight to meet him.'

'What does he do?'

I kept reading and slipped my ring to my fourth finger. He looked down.

'You are looking very nice.'

I kept reading, but now goosebumps peppered my skin.

'Am I making you uncomfortable?'

At that moment the sweeper's broom swished by the doorway and it took spasms of restraint not to leap on the little man and kiss his grey stubble. The inquisitor sloped off.

'Are there any hotels near here?' I asked.

The sweeper picked up my smaller bag, swayed his head around, and began to walk off at a pace towards the station exit, so I followed. Wherever he led me, it had to be safer than Arserape Junction.

❖

It was the worst hotel room in India.

Mould marbled the walls and if I stood in the middle I could just reach both sides with my fingertips. A child's desk wobbled in the corner by a low bed slung with a baby's blanket, a human outline creasing the sheets. Just below the ceiling a rectangle had been cut out of the wall – either to fit an air conditioner or to remove corpses – and a light bulb had already hanged itself from a thread of wire.

The Rambagh Palace this was not.

I shut the door and a shower of plaster greeted me from above. Bolting the door, I curled into a ball on the bed. It was almost 9 pm.

By 11 pm my eyes were dry and blinking and I needed the toilet. Tempted to use the bin rather than risk opening the door, I tipped it towards me and found a wad of human hair at the bottom. Easing back the bolt, I peered around the door and looked down to find a man in khaki flat on his back with one hand in his trousers, lying next to a thali filled with half-eaten wigwams of dal and rice. He had lost interest midway through both activities and succumbed to sleep. The corridor was lit like a dungeon and I could just make out another man on the floor cradling a bottle of what could have been kerosene. I padlocked my door and tiptoed around them, trying not to detonate a landmine of potential rape.

On my return, both were still comatose. Slipping back into the room, I bolted the door and leapt onto the bed, taking a spring in my shoulder blade. Finally I began to doze and the power cut out. This was it: this was the night I was going to die. Nobody knew where I was. I did not know where I was. Fishing the photo of Shirdi Sai Baba out of my bag, I lay on my back, pressing it between sweating palms in the hope that I might see another sunrise.

Suddenly I flicked it away and sat up. No God or saint was going to save me unless I saved myself. Swinging my legs off the bed, I loaded up my bags and threw open the door. The men had gone. Stumbling down the stairs I lunged for the door, tripping over a body that lay like a rug across the threshold. Yelping, the man jumped up in a fog of dirty rum, scratched and yawned, then fumbled for a key. Yanking up the grill, he rearranged himself as I fell out into the street, shattering the midnight stillness, and ran in zigzags down the hill towards the light of the station.

16 | God Bless the NHS!

'May I tell you something, ma'am?'

'Of course.'

'You are selfish.'

A horn blasted through the air and a sea of sinewy necks swept past balancing baskets, boxes and other bits of battered luggage tied with string. A battle had broken out, roaring its way towards the severely delayed Bilaspur Express as it came to a halt. A trio of sadhus pushed me sideways in their haste to clear away the puja area they had built out of boredom. Taken aback, I stared at Sandeep, who faced me, expressionless but for a growing upward curve of his bottom lip.

'So,' Sandeep continued, 'are you wanting to go to your AC carriage or to come to the general class?'

'I'm coming with you. I want to know why you think I'm selfish.'

Since I had left Londa on the Hubli Link Express, a cluster of trains had pushed the number up considerably. The Mandovi Express from Madgaon to Ratnagiri had marked 55, followed by the Jan Shatabdi to Mumbai. A local from Jogeswari to Churchgate had brought the total to a respectable 57, and earlier in the day I had arrived on the overnight Kolkata Mail from CST into Katni, a junction in Madhya Pradesh, which made 58. A passenger connection to the relatively unknown town of Umaria was due within a couple of hours, so I had squatted by a wall with a copy of *Heat and Dust* and a ladoo. As I was finishing the last pages, a man had arrived on the platform and patted me on the head. He wore a black topi and several rows of beads and had an orange beard that flamed like a gulmohar tree. He began to unpack his holdall. Carefully unrolling what looked like a tightly wrapped bed sheet, he appeared to be preparing for an afternoon nap. But after inspecting every inch of the sequinned cloth and grunting in approval, he flapped it like a dhobi, swept it around his back and onto his shoulders, and began to dance a little jig. Waving the sheet behind his head, he cackled and his face cracked into wrinkles as he shimmied along the platform, until I realised two things. Firstly, that he was quite mad, and secondly, that my train had departed from the platform behind me.

While waiting for the next connection, Sandeep and I had begun chatting. Sandeep was a 25-year-old engineering student from Puri, in Orissa, who never ate food cooked outside his house and wore trousers so tight that impotence was inevitable. He was odd, but my affinity for oddness had grown over recent weeks and I entertained any opportunity to indulge it. Now the delayed train had arrived I trailed after Sandeep, who sailed ahead on a cloud of smugness. Squeezing through the doorway of train number 59, I picked my way through the carpet of crossed legs, conscious of the aura of angst that hung around my sweating body. Sandeep was sitting by the window, his powdered face a perfect circle of pale grey, his side parting slicked into place.

'Go on, then, tell me why I'm selfish.'

He raised his index finger. 'How long were you talking to me on the platform?'

'About half an hour.'

'It was almost twice that time,' he replied, baring an alarmingly white set of teeth and now holding up a pair of fingers fitted with gold rings, both embossed with an image of Lord Krishna.

'Why did you ask then?'

He ignored me.

'In that time that I was standing and talking to you, you did not ask me to sit down.'

That was it.

I had not asked a grown and able-bodied man to sit down on a bench that had space for two extra people, after I had made room for two mothers with babies.

'If you wanted to sit down, why didn't you just sit down? I like stretching my legs in between journeys. For all I knew, you wanted to stand.'

'That is not the point.'

'Try getting on the tube in London. You wouldn't last two minutes if you expected people to invite you into spare seats.'

'Then you are living in a very selfish country.'

He was right. It did make me wonder about the indifference of travellers on the Underground: passengers only unite in the face of disaster or in the presence of a wasp – or if an unaccustomed tourist fails to find a handhold and falls into someone's lap. Even then, giggles are stifled behind newspapers and all eyes avert in denial of the incident.

'You should not worry what people tell to you,' he grinned. 'Why are you caring if I am telling such a thing? Is it not wiser to leave this comment on the platform when you are getting on the train?'

He was right again, but my ego would not allow him the satisfaction of knowing I agreed with him.

'You mustn't form attachment to ideas or things; this can only lead to misery. You must learn that we are not those things or those ideas, we are only owning them. They are not owning us.'

Sandeep reached into his backpack and pulled out a stout book, which he touched lightly to his forehead before opening it up to read out a passage:

'The nature of the mind is flickering and unsteady. But a self-realized yogi has to control the mind; the mind should not control him.'

It was the *Bhagavad-Gita as It Is*, a translated version of the original text.

'If you read this you will see that it is possible to calm these thoughts you are currently allowing to affect you.'

'If you have no attachment to things, then you won't mind if I take your copy?'

Sandeep fell silent and my heart wriggled with delight.

'You keep it, ma'am, but you promise me one thing. You promise me that you will read it properly.'

Sheepish, I promised, thanked him and dropped it into my backpack as the entire compartment announced to me that we had arrived at Umaria station in Madhya Pradesh, the home of the Lifeline Express.

Night had fallen and the station cowered beneath a depressing blue light. Beyond the four empty tracks was nothing but blackness. For an Indian town it was spookily still; even the crickets rubbed their wings with reluctance. A band of dogs sauntered down the platform on a mission, stopping briefly to sniff a sleeping family that had formed a protective circle around their cloth-wrapped belongings. On the fifth and furthest track, a train was resting, the rainbow on her side just visible under the light from a buzzing lamppost. Sliding off the platform, I stumbled over the tracks and banged on the door of the Lifeline Express, the world's first hospital train.

For many, Indian Railways provides little more than a mode of transport: a cheap and convenient way to commute, visit relatives or simply while away the day. For others, it is a place of employment where generations have earned their livelihood. But for some, it is the bloodstream that keeps India's heart beating. Nehru had once suggested using the railways to reach those who could not get to hospitals, but little surfaced until 1991 when a lady named Zelma Lazarus kicked the idea into action. Lazarus, who is the founder director and currently the chief executive officer of Impact India Foundation, an NGO, had loaned a minibus to a team of foreign surgeons travelling to the Himalayas to offer medical care to hill-dwellers. Having never visited the Himalayas herself, she travelled with them to observe their work.

One night a man came running towards the doctors carrying the body of a dead child. On inspection the child was not dead, but had suffered a burst appendix that had infected his whole body. The doctors worked all night and saved the boy's life. The following night the team sat around a campfire discussing how they could bring medical care to the corners of the country, when a mountain train rattled by, hooting as it passed. Lazarus went to the Rail Bhavan in Delhi the next day and asked to meet the railway minister. His secretary shouted at her, told her to write letters or make an appointment and shooed her out – but she waited. George Fernandes, the railway minister at the time, spotted her and called her into his office, where she proposed the idea of using a train as a mobile hospital. Impressed by her persistence, Fernandes gave Lazarus an engine and three coaches and on 16 July 1991, the world's first hospital train began its journey around rural India to bring free medical services to the neglected poor.

Initially, patients were invited on board for cataract surgery, treatment for hearing afflictions and orthopaedic disabilities – particularly children who had suffered polio. In 1999 cleft lip surgery was introduced, followed by treatment for dental and oral problems, epilepsy and neurological disorders. Gynaecological check-ups had recently been introduced and the possibility of laparoscopic surgery was also on the cards. On average the train spends four weeks on each project at locations deemed worthy of medical attention and patients are welcomed aboard for on-the-spot treatment. Each project costs around ₹30 lakh, which covers medicines, travel and lodging for volunteer doctors, patients' food and accommodation, ambulances, fuel and water. The fee is met entirely by one sponsor, which in the past had included the Rajiv Gandhi Foundation, Tata Steel and Dr Michael Chowen, a private sponsor in the UK. Lazarus hoped that the services offered by the train would push the poor to generate a demand from the government for a more efficient health system. Despite being behind on my schedule, the Lifeline Express was one train that I could not miss.

As I reached to knock again, a face appeared at the kitchen window and the door was heaved open by Rai, a driver who ferried staff around throughout the four weeks. He led me towards a jeep that bounced down Station Road to the Hotel Surya, where I could sleep off my journey and wake fresh for what was to be a gruelling first day. What I did wake to was a timid knocking on the door at 6 am.

Passepartout was back.

The following morning we met Gaurav, who manned the hotel's reception. He had an endless supply of bottled drinks behind the front desk that he readily offered, along with cautionary tales about bad western people, none of whom he had ever met. He and his staff were keen to clean my room, change light bulbs and service the air conditioner on a regular basis, which tended to coincide with when I was in nightwear or emerging from the shower. At precisely 8 am a gentleman with soft jowls and closely cropped white hair appeared in the lobby. Randhir Singh Vishwen was a retired colonel from Lucknow and the CEO of the Lifeline Express, who oversaw every project. Punctuality was second nature to the colonel, who herded us towards the jeep and back to the station, where a scene wholly different from the previous night awaited.

Against the backdrop of a baby-blue sky, train number 60 looked like a mobile kindergarten. A rainbow arced over five windows, threaded marigolds looped beneath the ledges and chunky red and yellow flowers swirled around the base. A stage had been erected alongside for the Umaria project's inauguration ceremony and a canopy stretched overhead, creating a makeshift auditorium to keep out the heat. It was barely 8 am but the sun was already burning the ground and turning the jeep to molten metal.

Hundreds of parents wandered around with dusty-haired children on their hips. The elderly squatted on plastic chairs, while others crouched on the cheap green matting, spreading out their food, sheets and babies. They knew it would be a long wait. A man with no legs from the knee down paddled by on a makeshift skateboard, watched by men idling in dhotis. A lady in a sunset-coloured sari carried her teenage son like a sack of rice, his withered legs bouncing off her with every step. A shy lady brought over her baby boy who squirmed and laughed in her arms, even though he had none of his own. Colonel Vishwen steered us onto the train.

To the left was a kitchen where Rajdeo, the chef, was sweating in his vest over a karahi of masala potato, while puris fizzed and swelled in another. To the right was a toilet complete with toilet paper, hand soap and an embroidered towel. An air-conditioned, carpeted room served as both a dining area and a lounge and was hung with articles about the train, certificates and an obligatory photo of Gandhi. Further compartments included the colonel's office, changing rooms stacked with scrubs and two operating theatres – one with two tables, the other with three. After the tour, Passepartout and I stood in the lounge as the colonel explained the format of the day, adding that two more volunteers would be joining us.

'There is Helen, a medical student from Nottingham University who is going to be assisting, and also...'

The door slid back and a tall, tanned figure in a blue T-shirt and grey suit trousers entered. Ben was half Welsh, half Indian and lived in Hackney. He had a warm Scottish accent, tipped his head to one side when he spoke, and produced deep, dirty laughs from the pit of his stomach that lit up his eyes. He was also a photographer. The air in the room stiffened.

After breakfast, Passepartout wandered off to photograph the crowds while Ben and I strolled along, taking in the pomp and fanfare surrounding the chief guest, whose head was walled in by garlands. Local cameramen pushed patients out of the way, the jobless jerked the garlands into place and the chief guest sat centre stage, flanked by nobodies.

'I'm dyin' here,' Ben sighed, pulling at his trouser legs.

It was hot. Not tiring, humid heat, but heat so dry that sweat evaporated before it even appeared. It was nearing 48 degrees and emerging from the air-conditioned carriage was like walking into the barrel of a giant hairdryer, so we made a detour to the local sweet shop for a couple of Cornettos and a Sprite. It was a relief to have someone else for company. One week ago Passepartout had got in touch. He was keen to photograph the Lifeline

Express and had arrived of his own accord, but to me nothing had changed. My plan was simply to crack on with my own business and allow him to do the same. Ben reached down and helped me up off the tracks and onto the platform as a toast-coloured mongrel trotted by and decided to join us for the day.

At the district hospital across town, Dr Ashok Kumar Agarwal and his colleague Dr Vikas Verma had begun assessing patients for corrective surgery. The hospital was painted in duckling yellow and smelt of Dettol. Sunlight beamed through open windows and balconies, reflecting off the polished floors, but upstairs was a scene of wall-to-wall desperation. A tangled mass of sari-covered heads, misshapen limbs, mirrored bangles, sleeping babies, bent backs, cracked feet, moist eyes and pleading voices jammed the corridor leading to the screening room. Faces pressed against the glass door, hands gripped medical documents and bare feet stood their ground as the crowd heaved from all sides.

Screening took place in an unused classroom where several chairs were lined up against the wall around a rectangle of desks, at the front of which sat the two doctors and Helen. Dr Agarwal was a volunteer orthopaedic surgeon from Lucknow, who was on board for his sixth year. He was a slight man in his early 60s with a light frown of concentration that remained when he smiled. He had a noticeable aversion to verbosity, so when he did speak, it was worth hovering to catch his pearls.

He beckoned in the first patient, an elderly man with eyes like a bloodhound, leaning on a stick as tall as himself. Dr Agarwal scribbled down a referral to Jabalpur Medical College for treatment, as surgery was not possible, and called in the next patient. An anaemic toddler with cerebral palsy was helped in by his mother, who held him up by his wrists, his toes trailing the floor like a puppet's. He was turned away before being seated. Cerebral palsy and other neurological problems were untreatable by the team, who could only offer surgery for orthopaedic afflictions. A teenager playing with her plait hobbled in and parked her left leg on the table. Even though her foot was bent in half, she had carefully painted each toenail crimson. She looked up and winked. Sixteen-year-old Roshni Gupta was given the first nod. After suffering polio as a child, her left foot had become severely deformed and she had already undergone unsuccessful surgery in Rajasthan, so the train was her last hope. She threw herself into one of the chairs at the back of the room and whipped out her phone to send a text.

The afternoon wore on and the line by Roshni eventually grew to include Yogesh, a clingy baby with floppy legs; Preethi, a 3-year-old narcoleptic in a party dress; and Mona, a 7-year-old who wept quietly into her dupatta, swinging her withered leg like a pendulum. Mona's mother was dead and she had come alone. Both ceiling fans slowed to a halt, the power cut deepening tensions. It was a far cry from the Accident and Emergency (A&E) ward at home. Babies suckled in peace, while others hopped and shuffled around the floor, smiling and clutching at parents who touched the doctors' feet. In two hours, Dr Agarwal and his team screened 90 adults, children and babies and selected just 17 who were invited to the train the next day for operations.

Just after 8 am, a line of saris curled its way up the ramp to the main door. Yogesh bounced on his mother's hip, Roshni grinned, Mona's grandmother was now by her side and Preethi had lost a little lustre, eyeing me from the crook of her grandmother's neck. They were shown into the waiting area by the theatre where they sat quietly, parents cajoling the frightened with whispers and hugs. In the lounge the doctors had finished their idlis and sambar and were scrubbed. The theatre door slid back and forth every minute, but little seemed to be happening. In his office, the colonel was an unhappy man. The start of surgery was delayed as a couple of doctors had gone to the tiger sanctuary at nearby Bandhavgarh and had not yet arrived.

At around 11 am the first patients were carried into the theatre. Jiten, a 2-year-old with a leg shaped like a hockey stick, was taken in while his mother waited, her turquoise sari pulled tightly over her shoulder, her eyes glued to the door. She sat motionless, her lips pressed together, magnifying her cheekbones. Although weathered, she was a defiantly beautiful woman. When the door opened again, Jiten was carried out in a blanket and placed behind her. The effects of the anaesthetic were still in place and she stroked at his hair and tapped his face. Her shoulders relaxed as he stirred.

'Preethi Chaudhuri?'

As one child came out another was carried in and the waiting area now doubled up as a recovery room. Babies who had neither eaten nor drunk since the early hours were beginning to cry and paw at their mothers' blouses, triggering a collective howling, while others lay in silence, limbs in wet plaster. Preethi was plucked from her grandmother's arms and carried away as the elderly lady dabbed her eyes with the corner of her sari.

Eerie beeping punctuated the silence as Preethi was sedated. At 1:20 pm her chest stopped twitching, her lids closed and her leg was cleaned and opened. At 1:50 pm her leg was sutured and plastered and she was carried out. Thirty minutes was all it took to change her life. Her grandmother shifted across the seat, her eyes wet, as her granddaughter was placed down. I turned to leave and Preethi's grandmother gripped my wrist and asked me a question in Hindi. All I could manage was *sab theek hai*, twinned with a thumbs-up gesture. Tears rolled into her wrinkles and she fanned herself with her sari, laughing with relief. As I left the train that evening, one thought filled my mind: God bless our NHS.

That night I sat on Ben's balcony finishing some work when he brought out a cup of tea for me. I had grown so used to angry silence and learnt to wade through hostile waters that he seemed an unusually calming person to be with. So calming that I asked him about it.

'Nothing really winds you up, does it?'

'I just try not to react to stuff. And I meditate every morning… at least I'm trying to.'

'Every morning?'

'I've come straight from a Vipassana course in Nashik and I want to keep it up, especially now that I'm here.' He leant back and rubbed his stomach. 'This place is pretty intense.'

I nodded slowly and he grinned.

'Have you done Vipassana?' he asked.

'No, but I have friends who have and I've wanted to for a while.'

Now more so than ever. If 10 days in silence could teach me not to react to agitation, it would be time well spent.

On the third morning a familiar scene was unfolding. Queues were growing, babies were bounced, tears were shed and the colonel was, once again, an unhappy man. This time, the anaesthetists had gone to the sanctuary and had not yet arrived. The colonel swivelled around in his chair and shook his head.

'This is typical. Nobody is saying "Don't go to the tiger sanctuary", but first do the job you came here to do and then go.' He allowed himself a weary smile.

'I know what will happen. *Aaram se,* they will take a long bath and have their breakfast and then turn up at midday. It kills everyone's enthusiasm.'

Once surgery was over, the children were sent to the district hospital to recuperate in one ward. Walking in felt like visiting family. Ben and I had stopped by the local English-medium school to find bilingual students who could help us interact with the patients, and with us now were two 17-year-old girls. Mine had a gentle bedside manner, while Ben's bellowed at the children, startling them with accusatory enquiries into their well-being.

Chattering, cuddling families and empty tiffin carriers filled the ward. Jiten lay on his side with his plastered leg on a cushion. He grinned with his tongue hanging out, one hand pressed firmly between his legs, which his mother kept pulling away. Yogesh gurgled in his mother's lap as she rocked him. His plaster – no longer than my middle finger – bobbed up and down over her knee. Preethi was back in her party dress and had dal and rice spread around her mouth as her mother tried to feed her from home-packed Tupperware. Roshni saluted and patted the bed so I could sit with her. She took my phone number – ringing me every month after I left – and explained in Hinglish that she would now find a husband quite easily. Her plan was to finish school, go to university to study music and then when the time was right, she would get married. She wiggled her crimson toes at me and tapped her plaster. 'No problem now,' she said, snapping her fingers. Marriage had also been a worry for Preethi's parents. Even though she was only 3, they knew that without surgery she would be doomed to a life of spinsterhood and ridicule.

The room fizzed with energy, but at the same time there was only so much the magic train could do. There were still millions of children who needed help. According to a BBC report, India spends £36bn a year on defence and £750m a year on its space programme, yet has more people in poverty than the whole of sub-Saharan Africa, to whom it even donates money. The Indian government had a lot to answer for.

After dinner one night, Dr Agarwal rubbed his hand across his face and looked at his fingers while the team ate in silence.

'It's the brain drain that is the problem.'

I glanced up. 'What do you mean?'

'We train good doctors and then they leave and want to work in the United States or in the UK.'

'Is it just because of better salaries?'

'No. The problem is that they just don't want to work in the rural areas. If they come here, where are the schools for their children? Where is the electricity and water supply for their homes? There is nothing incentivising them. The village and the city need to move closer together.'

Just above Dr Agarwal hung the photo of Gandhi. His determination to keep the village as the fulcrum of Indian life now seemed well and truly outdated. Over the last few weeks I had learnt in my train doorways that fewer and fewer villagers wanted to stay put. They would rather live in squalor on the edges of cities where water ran and lights lit up, earning more in a month than a year of pulling ploughs and sowing seeds.

'The big mistake Nehru made was to inject money into the middle classes instead of at the lowest level,' Dr Agarwal continued. 'He built universities rather than primary schools. So the middle classes steamed ahead, leaving the poor far behind and creating a gap that can't easily be filled.' He gestured out of the window. 'These people don't need shopping malls, they need schools and vaccinations.'

One week flew by and there were three weeks remaining of the project, but train connections from Umaria were few and far between and we needed to leave. As I packed on the last night, I found Sandeep's copy of the Gita and smiled. Ben was watching my television and Gaurav poked his head around the door every five minutes.

'Stay, Mrs Monisha,' he urged, tempting me with his half-drunk bottle of Mirinda.

'Knock on the door, man!' Ben shouted.

A large part of me wanted to stay to meet the cleft-lip patients and to follow up the progress of Roshni, Preethi and Mona. This was a happy place with good people and it felt, as yet, unexplored. Ben and I had also become quite content in each other's company. He was now watching me fold my things reluctantly.

'Why don't you just stay if you want to?'

'I can't. There are just 20 trains left.'

'Don't do something you don't want to do.'

'But I do want to. Just…'

'…not with him. You don't have to go with him. Finish the project here and I'll come with you up to Jammu and Assam and do the rest of the journeys.'

'I can't. I started it with him so I should finish it with him.'

Sighing, I shoved my clothes to one side and lay down next to Ben on my bed while the air conditioner spat droplets of water on my head. For our last supper, Rajdeo had made a thick, peppery chicken curry, which had found itself a cosy spot in my stomach. I soon began to doze. In the darkness *Batman Returns* was flickering on the television and the Penguin was firing shots from his umbrella, shouting in badly dubbed Hindi. Ben looked over.

'Do you want me to stay tonight?' he asked.

I nodded and curled wordlessly into the curve of his body, sleeping soundly for the first night since I had arrived, stirring briefly as he kissed my forehead.

Gaurav was wringing his hands when I checked out the next day and refused to make eye contact. But he soon placated himself, Ben told me later, after finding a group photo from the Golden Chariot that I had dropped in my room, which he then framed in reception.

The Narmada Express to Katni, Madhya Pradesh, was due to leave just after 4 pm, so Passepartout and I set up camp on the platform and watched as a family made its way across the footbridge carrying a toddler. She had kohl-rimmed eyes, slender gold hoops in her ears and a lightning bolt split her top lip into her nose. They put down their bags and boxes, slid off the platform onto the tracks and picked their way over to the train. It was the first day of the screening for cleft lips. Two men linking pinkie fingers made their way down the platform and flashed crooked smiles, before jumping onto the tracks and joining the group.

At the last possible moment we boarded, and as train 61 pulled out my heart thumped heavily against my chest, drowning out the clanking wheels. From the window I could just see the end of the rainbow on the side of the train, the pot of gold of the Indian Railways.

17 | A Taste of Rocky Road Ice Cream

In India things happen when you least expect them. It was part of what made travelling around the country a constant source of both shock and delight. As little as one cow lingering on the tracks could delay numerous services, and during bad weather it was not unknown for drivers of old trains to stop and wipe the windscreen with a cloth. For that reason, our plan at the start of the trip was to have no plan, to avoid constant battle against the country's orchestrated chaos. It was easier to take a deep breath and allow the current to drag us at will.

Arriving in Katni, we discovered that it was three days before the next available train to Delhi. Nineteen trains remained and we had still not reached Udhampur. The fixation on reaching the northernmost tip of the railways had begun to drain the dregs of my sanity. In the last few days Udhampur had morphed in my psyche into India's answer to the Elysian Fields, where, as Homer wrote in *The Odyssey*, 'No snow is there, nor heavy storm, nor ever rain ...', which for the Himalayas was most unlikely.

Rather than waste three precious days, we found a hotel and decided to take the Mumbai-Howrah Mail the following day to Allahabad, hoping that once we arrived we would find a suitable connection to Delhi. After watching a bit of TV, I placed water glasses over the family of cockroaches in the bathroom and climbed into bed just as the power failed. The fan came to a silent halt, bringing the night-time bumps and groans of the hotel to a crescendo. Gazing at the map by torchlight, I pulled the covers over my knees, using the hairy blanket to rub the welts left by mosquitoes humming around my ear. Even the purple patch representing the state of Jammu and Kashmir appeared to me now in the shape of a four-leafed clover, fields of which would fill the valleys where I could run in bare feet, strumming a lyre, chiffon caressing my ankles...

Passepartout thumped on the door and I sat up in the darkness, my torch on the floor. He had gone outside for a cigarette and got locked out on the balcony, while I had fallen asleep face down in my map.

'Rickshaaaaaaa ... rickshaaaa ... *tinglinglinglingling* ...'

Outside Allahabad Junction a cycle rickshaw driver rang his bell and swerved over, curling his bike around us as we walked towards the exit. A fresh ticket for the Allahabad Duronto Express to Delhi lay pressed between the pages of my logbook and momentary relief tempered my madness.

'Where going?' he asked, winding around us in a figure of eight.

'Just across the road,' I replied, as he swayed his head, following the curve of his wheels. He looked like an Indian version of Manuel from *Fawlty Towers*, a weasly mix of teeth, moustache and perplexity.

'I take you,' he said.

'No, thank you, we're okay,' I replied as Passepartout strode on ahead.

'I take you,' he repeated.

'No, we're fine, thank you.'

'Forty rupees,' he bargained.

Passepartout whirled round. 'We don't want your rickshaw!'

'Thirty rupees,' he continued, undeterred.

'No, thank you.' I giggled.

'Twenty rupees,' he grinned, pedalling alongside me.

'No, thank you, really.'

'For free!' he offered, standing up on his pedals like a 1980s BMXer.

We both knew that I had no excuse for refusing him. We both also knew that I was a pushover and would offer him baksheesh at the end of the journey. If anything, he deserved a reward for ingenuity. I shrugged and stopped. Beaming, he helped me in, struggling with my rucksack as it sank into the canopy of his rickshaw, causing the front wheel of his bike to lift up. He waved a hand behind to make sure I would not fall out and began to ride slowly behind Passepartout, keeping close to his ankles and jingling his bell softly. Refusing to overtake Passepartout, who walked ahead, he turned around and flashed me a wicked smile.

Eventually, we stopped before crossing the main road and Passepartout climbed in, hugging his bags. Less than 20 seconds later we pulled up outside the hotel and I went inside to ask for a room. A moment later I came out and hopped back in. It was almost twice our budget and had a crow in the bathroom. Taking it in turns, Passepartout tried the next hotel and was turned away. After nine attempts even the driver was beginning to lose his humour and breathe in alarming rasps. His once yellow T-shirt was now blotched with sweat, turning it a dirty mustard colour. It was a Friday night, but it seemed impossible that every hotel in Allahabad should be full.

'I don't think they like white people around here,' Passepartout declared finally.

By this point I had silently reached the same conclusion and decided to test out the theory. At the next hotel the driver dropped me off and parked away from the entrance.

'How many?' the owner asked.

'Two.'

'Where is the other?'

'Outside. Do you have a room?'

He refused to answer.

'Where is the other guest?'

'Outside with the bags. But do you have a room?'

Stepping out from the desk, the man peered out of the doorway and saw Passepartout smoking with the driver.

'No. We are full,' he replied.

Whether Allahabad's hoteliers had a revulsion towards white males or they were just more accustomed to recognising a psycho than I was, not one allowed us in. Desperation kicked in and at the next hotel I pleaded with the owner, whose idea of air conditioning was a window that faced a brick wall. It was now more than two hours since the driver had made the fateful move of engaging with two people who had, so far, managed to rack up a spectacular run of bad luck travelling together. However, if his internal pedometer was clocking up the distance, he was due a hefty donation towards his work. Gasping for air, water and release from our clasp, the man dragged round his rickshaw and took us back to the first hotel.

The room was still available. And the crow had gone.

Unravelling as many 100-rupee notes as we could find, we stuffed the money into his hands as he smiled through streams of sweat that could have been tears, and wheeled his bike off into early retirement.

The following night, after a visit to the old Nehru family home, a plate of chicken neck biryani and an obligatory fight at the holy ghat at Sangam, we boarded train 63, the Duronto to Delhi. Not a speck marked the walls or sheets. The taps shone and the floors gleamed with clinical levels of cleanliness. It seemed to have rubbed off on the passengers, who had placed all their rubbish in bags, slid between the sheets and gone to sleep without fuss. The moment my cheek touched the pillow I fell asleep and slept my first full night on an Indian train without waking once.

Delhi's sun had risen in far too jubilant a mood for my eyes. It was barely 7 am and the slumber was slow to wear off. At the station restaurant I spread out the map to plot out the onward route. Someone had once told me that the map of India looked like a lady wrapped in a sari, raising her left arm. Following her arm to the fingertip, my own finger arrived on the purple square marking Tinsukia in Assam. I had not heard back from the three friends with whom I had travelled to Chennai and was annoyed that the smug woman in the adjoining compartment had been right all along, but more annoyed with myself for believing them. Passepartout was unsure whether he wanted to come along and wandered off to nose around Delhi, while I had one final stop to make.

She took off her glasses and looked at me. 'Are you still here?'

'Yup.'

'Give me,' Anusha said, holding out her hand.

'I now need to get to Udhampur.'

'I thought you went?'

'No, we changed that and I went to Chennai.'

'Okay.' She typed in a few numbers and pursed up her lips, which I knew now was part of the performance. 'I can give you second-tier in the Rajdhani that leaves tonight.'

'Let's do it.'

'Then?'

'I want to go to Gorakhpur and then across to Tinsukia and then to Ledo.'

'Gorakhpur?'

'Yes, I found a scribble in the back of my logbook that says Gorakhpur to Nautanwa and I'm not really sure why, but I want to go and find out.'

'You will need to come back to Delhi and take a train up to Gorakhpur, but the other ticket you buy when you get to Gorakhpur, it will be a short journey.' She sighed, blowing her aniseed breath at me. 'Then?'

'Then I need to get to New Jalpaiguri and across to Tinsukia and then back to New Jalpaiguri, because I want to take the toy train up to Darjeeling.'

Anusha wrote down the sequence then eyed me. 'Heard from your friend?'

'Yes.'

'Oh-ho!' she whooped. 'Where is he?'

'Here in Delhi, actually.'

'Oh God, then he will come and ask for the same trains and I will have to lie and pretend I don't know.'

'It's fine, I really don't mind if you put him on the same trains.'

'I will give him different compartment,' she grinned.

With one final push her printer strained out the last of the tickets. It was on the brink of death, largely due to our visits. Handing over the tickets, Anusha pushed up her glasses and tipped her head to one side, the stripe of kumkum still flaming in her parting. I took the tickets and thanked her.

It was the last time I would see Anusha.

I speared a few pieces of chicken in white wine. We were sitting in the Big Chill café in Khan Market, beneath a series of framed film posters jammed alongside one another, paying homage to *Breakfast at Tiffany's*, *The Graduate* and *La Dolce Vita*. The restaurant was filled with couples linking fingers under the table, slurping from shared malt milkshakes, and bored girls stabbing at BlackBerrys. I looked up at the still from *Amélie* where an impish Audrey Tautou held up a silver spoon, as though poised to smack Passepartout on the head. He had summoned me to offer an apology. Since his arrival on the Lifeline Express we had not acknowledged the breakdown in Chandigarh. Expecting a squash rally of accusations, I found none.

'I'm sorry I made things so personal.'

I folded my arms and nodded, unconvinced by the apology.

'I don't really understand why you persisted down that route when you knew how much it upset me. We had a job to do and you seemed hell-bent on just ruining it.'

He closed his eyes and nodded in agreement. 'I know and I'm sorry. There's nothing I hate more than having to admit being wrong.'

He sat staring at me expectantly.

'Okay, apology accepted.' I glanced at his wrist, where a slim steel bangle sat.

'Are you wearing a kara?!'

'Yes. After you left I went on up to Amritsar, where I met these three Sikh lads. They took me off to their village for a couple of days and took care of me.' He grinned. 'They even tied me a turban.'

'And now you're wearing a kara? That's not really very in keeping with your beliefs, or lack thereof.'

'They gave it to me. And besides, theirs is actually a culture.'

I looked down at my chicken and said nothing. After Amritsar he had made his way to Varanasi and Haridwar, then spent time in Kushinagar. Whether or not his choice of holy sites was coincidental, he had certainly tempered since Chandigarh.

The rest of the afternoon was spent traipsing around Khan Market in search of a book Dr Agarwal had recommended called *Scoop!*, a collection of eyewitness accounts and insider stories tracing back to Partition. Fittingly, Khan Market's shops and residences had been built by the Ministry of Rehabilitation and given to migrants at the time of Partition. It had flourished into one of the most expensive shopping districts in India, favoured by expats, the upper class and cool kids. It housed independent shops selling incense, embroidered stationery and jewellery, alongside Nike and Benetton outlets. Coffee shops, Subway, Japanese restaurants and a Fab India spanned several floors. After little luck we came upon BahriSons bookseller, a booklover's dream. The shop had opened at the time of Partition and was crammed with crick-necked customers thumbing the rows of creased spines. It had the warm allure of a coffee shop on a rainy day. An assistant clambered up a ladder and, much to my delight, descended with dust on his jumper and a copy of *Scoop!*.

It was too late for Passepartout to reserve a ticket to accompany me that evening, so with my book in hand I gave him a hug, agreeing to meet him in Udhampur, and left him hunting for *The Greatest Show on Earth*.

Three men were sharing my compartment to Jammu. One lay in the side berth flicking through a copy of *Outlook* and two sat by the window, one reading, the other finishing a container of bhindi and parathas. As train 64

jerked and began to move out of the station, a rat appeared in the aisle. It went up on its hind legs, its wrists hanging limply, and looked at me. The rats at the temple in Deshnok had not bothered me, but this one did. Those rats were supposed to be there. This one was not. Madras had a lot to answer for when it came to my phobias, and my dislike of rats stemmed from another incident that had taken place in our Besant Nagar flat.

One afternoon, after finding chunks of Modern Bakery bread rimmed with teeth marks, my mum realised we had rats and enlisted the help of our maid, Devi, to capture them. Devi's normal ritual was to arrive half an hour late, citing a detour to the temple as her excuse, then fall asleep under the dining table, having barely swept one bedroom. Put out, she lumbered to her feet while I stood on the dining table watching them pull the sofa away from the wall. A rat shot out and darted into the record collection before Devi clamped a dustbin on top of it.

Through a combination of telepathy and hollering across balconies – a form of communication unique to the Madras maids' cartel – my grandma's maid heard about the rat and came over to inspect it. One-Eyed Mary appeared at the front door, her eye rolling in its socket like a marble, panting 'Show me! Show me!' and salivating through saffron-coloured teeth. Lifting the bin, Mary allowed the vigilant rat to shoot out and hide behind the fridge. Devi, exerting more energy in one movement than in the six months she had worked with us, walloped Mary with her broom while my mum waited for the two to finish and help with the recapture. Feeling guilty, Mary pushed everyone aside and crouched down by the fridge. Suddenly she yelped with delight. She turned around, her eye swirling with delirium, the rat thrashing around in a bulge in her petticoat. Needless to say, the rat bit her and ended up dunked in a bucket of water, while Mary ended up in hospital.

I lifted my feet off the floor as the rat strolled about, sniffing at puffed rice before disappearing under my seat. The gentleman finishing his dinner threw the box under the seat and picked grains from his teeth.

'You are travelling to Jammu?' he asked.

'Yes, but I'm not really stopping, I'm carrying on up to Udhampur.'

'But Udhampur is very small, you have friends there?'

'No, I'm travelling around the country by train and wanted to get to each end of the railways.'

'You have been to Kanyakumari?'

'Yes, I started in the South, then went to Dwarka and am now heading to Udhampur, then across to Ledo in Assam.'

'How many journeys have you taken?'

'I think this is number 64.'

'What is your profession?'

'I'm a journalist.'

'Oh, I am also a journalist!' He handed me a card saying NEWS BEAURO CHEIF, which I tucked into the back of my book.

'If you will excuse me I will retire, I have had a very long day,' he said, climbing up to his berth.

I stole his space by the window and leant against the glass, watching little more than the reflection of our compartment against the navy sky. Silhouettes of towns whipped by at longer and longer intervals the further we pushed out of Delhi. The occasional wail and jolt of passing trains snapped my eyes open and I went back to my book, when the gentleman sitting opposite me looked up.

'From where do you hail?'

'England.'

'I can see that, but where?'

'I live in London.'

'I read mathematics at Cambridge.'

'Oh, which college?'

'King's.'

'Gorgeous chapel.'

'Your Stephen Fry's alma mater.'

'Didn't he go to Queen's?'

'No.'

'I'm sure there was an episode of *Shooting Stars* where he says he went to...'

'Were you at Cambridge?'

'No, I read French at Leeds.'

'I have not heard of it. My son is at university in London,' he continued. 'It has changed too much.'

'In what way?' I asked.

'I can see that all the class has now gone from England. Their colloquial speech, their lack of finesse. It is shocking. They are no better than the riff-raff we used to see on the streets in Cambridge.'

'When were you last there?'

He darkened and turned to volume as his preferred weapon of defence. 'Cambridge had a uniqueness you won't find in your other universities...'

My lids began to droop as he continued his trip down memory lane.

'…the punter was a wonderful…'

'Oh, that's still a great pub,' I perked up. 'It does really good scallops and black pudding.'

'I was talking about the sport. This establishment of which you are talking must be something new.'

Sunday afternoon punting was about as much of a sport as sunbathing, but I allowed him to continue. In addition to their penchant for arguing, Indians love a good monologue, and I soon slipped into a coma of boredom and nodded off. When I woke, he had made up his bed and gone to sleep, so I shook out the contents of my own paper bag and began tucking in the sheets. Every time I pulled one corner another came out and I held the sheet down with one knee while trying to shove the edges down the back of the berth. Aware that I was being watched, I hid the ridges with the blanket, like a 6-year-old cramming toys behind a cupboard door.

'You have travelled on 64 trains and you still do not know how to make up a bed.'

The man in the side berth signalled for me to stand in the aisle as he tugged the sheets off my bed and started again. With Mary Poppins' proficiency he nipped, tucked and smoothed the sheets into place. All my bed lacked was an After Eight mint on the pillow. Taking up his magazine, he sat down, then scrutinised the windows and fan, which had begun to rattle unnervingly.

'I thought Rajdhanis were supposed to be new?' I asked.

'They are, but even then some of these are cut-and-paste jobs. The compartment will be from a mail train while the carriage might be new.'

I nodded in agreement, wondering how he knew. He eyed me suspiciously.

'You know how to calculate the age of a carriage?'

'No.'

'Do you know what the numbers painted on the outside mean?'

'No.'

'Do you know how to tell engines apart?'

'No.'

He put down the magazine, laid his glasses on top and leant forward.

'Do you know anything?'

'Erm, probably not.'

He exhaled with poorly disguised disgust. 'You have travelled on more of the Indian Railways than most Indians will ever do and yet you can't make a bed and you have learnt nothing. May I?' He turned to the back of my logbook and began to sketch a train. 'See, on the outside of every carriage there are five numbers painted.'

I had noticed them from the start, but assumed they simply provided insider information for train manufacturers and had never bothered to ask anyone what they meant for fear of a fabricated response.

'Let's say the number is 88432, that means the carriage was built in 1988. Then look at the last three digits. If they lie between 401 and 600 you have a general 2nd-class coach. Subtract 401 from 432. This means that it was the 31st coach built that year. Any carriage whose last three digits lie between 201and 400 is a sleeper-class carriage. So if the number painted on the outside is 97312, it was made in 1997.'

'And so if I then take 201 from 312, that makes it the 111st sleeper class coach made in 1997?'

'Correct.'

It was like learning a secret handshake.

'You'll find that in one long train there will be a whole mix of different numbers. It's a good way of choosing the carriage most likely to have nice new insides.'

Wishing this gem had been in my possession from the outset, I thanked him and closed my book. Arun was from Cochin. As a child he had lived by a railway track, waking to the sound of horns and watching from the windows as trains clattered past. His parents had been in the Army and had often been transferred from one city to another; constant uprooting meant that he and the railways had become firm friends.

'Now, do you know how to read the actual train numbers?' Arun asked.

Recollecting the chat with Mandovi Rick on the Konkan Railway, I recounted that the final digit changed for return trains, trains beginning with '2' were normally the fastest, and that the first number often indicated the region. Appeased, he bowed his head. 'And a number made up of only three digits generally indicates passenger trains. But I'm sure you have not bothered with those.'

'About 14 actually. And I'm counting half a dozen Mumbai commuters in that.'

'Oh, not bad.'

Indignant, I tied up my logbook and clambered up to bed, as he unrolled his sheets and disappeared to the toilets to change.

❖

Jammu Tawi station had the bleakness of Blackburn in November. The skies hung low in rumpled puffs of grey and rain stippled the platform as I sat waiting for the connection to Udhampur. Even the dogs looked bored with each other's back ends and lay on their sides staring at the wall. Every 10 minutes fellow passengers peered up at the signs, checked watches and murmured to one another, before eventually dispersing. It turned out that the train was delayed by an hour. In normal circumstances I would have busied myself in the city, but this being India, it was likely that the train would arrive ahead of schedule and cause fits of panic. I made my way towards the station restaurant and passed the time with my copy of *Scoop!* and the best omelette sandwich to be found in any of India's railway stations. Before I had mopped up the last blob of ketchup, the passenger train hissed and creaked into the station and waiting passengers began to hook themselves to the handrails before it had drawn to a halt. Foreign phones – which included any purchased outside the state of Jammu and Kashmir – did not work, as a security measure against militant activity, so there was no way I could contact Passepartout.

As train 65 began the ascent from Jammu, white-walled stone houses rushed the other way, then began to linger far behind until nothing but stepped hillsides rose on either side of the windows. The Shivalik mountain range loomed all around, its humps lining the horizon, the edges trimmed with trees. Soon the train began to rattle over gorges furrowed by rivers of chocolate milk and balding riverbeds piled with rock. Here plans were afoot to build the world's tallest single-span bridge over the River Chenab, 35 metres higher than the Eiffel Tower, but this terrain was not easy to manipulate. It had a mind of its own. Soft mud often caused tunnels to collapse and water seeped into drilled sections of the hillsides, forcing frustrated engineers to abandon projects. The land soon levelled as rain began to attack the carriage on all sides, fighting its way in through the shutters. Puddles grew on the seats and the sound of drumming on the roof heralded the arrival into Udhampur.

'No snow is there, nor heavy storm, nor ever rain…'

I leant out of the doorway as the Himalayan rain peppered bullet holes into my skin. The carriage cleared as passengers fashioned umbrellas out of carrier bags and leapt like frogs around the puddles on the platform. Hopping down, I wandered towards the end of the station. No trains were due in, so I took the liberty of sliding off the platform, landing with a splat where the rain had mixed mud and stones into a paste of Rocky Road ice cream. Shouts and waving arms tried to catch my attention, but I squelched on and eventually came to the final sleeper. So far I had travelled on over 28,000 km of this track and this was where it ended, as though cut off mid-sentence. Satisfaction flooded my stomach. It was long overdue, but much had happened in that time and not one moment was tinged with regret. A pincushion of green peered up through the mud and I tugged at the tuft of grass, putting a few blades into my pocket. Train 66 shuddered and heaved out of the station, shaking its puddles awake. I looked out across the hills where sunlight had begun to crack through the clouds, beaming down like spotlights lighting up the Earth.

Back in Jammu, I passed the time in the company of another omelette sandwich before boarding train 67, the Duronto Express back to Delhi. While scanning the carriage for my seat, my eyes flicked over a figure in a blue shirt, clutching coffee and fighting to keep his eyes open. What used to be Passepartout looked up and waved, his eyes shadowed by two grey crescents.

'Where did you get to?' I asked, squeezing in next to him.

'Anusha put me on a train that got to Udhampur at about 5 am. I don't think I actually slept at all, but this lovely man invited me to his house for breakfast and a shower and then he took me around Udhampur.'

'That's kind of him.'

'Yes, but I paid for it. I think I spent most of the day being shown his wedding photos.' He laughed. 'Just about every photo of him was fine, but his poor wife looked dreadful,' he squinted, then shut one eye. 'She looked like this in almost every picture, yet no one, not even the photographer, seemed to care and shoved the whole lot into the album. Poor woman. Anyway, where were you?'

'Eating omelette sandwiches and playing on railway lines.'

Shortly before lights out we both took to our berths and slept soundly, arriving in Delhi the following morning.

After shots of hot coffee and a wash in the station toilets, we ventured into the no-man's land of Paharganj to check emails. Touts hovered but ignored us. The virgin-fresh sheen of our first visit had dulled to a matted-haired, ali-baba-pant-wearing state of cliché and they knew better than to offer us tickets for trains, or their well-rehearsed performances. Wedged into a booth in front of a computer with a sticky mouse and a desktop covered in minimised windows offering sex with Lakshmi and her friends, I found an email at the top of my inbox.

'Dear Monisha,
I have already forwarded your message to Supertendent of Police, Dist. Tinsukia, for arrangment of your accomondation and other journey programme. Be assured your all arragement will be done and some one will be at Tinsukia Railway Station to recieve you.

thanks and best wishes, Sanjeev, Adil and Rohit.'

In India things happen when you least expect them, but sometimes, just sometimes, you cannot ask for a better time.

18 | Bullets over Brahmaputra

If there is one thing South Indians relish, it is declaring their superiority over North Indians. Wedding-Crasher Bobby had launched into a tirade of scaremongering while driving us around Chennai the first day we arrived in India.

'I swear... you'll find it awful,' he insisted, plucking rapidly at the front of his shirt as it stuck to his chest. 'Baaaas-tud I swear...,' he cursed, as a cyclist swerved dreamily in front of the bonnet, then braked and banged it with his fist, '...if you think Chennai is bad, man, you should check out the North, particularly if you go to West Bengal and Assam. What all you'll see, broken trains and such dirty people I tell you,' he added, winding down the window and chucking out an empty packet of Marlboro Reds. 'Animals... pukka junglees.'

Junglee is one of my favourite words: a Hindi term that literally means 'jungle dweller' and conjures up images of Mowgli types with uncombed hair, scratching themselves and foraging in bins for half-eaten kebabs. Needless to say, North Indians are nothing like this, but in turn will readily describe Southerners as a bunch of snobs. Indians are racist. They will not admit it, but paradoxically they are proud of it. While North Indians are classified as brash, undignified and vulgar with wealth, Southerners are deemed bookish, backward and black – wholly undesirable in a country where Clarins White Plus face cream is advertised as 'the magic wand you have been waiting for'.

After Bobby's warnings about the Northeast, its trains and its people, I was nervous by the time I arrived in Siliguri. It is a boisterous junction town connecting Bhutan, Darjeeling and Assam, well known for its Hong Kong Market, which specialises in imported goods and Delhi-made items stamped with 'Made in China'. Long before branded goods had found their way into mainstream India, most electronic items were snuck in through this corner and the majority of wares are still illegally imported.

A night rickshaw ride took us through the market, which was hung with tracksuits, earmuffs, cross-eyed dolls and wicker baskets plump with fruit that glowed under hurricane lamps. While waiting at a red light, a rickshaw broke free from the pack and veered towards a no-entry. Not quick enough, the driver was collared and slapped repeatedly by a white-gloved traffic cop, who then let down his tyres as further punishment. His passengers were left standing in the middle of the road, holding their shopping and looking for any takers. So far, the Northeast appeared no different from the South.

The following morning, we hailed another rickshaw to New Jalpaiguri, Siliguri's sister town, to catch the 11:45 am Dibrugarh Rajdhani, which was due to arrive at Tinsukia in Assam at around 5:30 am the next day. Anusha had booked Passepartout onto the same train, but could only find him a ticket in third-tier, while I was up in second. Fortunately, we were separated now only by a pantry car, rather than several states, and were content to nip back and forth to keep each other company. Down in coach B9, he appeared happy enough, engulfed by singing children, curious children, large mothers and indifferent fathers, so I picked my way back to A2 where my family for the next 18 hours seemed relatively docile.

In the side berth a lithe gentleman lay dozing with both legs crossed at the ankle, sporting a futile attempt at a combover. His head was as smooth as a freshly shelled conker, but for six strands of overgrown hair that stretched from one side to the other like an Alice band. Underneath my berth lay a mummified figure whose face I was yet to see, while the other three berths were still unclaimed. The only other characters were policemen in khaki, who clumped along the aisles every few minutes carrying rifles. Each wore a long black bandanna, tied behind the ears and hanging down the neck, giving them an air of vigilante menace.

I climbed into my berth and began to update the list of trains. Intrigued by the elusive scrawl *Gorakhpur to Nautanwa*, I had taken train 68, the

Gorakdam Express to Gorakhpur in Uttar Pradesh, only to find that the train to Nautanwa, on the border of Nepal, had ceased to exist. After many warnings from Bahadur, my cousin's Nepali butler, of 'No baby, Gorakhpur very bad, baby. Bad! Don't stay, careful being!', I had left immediately on train 69, the Avadh–Assam Express to Siliguri. Passepartout, meanwhile, had decided to stay behind to look around Delhi and agreed to meet me in Siliguri, so we could take the train together to Assam. We were now on board train 70.

Pleased with the progress, I leant down from my berth and gazed at the greyness outside the window. The Rajdhani was now getting into its stride, tearing along waterlogged fields of green, passing woods, lakes and mud houses with swirls of smoke rising in the yard. Feeling fidgety, I decided it was time for a wander. Swinging both latches round, I heaved open the train door and was shocked by the thump of cold air. Crouching down, I watched as endless paddy fields flew by. Unlike the South, the expanse was flat and ran to the horizon, eventually disappearing into a blanket of cloud.

The 'too many people' adage, a favourite of complaining Indians, held no weight here; the road running by the track was filled with nothing but ruts and puddles and scarecrows crying out for company in the fields. Gone was the kaleidoscope of colour alluded to in tourist-board blurb. Northeast India's contrast button was held down to the minimum, muting the scene to a palette of greys befitting a James Joyce novel. A horn blasted through the fog, signalling entry into the first tea plantation. Plump and plucked to perfection, the rows of bushes stood no higher than my waist. Women wearing headscarves carried baskets like wicker drums on their backs, the straps fixed across their foreheads. Stony-faced, they watched as the train intruded on their work. Embarrassed, I waved gingerly from the doorway and they broke into giggles, white teeth flashing like camera bulbs, and they waved back until we were out of sight.

Rain began to whip the windows, not in wispy English streams that dampen spirits, but with the kind that lacerate human skin. Shivering, I zigzagged back through the pantry car. At one end a man wearing a T-shirt filled with holes tossed smoking cauliflower in a karahi the size of a satellite dish, while at the other a pair of boots attached to a sleeping policeman stuck out over a berth, his AK47 propped up against the wall. It was a far cry from *Hello!* magazine, packets of Quavers and the balloon-red blazers of a Virgin Pendolino.

I settled down to read when the compartment resounded with an almighty 'BAM!' and I peered over the edge of the berth to see who had been shot. The Human Conker was crouched on the floor, running his hand over a hole in the window that was now splintering into a spider web.

'Rocks,' he said. 'They throw rocks sometimes to cause problems. Sometimes bullets.'

Hoping nobody chose that moment to throw bullets, I jumped down and inspected the web. 'Who does?' I questioned, as he smoothed his strands back into place and ignored me.

Curious, I got back into my berth just as Passepartout appeared with his book and the haggard look of a sleep-deprived mother. He clambered into the empty berth as the ticket inspector waddled into sight. He was an unpleasant man whose top lip curled up as he peered at our tickets, revealing dark, sticky-looking gums.

'Tell him to go!' he shouted at me, gesturing at Passepartout with a pair of pantomime eyebrows.

There was nobody in the berth and since the rail passes included second-tier, I saw no reason why he should.

'Someone is coming at the next stop,' he barked.

Passepartout slid down and walked off. Nobody came for the next four hours.

I must have fallen into a deep sleep, as when I looked over, the bed was made and a skeletal man in a cross-legged position was cupping his elbows, engaged in breathing exercises. Chandan was a 31-year-old English teacher from Dibrugarh in Assam who studied naturopathy and drank two glasses of hot water with every meal to prevent fat absorption. His eyes flicked open and he looked straight at me.

'May I ask what it is you are writing?'

I showed him the list of train journeys and he pulled out a giant encyclopaedia on the history of Assam and tossed it across to me.

'Why are you carrying this?' I asked in bemusement.

'I was teaching in Delhi.'

He closed both eyes, but continued talking.

'It's peaceful now,' he said. 'Earlier, young people were feeling that the central government of India was neglecting Assam since independence. Compared with other parts of India, you will see that Assam is underdeveloped, there is no investment and huge unemployment. There is also the problem of infiltration from Bangladesh. Immigrants come in and settle on the banks of the Brahmaputra and then gradually they make their way up to the main part of Assam and start occupying. Rajiv

Gandhi signed the Assam Accord in 1985, but no section of this has been fulfilled yet.'

He paused to inhale while I scribbled, thrilled at this uninvited explanation of Assam's unrest.

'What did the Accord include?'

'They had promised to clear out illegal immigrants and to help industrialisation, but all they do is take advantage of our tea and oil.'

'Why haven't they addressed the demands?'

'Assam youth are fed up of being exploited and are demanding independence as a state, but India wants to keep us attached because we're useful.'

He placed the index finger of his right hand against his left nostril and exhaled.

'Mainland India is full of terrible people. They complain that you Britishers came and raped the country, but Indians do no better among their own people.'

'What can you do?'

'Not much. We often kidnap foreigners, make off explosions and no doubt you will be reading of dastardly behaviour: we are just trying to get the attention of the Indian government.'

Whether or not he meant the royal 'we', I now had no intention of falling asleep in the berth next to a self-confessed kidnapper. He hugged his knees to his chest and rolled onto his back, before sitting up and watching me drain the dregs of my tea.

'You mustn't drink tea in Assam,' he grinned.

After drinking over a thousand paper cups of tea-flavoured treacle, the trip to Assam in search of the finest cuppa was like pilgrimage. Whether my tea obsession came from my Indian genes or from growing up in Yorkshire, travelling to Assam felt to me what a trip to Colombia must mean to Charlie Sheen.

'All tea in Assam is full of pesticides, so don't drink it. We call it *saalu chai*, or "dirty tea". Good tea is exported to you people and to Germany.'

I wished I had packed a bumper box of Twinings.

A man arrived wearing a grey anorak, a grey cardigan, grey trousers and a grey tie, with a shock of orange hair. He and his young son took over the bottom berth just as the mummified figure had crept out from beneath her blanket, revealing a slender face flushed with the glow of a good sleep. The Conker had gone and an elderly doctor with rosy cheeks lay in the side berth, repeating *saalu chai* and laughing. Now was a good time to ask why there were so many policemen on board.

'Why do police keep walking up and down our carriage? Is that normal?'

The doctor smiled as though he had not heard me. The grey-clothed, orange-haired man repeated the question, staring out of the window as the others looked away. I had committed the Assamese equivalent of farting in public. Still gazing at the blackness, he replied:

'They are thinking that there might be a bomb on the train. This is a prestigious and very nice Rajdhani train, so it is of special interest to militants.'

Inwardly I cursed Anusha and her love of Rajdhanis.

'You shouldn't worry,' he said, 'but one way to know if this is true is if they bring sniffer dogs onto the train.'

As the train shook across the bridge entering Guwahati, the Brahmaputra river drifted in the dark, a wide-mouthed beast, rippling and sparkling beneath a full moon. Moving into the doorway, I squatted to watch the show playing at arm's reach. Huts lit by oil lamps and candles slid past, while fires burned beneath pots of food, the smoke flitting across the train doors. The city flickered like a fairytale kingdom as the train clanked and rolled past open homes and families winding down for the day. A body pressed itself against me and I jumped back to find a boy in an anorak, lighting a cigarette. He fixed me with a pair of slanted green eyes as his friend cleaned his nails with a blade. They were both Naga.

'You are Christian?'

'No, I'm a Hindu,' I replied, wondering what that even meant any more. They raised their eyebrows and glanced at my clothes.

'No, you are Christian,' said the second boy, pressing his blade against the sleeve of my fleece.

I assured him I was not, then added that my granddad had been stationed in Nagaland in the 1960s, building roads with the Indian Army.

'Not Christian?' he said, pulling his blade back.

'No, not Christian,' I snapped.

'Sorry, ma'am, we see you with Christian man, we think you also Christian.'

The thought of the 'devout atheist' being mistaken for a Christian was laughable and not at all worth getting into, so I pulled together a few lines of Hindi, much to their delight, and wandered back to my seat as a pair of Labradors were led through the carriage.

❖

'English ma'am, English ma'am, the train is arriving early.'

I sat up and squinted out of the window. There is a type of greyness that saves itself for days of early-morning travel or after sleepless nights. It was in place, hanging from the skies and draped over the river. I raced down to B9 where, amid the neon lights, sari tying, catarrh clearing, toddler whacking and hair combing, Passepartout was curled up like a question mark, still asleep. As the train drew into Tinsukia, the morning dampness drifted through the open doors, bringing with it the smell of moss, mud and rain. It was certainly colder than West Bengal, but not cold enough to warrant the kind of attire that looked more suitable for a ski trip. A pair of newly-weds wore matching balaclavas – the man also wrapped in a checked scarf, while his bride was wearing a pair of fingerless gloves revealing the maroon of her wedding henna.

I looked down hopefully at my phone. As in Jammu, foreign phones did not work here and I was worried we would not find our hosts. I was already nervous that the Rajdhani trio were professional con-artists, and I – naive and trusting – had fallen prey to an elaborate plot to lure foreign bait into the clutches of militants looking to take hostages. Or perhaps I had been reading too many books.

As we hovered, a stocky man with a square head, wearing a Pringle jumper, approached. He looked like a little brown Legoman and shook my hand, smiling to reveal rows of teeth that looked as though they were fitted from the mouth of a 4-year-old. Nirmal was the detective superintendent of Tinsukia police who was to take care of us for the next two days.

A jeep waited in the forecourt, with five armed police standing to attention, more of whom saluted from the roadside as we drove to the Circuit House, a colonial building set back from a lawn being mowed by two hungry goats. A bundle of overgrown puppies rolled around the porch, suckling at their mother, as Nirmal showed us to our rooms and left us in the care of Paulie, a lanky boy, no more than 15, wearing an oversized shirt and a smile that formed two dimples. It was Paulie who brought the first of many cups of tea. Dirty or not, it was like nectar from the Gods. Clay red, with neither milk nor sugar.

It was still barely daybreak and orange slivers were just beginning to crack through the grey, so we took to our beds for a couple of hours, crawling between damp covers that bore the mustiness of boarding schools, waking eventually to adamant quacking. Pulling back the curtains, I was greeted by the blue skies of a primary-school painting. Cotton-wool clouds and an egg-yolk sun shone overhead and a motley crew of ducks and one goat splashed around in leftover puddles. The oedipal puppies had vanished. A man was sitting in a wicker chair in a tight red polo neck and flares, smiling from under a fine bouffant. He spotted my head in the window and waved.

Pradeep had a wide face and gappy teeth and thrived on gathering useless trivia. His specialist interest was cash points, but this also extended to enquiring about rucksack straps, our blood types, the expiry dates on English breakfast condiments and star signs. At one point he tried to scratch a mole off my right ankle, insisting that it was dirt. Pradeep was Nirmal's best friend and an accomplished guide, who spent the next two days ferrying us all over town to meet his family, interspersed with visits to tea estates, oil refineries and collieries. But mainly to meet his family. After another cup of tea, we left the house, the jeep straining over ruts before Pradeep made a pit stop. A policeman climbed wordlessly into the front seat, balancing his AK47 over one shoulder. Passepartout turned pale in the back.

'Nakul is your escort while you are here,' Pradeep explained, driving in the middle of the road, ploughing through pedestrians and turning on the siren at the slightest indication of traffic. Nirmal had arranged a tour of one of the 13 estates owned by a British company that produced 900,000 kg of tea per year, 70 per cent of which was exported to Germany and Britain. Passepartout turned to me.

'Isn't it going to draw more attention to us, walking around with an armed guard, than if we were just on our own?'

'Maybe, but I don't particularly fancy our dastardly killings appearing in *The Hindu* next week.'

Navigating the bright green rows of bushes was like winding around Hampton Court Maze, at the heart of which lay an oasis of blossoms and dogs gambolling around the home of the estate manager. Ranjit was a beast of a man who stood on the steps, his thighs bulging in his shorts. He immediately ordered tea, which arrived in delicate china. Passepartout and I had begun to tremble from the caffeine and wobbled into the back of Ranjit's jeep, which bounced and slammed along the dirt tracks to the factory. Row after row of geometrically perfect bushes stretched on for miles as pickers plucked the old leaves to make way for the second flush – provider of the purest tea. Inside the factory, Ranjit lined up a row of cups and began to slurp and hiss his way through each batch, before spitting like a cobra into a wooden column. He had the bull's-eye precision of a pro and stepped back, gesturing towards the cups.

'Please, you must taste them yourself.'

I sucked in a mouthful of what turned out to be cold, unsweetened tea, so potent that my eyes began to water. Gagging and dribbling, I sprayed most of the column and, much to Passepartout's delight, snorted a stream from my nose. Thrilled by the mess, Ranjit delved into an explanation of leaves, potency and oxidisation and gave us a tour of the sifting, drying and packing processes. It was barely 4 pm but, bored with niceties, Ranjit wanted to give us a proper Assamese welcome.

'What do you drink?' he asked.

'Normally tea with milk, but I don't mind it without.'

Ranjit chuckled. 'No, I meant what do you *drink*? Whisky?'

By 5 pm we were back in his living room, flushed, giggling and flicking through his wife's copies of *Femina* magazine while he emptied every bottle of whisky in the house. Pradeep was jiggling around in his chair, desperate for us to meet his wife and children, but Ranjit beat him to it by extending an invitation to the estate managers' social club. Having been turned away from the Gymkhana Club in Chennai for wearing flip-flops on the verandah, I was worried about our scruffiness, but arrived at the club to find one barman, an out-of-tune piano and a carom table on a plinth.

On the way back to the Circuit House, Pradeep swerved into his own driveway, bundling us out of the jeep and into his home to meet his wife, two daughters, mother-in-law and seven puppies. After two cups of tea we got back into the jeep and carried on to the home of his wife's parents, where we were given two more cups of tea. My bladder could not handle any more relatives, so eventually the jeep sped back to the Circuit House for the night.

The next morning we boarded train 71, a passenger train to Ledo, the easternmost tip of the Indian Railways. In 90 minutes we would have completed the four corners of Indian Railways' geographical diamond (if we ignored the confusion at Dwarka). Nirmal had instructed Nakul to accompany us, but nobody batted an eyelid as he squeezed onto the end of the row of kids and fruitsellers, clutching his rifle with one hand and picking at his ear with the other.

For the first 20 minutes the train collected women on their way to vegetable markets, or men who were their own vegetable markets, carrying sets of scales over one shoulder and sitting on the floor, measuring their wares. Here the contrast button was set to high. Overnight rain had washed the scenery clean and now the grass gleamed beneath a Riviera-blue sky and bundles of blossom throbbed with colour. As fast as the train left one town, it came upon another until it began to squeeze through the tightest of passages, pushing by the backs of homes as children grimaced on doorsteps, their mothers oiling their hair. Men in vests read the morning papers and women aired laundry, ignoring the voyeurs peering over their walls. Hooting and clanging, the train curved around a row of houses coloured like jelly beans, below which sat an amputee on the edge of the track selling fruit in twists of paper. He waved up at the windows as the train thundered past, inches from his face. For all the talk of the new India, the old is never far away.

As we reached the end of Mother India's fingertip, China to the north and Myanmar to the south were closer than mainland India. Just inside the open doorway, a sapota seller with sores on his ankles squatted with his wares and pulled out a wad of money from his basket. Unaware that anyone was watching, he unravelled the notes, which wilted with dirt, and counted the pitiful amount. Closing his eyes, he pressed the money between his calloused palms and brought them gently to his forehead. At that moment it became clear why the Indian Railways had earned its name as the lifeline of the nation.

19 | The Temple of Doom

With the exception of the Indian Maharaja and the Golden Chariot, we had bypassed luxury travel and largely opted for second- and third-tier for overnight journeys and general class during the day. For our journey from Tinsukia back to New Jalpaiguri to catch the toy train to Darjeeling, Anusha had convinced us to stump up the extra fee and had booked us into first class, ignoring my protests with a blank stare and convenient deafness.

'Always you are travelling in these classes. See, my book is filled with your journeys.' She flicked through her logbook. 'So boring.'

'I know, but they're comfy enough.'

She stared at her screen. 'I am booking you in first-class cabin, it's very nice.'

Anusha was eligible for the award for weakest sales pitch, but at this stage in the journey a little luxury would not hurt, and besides, she was right. Among the many trains, we were yet to travel in a first-class cabin, so train 72 was a treat. As we squeezed through the doors of the Dibrugarh Rajdhani Express like two packhorses weighed down by books, bags of tea presented by Ranjit and scarves presented to us at every home we had visited, we came upon a problem. Passepartout had been allotted a berth in a cabin of four, while I was in a cabin of two with a businessman named Frank. He had made himself at home in a pair of blue flannel pyjamas and bed socks and looked dismayed when I pulled open the door.

'Oh good grief.'

'What's the matter?'

'Are you in this cabin?'

'Yes, I think so.'

'Then I have to move.'

Offended, I put down my bags. 'Why?'

'A man and a woman are not allowed to share a first-class cabin if they are unknown to one another.'

'Oh. Well, I don't particularly mind. I'm only going to climb up and go to sleep.'

He sighed and pulled out his bags from under the seats. 'Well, I don't have a problem either, but those are the rules. Where is your friend?'

'In the next cabin along.'

'Then I will have to swap with him.'

Thinking back to the journey from Delhi to Chennai, I found it strange that it was acceptable for me to travel in a cabin with three strange men, but not just one. Frank shifted his bags out into the corridor, pressing his back to the wall and holding in his paunch as Passepartout slid past and joined me. Muttering and sighing, Frank poked his head back in to collect his knitted hat and then bade us goodnight.

Unlike the blue vinyl of the other classes, the charcoal-grey berths had the softness of car seats and, like sponge, sprung up when pressed down. There was even space to lie spread-eagled on a bolster pillow and soft red blankets. Dinner arrived on full-sized plates with polished cutlery, which we finished, placed outside the door for collection and then fell over in the morning. The class may have been upgraded, but the service was still the same.

As expected, the toy train from New Jalpaiguri was fully booked, so we took a minibus up to Darjeeling cramped next to two honeymooners who slept for the full four-hour journey while a leaking roof dripped rain onto their foreheads. Outside, the sky had darkened. Indigo clouds descended on the horizon and pale plumes floated into the valleys, obscuring the outlines of the mountainous humps hemmed in with tea bushes. Halfway up the hill the headlamps failed and the driver opted to drive in the blind spot of the car ahead, using its headlamps to guide him, while ploughing oncoming drivers off the road.

Sheets of rain blew sideways on arrival in Darjeeling. Water tumbled down the road in rapids as we trudged uphill through poorly lit alleys to the sound of hammering on tin roofs. Arriving outside the hotel, we waded through mud slithering past and fell up the steps, just as the rain stopped. But it was too late. All our things were drenched, the tea leaves stewing among my socks and T-shirts. There was no heating, so wrapped in towels and bed sheets we made our way up to the restaurant, where a fire burned in a corner and wooden tables were lined with diners hunched over steaming bowls of chilli noodles. A bowl of meaty *thukpa* and a frisbee-sized piece of sweet, deep-fried Tibetan bread brought the pulse back into my veins before we slid mournfully back into wet trousers and made our way down to the town to buy some dry clothes.

'The last thing I want to do is to load up with more clothes before going home,' Passepartout complained, skidding over muddy verges in the darkness, following the direction of voices from below.

'And the last thing I want is for you to catch pneumonia and for me to have to put up with your whingeing for the last few days.'

He grinned and helped me down the slopes as we emerged at the back of a stall in the middle of the night market. Much like the market in Siliguri, the stalls were hung with tracksuits, fake-fur jackets and cardigans, at least two decades out of date. It was now the first week of May and shoppers were buying up balaclavas and earmuffs as though a Siberian winter was en route.

'Paaaaaanties!' sang a man waving around what looked like a pair of doll's knickers. Sifting through the stack on his table, trying to find some dry underwear, I held up the least offensive-looking pair under a hurricane lamp. They had a picture of a cowgirl on the front and as I turned them over the vendor snatched them from my hand.

'These no good. You fat!' He ripped open a packet that I had thought were T-shirts and threw a pair at me. 'Take!'

Passepartout found a couple of long-sleeved tops that looked more like leggings, and I bought a pair of comfy-looking trousers that would have fitted a hippo. With our new autumn/winter haute couture we made our way back up to the hotel for a cup of Darjeeling tea.

James Shakespeare had been right: the toy train took just over seven hours to descend to New Jalpaiguri. He had also informed me that I would want to kill myself by the time we reached the bottom, so to be on the safe side we opted for the joyride, a two-hour journey that looped around to Ghum, the highest point of the railways. Launched in 1881, the Darjeeling Himalayan Railway, nicknamed the 'toy train', was the first of the hill passenger railways in India and many of its original features remained intact. It looked like one of Thomas the Tank Engine's little blue friends trundling into the forecourt. Steaming from its chimney, as though exhausted by the children tumbling out of its doors, all it lacked was a pouty face.

Eight children, eight adults and two babies shared our carriage, clapping and singing their way through as many Bollywood songs as they could remember while Passepartout and I leant over the back of rainbow-striped seats, watching the engineers shovelling molten coals. Train 73 travelled along the main road, passing cars and sliding so close to the edges that passengers could reach the eggs and bananas on roadside stalls.

'Dead body! Dead body!' one of the children shouted, pointing as a procession of mourners made its way alongside the train.

After the previous night's downpour, Darjeeling was now washed and wide awake, the snow-covered Himalayas sparkling in the distance. As the train approached the Batasia Loop and began to curve along the edge of a drop, I peered down into the valleys, taking in the panorama. Homes, hotels and shops looked like precariously balanced building blocks, stacked one above the other, with trees popping up in between like green lollipops. At the beginning of the trip, the seas swirling beneath the solar eclipse in Kanyakumari had been the first of many extraordinary sights. Now, staring at the white crags of Kanchenjunga glowing in the sunshine, after what had felt like a journey to the ends of the Earth, I could barely believe that one country could lay claim to such extremes of beauty. Despite missing trains, sleepless nights, long waits, being jostled in queues, surviving stampedes, fighting against illness and exhaustion, these moments made the journey worthwhile.

Worn out by the children, we slept soundly on train 74, the overnight Darjeeling Mail from New Jalpaiguri to Kolkata. The only train available out of Kolkata that week departed that very afternoon, so we made do with an indulgent breakfast at the Oberoi hotel and a wash in the luxury bathrooms, before boarding the Coromandel Express to Bhubaneswar. Throughout the four months I had remained very aware of the incidence of fatalities from train accidents, but had shoved the likelihood of a crash to the darkest corner of my mind and locked the door. However, in February 2009, within hours of the railway minister Lalu Prasad detailing the 'steep reduction in the number of railway accidents' during a parliamentary speech, the Coromandel Express had derailed 100 km from Bhubaneswar, leaving at least 15 people dead and more than 140 injured. Despite having escaped theft, injury, death and derailment in over 70 journeys, I incorporated the policy normally reserved for bus and taxi rides: I put my head down and went to sleep – waking at midnight as the heavily delayed train, number 75, rolled into the capital of Orissa.

The coastal town of Puri, like Dwarka, was one of the four *dhams*. It was home to the Jagannath temple and was famous for its annual Rath Yatra festival, when idols of the deities are placed on decorated chariots resembling temples and pulled through the streets by priests and devotees who flock from around the world for the privilege. It was from Lord Jagannath's chariot that the term 'juggernaut' came into use. The twelfth-century temple complex was hidden behind walls, but its tiered centrepiece was elevated on a pedestal with a red flag waving from the tip. Much like the Royal Standard over Buckingham Palace, it indicated that the lord was in residence.

A two-hour trip on train 76, the Dhauli Express, brought us to the town, thronging with visitors to the temple. Halfway down the road a man ran up to us, jogging backwards to keep up, and pointed to a building next door.

'Non-Hindus not allowed,' he declared. 'But you can take nice photos from Raghunandan library rooftop, best view, only a hundred and fifty rupees.'

Passepartout glared at him. I flashed him a look that suggested that if he valued his life he would try his luck elsewhere. Familiar with the ritual, Passepartout took my handbag and water bottle and crossed over the road for a cigarette and a coffee. I kicked off my flip-flops and joined a queue that led to the entrance, where a khaki-clothed guard sat on a stool. He put his hand out as I approached.

'*Naam?*'

'Monisha.'

'*Gotram?*'

I had learnt at Dwarka that this referred to lineage or clan. 'Pala.'

He looked me up and down, then beckoned me out of the queue with two fingers and led me to what seemed to be a ticket office. A balding man with a grey moustache sat inside the window shuffling paper. Without looking up, he held out his hand.

'ID card?' he demanded.

'I don't have one.'

'All Indians have ID card.'

'I'm not an Indian resident.'

'Where is your passport?'

'I don't have it on me.'

'You are not a Hindu.'

My palms tingled. 'Excuse me?'

'You are not a real Hindu. Show your passport.'

Heat crawled up my neck. 'My passport doesn't have my religion on it.'

'Show your passport.'

The tout from earlier was still hovering. He edged his way over and piped up 'Husband has passport', pointing across the road.

The man peered out at Passepartout. 'That white man is your husband? Then you are not a real Hindu. Hindus do not take another in marriage.'

A volcanic eruption of anger rose with such force that I did not even bother to correct him. 'You show me where it says that a Hindu cannot marry someone who is not a Hindu.'

'Even Indira Gandhi, Prime Minister of India, was not allowed into temple,' the tout said, with infuriating smugness. 'She also took *another* as her husband.'

Passepartout, realising something was afoot, stubbed out his cigarette and hurried over. I took my passport from him and handed it to the man in the window. He examined my picture. Contorting his face into an expression of incredulity, he waved the passport at me.

'Rajesh? What name is this? And British?' He threw my passport at me and it bounced off my forehead and onto the floor. 'Look at how you are dressed. You are not a Hindu. Get out!'

I looked down at my trousers, swinging low at the crotch, and the full-sleeved Fab India kurti. In normal circumstances I too would have been embarrassed to be caught in such a state of sartorial disaster, but the man had now stoked a fire that for four months I had managed to contain.

'What would you prefer I do? Come here wearing a sari, tailing behind my husband like a good Hindu? Or smear myself in ash and heap you with donations? You disgust me.'

Like moths to a flame, Indians love a good drama, and many drifted across the road and came out of shops to watch the show. They circled, hand on hip, trying to secure a prime viewing spot – including the priest. One man looked me up and down and then poked the priest in the arm.

'She is Hindu!' he exclaimed.

In reply, the guard slammed his stick across the back of his head.

'You're going to hit him now because he's saying a truth you don't want to hear?' Passepartout demanded.

The priest, the guard and the fanatic behind the window started to laugh at me.

'You're a bunch of hypocrites!' I shouted, half fearing they would douse me with kerosene and set me alight. I later found out that these were the same priests who had burnt an effigy of Srila Prabhupada, the Founder of the International Society of Krishna Consciousness (ISKCON), for celebrating the Rath Yatra festival on the wrong day in 2008. 'You can take your temple and shove it up your arse for all I care. Do you think that your God isn't watching you all right now?'

'You are not a Hindu,' the priest insisted.

'Who the hell are you to tell me I'm not a Hindu? You're so caught up with making money from your wasteful, pointless rituals that you don't even know why you do it, and what it means to be a good person. People like *you* are what is wrong with religion!'

'At least everyone is welcome into a church,' Passepartout added.

Reeling both from the accusations and from Passepartout's defence of a church, I pushed through the crowd, my cheeks flaming, and strode up the street, snatching a cigarette from Passepartout as he jogged alongside.

'Come on, let's at least go to the Konarak temple,' he offered.

'No.'

'Why not?'

I flagged down a rickshaw and we climbed in. 'I think I've had enough of temples. For good.'

For the first time, Passepartout had nothing to say.

Slumped in a corner of the Puri-Talcher passenger train, embracing my first real sunburn, I took out my logbook. I was still fuming and scraped 77 into the parchment as the ticket inspector arrived. Our passes had recently expired and we had been buying tickets, but having never met a ticket inspector on a passenger train, we had become casual. Hiding in the toilet was not an option that I was willing to entertain. He held out ringed fingers.

'Where are your tickets?'

Passepartout tried to distract him with his camera. The inspector put down his clipboard, pulled his moustache with both hands and waved a pair of jazz hands, thrusting out one leg.

'Thank you,' he said. 'Now where are your tickets?'

I swung my legs round and sat up, my shoulders sagging. 'We haven't got any.'

'Would you like a fine?'

'Not really.'

'Do you think you can run quickly and avoid the ticket collectors in the station?'

'Probably.' I sat up. This was no ordinary inspector.

'To be safe, let's just give you the fine.'

Passepartout pulled out ₹500 for each of us. Once the inspector had gone, he waved the inky foil at me.

'Cheer up, it's great! Imagine how fun that will look amid all our other stubs.'

I scowled. 'I know, I might find it funny one day, but right now I'm not in the mood.'

'What's the matter?'

I had a migraine. I had only ever had two in my life. One was when we were moving to India. I remember sitting on the back row of the Air Lanka plane with my forehead pressed against my palms while my mum asked the air hostess for paracetamol. All she could reply was 'see-tamole?', 'see-tamole?' until I passed out from the pain and the lack of 'see-tamole'. The other was when I messed up my A-level results and let down my parents. This new migraine was not the result of dehydration, nor was it due to a lack of food. This migraine was not induced by heat. This was something else. I turned to Passepartout.

'Please don't be upset, but I have to go and do something.'

'What, when we get back to Bhubaneswar?'

'No. I'm not sure where.'

'What do you mean?'

'This has nothing to do with you, but can you just give me a week or so on my own?'

'Are you all right?'

'Not really. But it's nothing that you can help with.'

'Are you sure?'

'Absolutely.'

'I don't mind. I have friends whom I wanted to visit in Jaipur, I may head back up there again if you're OK with that?'

'Yes, that's fine. I can meet you back in Chennai.'

He paused. 'Why don't you go ahead and finish the last three trains.'

'On my own?'

'You've done a hell of a lot more than me and I can spend this time playing catch-up.'

I frowned. 'Are you sure you're OK with not finishing them together?'

'Sure. There are a couple of places I'd quite like to see myself and I want to genuinely complete all 80 for my own satisfaction before we head back home.' He smiled. 'Besides, I think this is something you need to finish by yourself.'

'Thank you.'

'Just promise me you will be all right on your own.'

'I will, I promise.'

20 | Losing My Religion

'Ten days in complete silence? I could never do that, I'd go completely crazy.'

This was the typical response when I described the meditation course I was about to attend.

'Why on Earth would you want to do that? No phone calls, no texts, no emails, no Facebook, no books, no writing materials and no iPods? And you can't speak to anyone? Or even make eye contact? You're insane. It sounds horrendous!'

To me, no communication with the outside world sounded like bliss. After almost four months, constantly on the move, a part of me had begun to go crazy. I had spent more nights contorted in a rocking berth than I had stretched out on a stationary bed. My back was filled with knots and the May heat was making me irrational and snappy. My thoughts were running riot. Snippets of conversation in my head had now swelled to constant jabbering, growing ever louder to drown out irritations from all around. It was once endearing – in the silly way that journalists on their first freebie to India describe 'the smell of sweet chai and spices' – but the honking of horns, the stench of sandalwood and shit, and the close proximity of sweating skin had begun to batter my senses. I needed somewhere quiet, to sit still, to breathe.

I had no intention of embarking on a spiritual journey and becoming the parody I readily mocked, but my militant atheist sidekick had dragged me down that path and dumped me at a crossroads. This society was built on religion, but over the previous months my faith had eroded. Observing the VIP queues at temples, the sale of spirituality and surface displays of piety from the rich and famous – who, when not dodging tax, publicly fighting over money with their siblings or inciting religious riots, were sure to be photographed mollifying a statue with a handful of sweets – had steered me towards reconsidering its significance in my life. Whether or not God existed was not for me to answer, but what I did know was that placing responsibility for myself in the hands of an unknown entity was over. From all around I was being fed a variety of unappetising comments: 'So sad you've lost hope.' 'Don't worry, you'll believe again.' 'Just pray to Hanuman and he will comfort you.' 'God has a plan.' On the contrary, I was not sad at all. I was cheered. Stepping out onto India's streets and looking down at the slums or up at The Oberoi was evidence enough that bad and good things happened to both bad and good people, and the sooner I stopped looking for reasons, the more palatable life would become.

Throughout my time in India, Vipassana meditation had cropped up in conversations and it sounded ideal: a non-religious method of mental purification that allows one to face tensions and problems in a calm, balanced way. Vipassana, a Burmese technique practised by the Buddha, means 'to see things as they really are' and involves 10 days without external distractions to sharpen the mind and learn self-control. After talking to Ben and browsing online, I chose a course run by a man named S.N. Goenka, who had found the technique useful in alleviating his debilitating migraines, and after 14 years of training had decided to share the wealth. He began teaching Vipassana in 1969 and had established centres all over the world, even introducing courses to prisoners in Delhi's Tihar jail. They resulted in such positive benefits that the Indian government was now considering the meditation as a permanent tool for reform. My mind was yet to join the ranks of those belonging to murderers, rapists, drug smugglers and senior politicians, but a little realignment could do no harm. One appealing aspect was that the course was free of charge, so no bogus guru was going to line his orange pockets with my cash.

I took train 78, the Konark Express, from Bhubaneswar to Hyderabad and arrived at the retreat, where I handed in my passport, my phone and, for all I knew, my sanity, and was shown to my room: stone walls housing two stone beds with inch-deep mattresses. Two? How could I share a room in silence? I made up my bed and sat down, reading through the pamphlet, which outlined five rules:

1. To abstain from killing any being.
2. To abstain from stealing.
3. To abstain from all sexual activity.
4. To abstain from telling lies.
5. To abstain from all intoxicants.

Easy enough – at least until I returned from dinner to find my new roommate Inga staring at four cockroaches on the bathroom floor, their fat bodies shining like medjool dates. I wanted to smash them to bits. Inga shrugged as we went in search of a broom.

'My mother claims that if you leave a problem completely alone, 50 per cent of the time it will disappear by itself,' she said.

By the time we returned, two of the cockroaches had vanished down the drain. We swept the other two out of the door and flicked them into the grass. That night, a mosquito found its way inside my net and began humming by my ear. I took a deep breath and gave it a slap. Technically the meditation only began the following morning.

In the still of the night a low gong sounded. 4:20 am. My heart sank. It sounded again. Peeling one eye open, I could just make out Inga, cocooned in her blankets. She was not about to move. I turned over as the gong sounded for a third time. Maybe if we ignored it, like the cockroaches, it would go away. Suddenly a shrill tinkling entered the open window as a bell-ringing sadist went from room to room rousing the dead. Flipping on the lights, I washed my face and dragged myself outside. The tree-lined gardens looked like the set of the *Thriller* video. Mist curled around the trunks and from the shadows shuffled glassy-eyed figures, silent and shivering in the morning damp.

At least 100 people filled the meditation hall, most of whom were Indian. Men outnumbered women by at least three to one. For two hours we sat cross-legged on cushions, eyes closed, observing our breath – a practice that is supposed to focus the mind. Goenka is based at the main Vipassana centre at Igatpuri in Maharashtra, but his voice periodically croaks from a crackling tape player, manned by a teacher at the front of the room:

'Be aware of your breath on your upper lip. Don't change it, just be aware of it. Does your breath enter the right nostril? Left nostril? Is it warm? Cool? Deep? Shallow? Be aware.'

I was aware that if I closed my eyes and watched my breath, I fell asleep. My head jerked up every five minutes and I looked around grinning, to see

if anyone had noticed. Everyone else looked so calm. Or they had perfected
the art of sleeping upright. When the two hours came to an end, I bolted to
the breakfast hall, wolfed down a plate of idlis, then crawled back into bed
and slept until the next session.

At 8 am we were back on the cushions. I soon realised that my breath
was a great indicator of my mood. My mind started wandering to my best
friend's hen party that I was upset to be missing. I sighed heavily, my breath
sharp and forced. A few moments later I could see an orange hue forming
in front of my closed eyelids as the sunshine came in through the windows,
warming my arms. My breath became so light it was barely detectable. For
what could only have been eight seconds, but felt like an hour, my mind
quietened. As soon as I realised, I gave myself a mental pat on the back and
then sulked for breaking the stillness. My thoughts now turned into two
voices arguing in my head:

Voice One: *What's wrong with you? You've got the attention span of a
3-year-old.*

Voice Two: *Look, I'm trying. It's not my fault. It's hot in here. Now go away.
Warm air on my upper lip… breath out of the right nostril… slightly twitchy
eye… God I hope lunch is better than breakfast…* '

Voice One: *You need help – maybe some Ritalin. Everyone else is so quiet
and still. Especially the girl to your left, I think she's called Annie. Look how
perfectly focused she is. Back straight. Fingertips gently touching.*

Voice Two: *She's probably been meditating her whole life.*

Voice One: *Or you're just rubbish at this.*

Voice Two: *Piss off!*

For the entire day the thoughts collaborated with each other to torment
me. From time to time Goenka's voice calmed them, reminding me to
observe them but not to attach myself to them. Just observe. But the thoughts
soon came out of hiding, ready for action. They mocked and bullied me:

'It's going to be so hard finding work when you get back to London…'
Four weddings to go to and you're still single? How awful, everyone will pity
you, Bridget Jones…' 'Remember that letter you sent Fiona Lanes in middle
school calling her a two-faced cow? You still feel bad about it, don't you?'

But sometimes my thoughts paused to play nicely: together we watched
a clip from *Coming to America*, then we decided that the blonde hippy
sitting on a rainbow cushion in the front row was actually a white witch
called Liberty. Just as I managed to coax my thoughts to bed, tucked them
in and turned out the light, they leapt up and squeezed my knee joints and

the base of my spine until they hurt so much I was sure I would explode. To
top it off, they invited Robert Palmer to join us and throughout the rest of
the day he crooned 'Addicted to Love' on a loop.

'Your lights are on, but you're not home

Your mind is not your own... '

The lights were on, but by the time I crawled into bed that night,
after observing my breath for 11 hours, I began to wonder if anyone really
was home.

Each day began at 4:30 am. After the first two-hour sitting, breakfast was
served in a communal dining hall with tables running around the edge of
the room, so everyone faced the windows, as though banished to one big
naughty corner. At 11 am we came back for lunch and for the next two
hours were free to nap, roam around the gardens or ask the teachers brief
questions about the meditation. It was the only time we were permitted
to speak and they offered beatific smiles and the same response to every
question: 'Just observe the breath...'

Helpful.

On the first evening I was shocked to find that no dinner was served after
the tea, fruit and puffed rice offered at 5 pm, and made a mental note to
load up at lunch on the rice, dal, butternut squash and beans, which made
me feel sick the next day and even more desperate for a cheeky afternoon
nap. The sittings ended at 7 pm with a 1980s video discourse from Goenka:
he was a podgy man with a side parting, free from ash, beads and robes,
who smiled knowingly and summarised the day with a freakishly incisive
understanding of the spectrum of thoughts and emotions flitting in and out
of us. He also warned us not to overeat at lunch to compensate for dinner.
It was the only hour of the day when I relaxed completely and slumped
against a wall with something other than my own dull breath to entertain
me. Goenka likened the 10-day period to a surgical procedure. An incision
had to be made on the surface of the skin to dig deep and find the cause of
an infection. The probing would be painful, produce pus and discomfort.
But once the root was discovered, it could be pulled out and the wound
would then be allowed to heal over.

'This will be a difficult period. But if you begin the process, please do not
leave in the middle with your wound half open, it will be worse than if you
never came here at all.'

Two red-eyed girls dabbed at their tears and snot and I made my way to bed, reassured that I was not the only one undergoing a real-life *Groundhog Day* and teetering on the edge of a nervous breakdown.

Three cushions were empty on the third morning and after lunch they had been removed. A warm cloak of smugness enveloped me as I realised that I was not the weakest in the fold and shuffled on my cushion, closing my eyes. I had not expected to, but I was beginning to enjoy the sensation of my breath being the focus of every moment. My shoulders were relaxed, my back ached less; or maybe the aches and pains were still there and my mind had just ignored them for the sake of observing my breath. A sudden shout ricocheted around the room and a spasm of shock swept through my chest. A lanky man in a red T-shirt was picking his way between the cushions, holding his head between his hands and yelling in Québécois French:

'That's it! How have I never seen this before? It's amazing!'

He grabbed the teacher by the shoulders and shook the little man, who did no more than smile as his combover came unstuck and flapped around. The man then bounded out of the room, punching the air. Old students of Vipassana went straight back to their lotus poses, while the rest of us, with minds like pinball machines, glanced around, shifted and thought:

'Bastard, how has he reached nirvana *already*?'

He had not reached nirvana. By tea-time he had soiled himself and was tearing up and down the orchards, caressing flowers and picking fights with the gardener. We hovered around watching like a brood of tongueless hens, wanting to cluck but unable to. It later transpired that he had been on medication before coming to the retreat, but had stopped it hoping the meditation would cure him. By sunset he had broken into opera and was streaking up and down the lawns, running after the herd of cows that had, so far, lurked peacefully around us. Before bedtime an ambulance arrived to take him away and as the last notes of 'Nessun Dorma' drifted out of the gates, I sat between the blades of tall grass, feeling them flick against my arms, and gave silent thanks. Praying was not allowed during the 10 days, to teach us self-responsibility, but it did not hurt to acknowledge the gratitude I felt for my health and well-being.

On the fourth morning we learnt that the breathing was a warm-up to the actual technique of Vipassana, the mental equivalent of lunging and stretching before a pole vault. The technique involves scanning the body from head to toe, observing any sensation: heat, itching, prickling, pain or pleasure. Whatever it is, you observe it with equanimity: no aversion to the unpleasant, nor craving towards the pleasant. The technique was much easier than the breathing, as I now had something to do. There were pins and needles in my feet, drops of sweat in the crooks of my elbows, blocks of pain in my left shoulder and mosquito bites itching everywhere. Halfway through the hour Robert Palmer returned and picked a fight with Peter Cetera, who kept trying to change the tune to 'Glory of Love'. I started not to mind. At least both songs were about love. While undergoing the mental MRI, both the music and my mind began to quieten down. For the first time in my life I listened to my body. To me it had always been a shell. But the closer I listened, the more I could hear.

Just before lunch on day five I felt a tingle in my forehead. It was so delicate it was like a filament flickering inside a light bulb. Intrigued, I sat as still as possible. There it was again. The flicker then appeared across the apples of my cheeks and moved into the tip of my nose. I had never felt this in my body before. I moved systematically down to my neck and felt the same flickering that soon grew to a thumping beat.

Woooohoooo!!!!!!!!!!!!!!

Goenka's voice crackled to life again, signalling the end of the sitting, and I realised that I had passed almost two hours without any niggling thoughts. See ya later, Robert Palmer! Of course, he was immediately back in the room singing with gusto.

'Your heart sweats, your body shakes...'

Silence is the most beautiful sound. Not once did it feel restrictive to stick to the rules. There was no need for small talk. It was liberating not to have to compete with, impress, feign interest in or be answerable to anyone, but just to be present for the sake of being present. Despite the lack of communication, we adjusted to one another quite naturally and, dare I say it, Inga and I became friends. She left me a towel when she saw I had misplaced mine. I left her bottles of water when I noticed she had run out. Through body language and intuition, we became sensitive to each other's needs. It was not a sixth sense but a heightening of the five I already had. Instead of allowing them to linger in the past or drift into the future, they had become focused on the present.

Leaping out of bed became the norm. After 11 hours of daily meditation, I slept straight through the night and rarely had dreams. The flickering soon branched out across my skin and swept over my body. It was like being on an Easter egg hunt. Scouring patches closely would soon turn up new goodies that I could add to the basket. My favourite flicker was the vein in my forehead. Growing attached to it was against the rules, but it was hard not to be thrilled by the discovery of my body. One night the flicker became a stream that connected my nose, cheeks, chin and neck, until my whole face throbbed gently in time with my arms and legs. My upturned hands felt as though 10 tiny heartbeats were living in the fingertips. Eventually they all connected, the inside of my wrists pounding so hard that I opened one eye to see if I could detect a movement on my skin.

But during the sittings there was one recurrent image: the night I fought with Passepartout in Chandigarh crept up on me, making my shoulders stiffen, my chest tighten and my breath rasp. I kept it under lock and key and pushed it out of my mind, but just as I had settled it would resurface. Goenka's voice smoothed over the creases with a constant reminder about impermanence:

'Everything in life arises to disappear. Do not become attached.'

But the memory refused to leave. It climbed out of my head, made itself comfortable in front of me and stared at me. Just as I found a state of calm, a bony finger poked me:

Hey, I'm still here, you still hate me, I still make the back of your neck hot and itchy every time you remember me.

The inside of my nostrils began to tingle and an ache grew behind my eyes as they filled. I started to cry, heaving with sobs on my cushion. Furious, I uncrossed my legs, left the hall and ran into the gardens, where I sat on a rock weeping onto my knees. The resident pye-dog trotted up to me and cocked his head to one side as if to say, 'Another one of you weirdoes on my patch.' He snorted, then lay down at my feet and began to lick himself.

As I watched the sun descending on the hills, I thought about how I normally dealt with upset: I phoned my best friend; watched *Anchorman* for the 50th time; played with other people's dogs on Hampstead Heath; or devoured Shanghai dumplings in Royal China. They were avoidance tactics. They briefly alleviated the symptoms, but suppressed the root cause of my woes that would soon push shoots up from the ground again. It had to be found, dug up, pulled out and thrown away. By dealing with the thoughts head on, there was nowhere to hide. I looked around and caught sight of Inga sitting against a tree, her face stained with tears. Against the rules, she flashed me a watery smile. After six days of no real human contact, it felt like the mental equivalent of a bear hug.

I settled back on my cushion and listened to Goenka's voice:

'When a thought originates from hatred, hurt or anger, an unpleasant sensation arises in the body. Just accept that anger is there and now heat, or tension or palpitations. Just accept that the mind is full of that negativity. You will come out of it. You have not suppressed it, you just observe and observe and one comes out of it.'

Michael Stipe had managed to oust the boys and was now sitting on my shoulder singing 'Losing My Religion'.

'That's me in the corner
That's me in the spotlight
Losing my religion
Trying to keep up with you'

I realised that the only person I was trying to keep up with was myself. In my first year as a journalist I decided I would only be happy when I got my film reviews quoted on posters on the Underground. Then I saw them on the Jubilee line and I was soon bored. I wanted a byline in a national paper. I had three back to back. But then I wanted a byline in *TIME* magazine, then another. I was overjoyed at the time, but it was short-lived. What next? Where did it end? Why did I care that Passepartout did not think I measured up to his standards? Why did I feel guilty for not getting my grades at A-level? It meant nothing now.

The hum of a plane passing overhead grew louder and louder until it screamed by and then faded away. *Everything arises to disappear. Learn to face both pleasure and pain with equanimity.* The truth was that they both hurt: one when it disappeared and one when it arrived. But by remaining a passive observer to both, perhaps day-to-day events would become more manageable. With this in mind, on the seventh day after lunch something strange happened.

I had traced the pulsations through my arms and legs and was sitting in what felt like a ball of warmth when the Chandigarh image sprang into my head – but nothing happened. No prickling along my skin. No tensing in my shoulders. I forced myself to play out the entire scene in slow motion in my head. Nothing happened. My breath was almost invisible. Meditation by its very nature is experiential. It is not open to description. It recoils from language, shrugs off explanation. Nor can it be a target of cynics or criticism: we cannot criticise what we have not known. But while still sitting cross-legged, my body underwent the most intense physical sensation I have ever experienced. My stomach muscles tightened, my arms burned and I felt as though a plug was being pulled out of the base of my spine, draining me of all my bitterness towards Passepartout and myself. At one point I thought I had risen off the cushion and panicked, blinking open my eyes and expecting everyone else to be staring. Nobody paid any attention. I ran from the hall, found my rock and sat down, surprised to feel my T-shirt drenched in sweat, tears streaming down my face. My body was crying, but my mind was still and had never felt so at peace. Those roots had finally been torn up.

Liberty the White Witch broke her silence the next morning. While on an amble through the orchard, she spotted the gardeners spraying the plants with pesticide and turned to me with her mouth hanging open. She willed me with her eyes to join her in uproar. I flared my nostrils in sympathy and slunk off to the dining hall for a cup of tea and a banana, while she argued with the teachers. With the final days approaching, people were becoming casual and smiling, nudging each other towards the bundle of puppies discovered in the bushes and standing in huddles to watch the sunset. On the tenth day we learnt the final stage of the meditation process. For the last ten minutes of every sitting, we were to imagine that our bodies were generating nothing but love and peace and happiness.

Where once I would have smirked, rolled my eyes and made jokes about tree huggers and hippies, it made sense to me. Over the last ten days I had done nothing but observe my breath and watch my own body. I had not been force-fed literature or doctrine, or been asked to engage in rites or rituals. I had not placed hope in an unknown entity. I had not asked for anything, from anyone. I had not paid money, or offered gifts as a bargain for my well-being. I had sat still, let my body do the talking and listened patiently. I no longer needed or wanted any kind of God or religion. Goenka's last piece of advice was this:

'Please don't leave here calling yourself a Buddhist. If the technique works, then please practise it to reap the full benefits. If not, then throw it in the bin and put it down to experience.'

We were then permitted to break noble silence. It was as though someone was slowly increasing the volume on a muted scene. Murmurs of relief gave way to the exchange of names, nationalities and a general release of joy. It turned out that Liberty's real name was Zooey and she was an ex-drug mule from Brooklyn who used to swallow condoms of heroin until her periods stopped and she almost died. Malini from Bangalore was here for the twelfth time. I could not help but assume that she had failed to learn anything on the previous eleven occasions. A contingent of Slovenians grabbed each other in excitement, then decided to travel to Pondicherry together. Perfect Annie to my left had never meditated in her life; and it turned out that Inga had tired of the meditation after three days and had torn open a big paper shopping bag and spent the last six days making notes all over it – so much for my heightened awareness. After packing our bags, gossiping about the Canadian outburst and cleaning our rooms, we were invited to make anonymous donations to the course based on what we thought was appropriate for ten nights' food and accommodation, or at least enough for someone else to benefit from the course.

I walked out of the gates bringing with me a lighter heart, a quiet mind, and two new friends in Inga and Annie.

21 | Answered Prayers

At Hyderabad Kacheguda station, I joined the queue to buy a ticket for the short hop to Deccan Nampally, from where I was going to catch the Charminar Express to Chennai. As I stood sandwiched between fellow passengers, a finger poked me in the base of my spine. An elderly man in a dhoti and Nehru topi stood behind me, applying steady pressure to my back with the tip of his index finger, as though this would make the queue move faster. Ten days ago I would have turned around and fumed. But now this man was only as annoying as I allowed him to be. In a few moments we would reach the front of the queue. Was it worth spending the next five or six minutes pulling my forehead into a scowl and tutting at a man who was completely indifferent to the effects of his poking? Not really. Instead I turned around, looked at him and started to laugh. He smiled back at me with a set of teeth like broken tombstones and muttered in Telugu about the wait. At the same time, he removed the finger to pick his nose. Everything is, indeed, impermanent.

After the 45-minute journey to Nampally, on the penultimate train, I wandered down to platform five, where the Charminar Express was waiting to take me back home to Chennai.

Home. Chennai.

Those were not words I normally associated with each other, but before I had a chance to ponder, a dark-haired man with a pair of Oakleys perched on his head stopped by me.

'Is this the train through to Chennai?'

'Yup, the Charminar Express.'

'OK, cool, I think this is my carriage but I'm not sure what W/L means.'

'W/L means that you're waitlisted. Can I see your ticket?'

He handed it over.

'It's only W/L 2, which means that you're second in line, so you should be fine. Check the list stuck up by the door to see if your name is on it, and good luck!'

I took a deep breath and made my way on board, finding my seat as a family of five entered the compartment, bringing with them the strong smell of Mysore sandalwood soap. The parents fussed over a small boy in a pair of shorts as his younger siblings climbed over the seats and hid in the overhead berth. His mother turned to me, the lightness of jasmine lifting off her plait.

'You are going to Chennai?'

'Yes.'

'Please, ma'am, he is travelling alone. My sister is going to meet him there, but will you do one thing? Will you keep one eye on him?'

'Of course.'

She took my hands in hers, which were warm and dry against my own, and shook her head, pulling round her sari pallu that kept sliding off her shoulder. Its cold silk slipped across my bare knees as she turned back to her son.

'Now this aunty will take care of you, OK? Be good for her.'

She held his chin between her fingers, then kissed the tips, before she and her husband retrieved their other two children from in hiding and collected on the platform. Referring to me as 'aunty' would normally have made me chuckle, but for some reason it seemed right. After four months and 79 train journeys, these trains had become my home and its passengers my family. I moved up to the window and looked out as Hyderabad began to slip from view. Beneath the sound of the wheels on the tracks was a softer grinding. Had it always been there? I realised that this was the last time I would watch the edges of a city slide from my vision and the thought bored a hollow into my stomach that filled with sadness. For once I did not reach for my iPod to drown it out, or flick open my book to distract my mind. I got up and went to find the only place where I knew I wanted to be.

Sitting on the steps in the doorway, I looped both arms around the handrails. I adored being here, and even though it was not in tune with my new philosophy, I had grown rather attached and was going to miss it. The train was rolling at little more than a walking pace through the outskirts of the city. On the verge of setting, the sun was stretched out across rooftops, spilling a papaya glow across the slums. I had always watched sunsets from the doorways, but this time I finally saw the spectrum of tones blending from yellow into orange into red, ever-changing, before there were little more than a few sprays of pink across the horizon. My ears pricked up at the sound of gushing water and as I leant out of the door I saw a burst water hydrant at the end of the tracks, shooting a jet into the air. As we drew closer, I noticed that a man was sitting at the base of the jet – the embodiment of Indian opportunism, he had brought a piece of soap to the broken hydrant and was squatting on the wall in his shorts, scrubbing himself all over and making the most of the free power shower.

If you give an Indian a chance he will take it. A history of struggle has instilled within Indians an inimitable instinct to survive, but with opportunity they can flourish. After four months of observations, conversations and first-hand experience, I realised that India is not shining – at least, not yet. The notion is an image, a façade built up by the powerful elite, who hope that if they shout it loudly and long enough it will drown out everything else, grab enough headlines and start to be true. A country's greatness cannot be measured by its size, but by the standard of living of every individual. Pockets of the country are aglow, bathed in the light of gated mansions, malls and Mercedes headlamps, but, like the passengers on the Lifeline Express, hundreds of millions still stand in the shadows, waiting for the clouds to part. But I had hope. I could see that the next generation would make the changes and encourage India to really shine.

And how did I feel? Deep down I knew when I left home that my parents did not think I would see out all 80 journeys. But I had. And I loved the fact that I did not want to leave. Indian Railways would always stay with me and I knew a part of me would stay with them.

As the Charminar Express swept out of the city, it began to grow chilly and I leant out to allow one last gust of wind to catch my hair before swaying back to my seat. My waitlisted friend was now sitting in the opposite seat, still wearing his Oakleys on his head.

'So you got on OK, then?'

'I did,' he replied. 'This is my first Indian train experience, so I guess I'm going to have to learn the lingo.'

'Don't worry, you'll pick it up as you go along. At least you now know what W/L means.'

I yawned and he yawned back, then glanced across at my book, *Answered Prayers*, spread open beside me.

'No wonder you're yawning. Capote?'

'Nothing wrong with Capote! I've just finished reading *Breakfast at Tiffany's* on recommendation of a friend and this is pretty good so far.'

'I've read *In Cold Blood*, *Music for Chameleons* and *The Grass Harp*, but not *Breakfast at Tiffany's* – I've seen the film, of course.'

'I like the title of *Answered Prayers*,' I held the book up, 'and this illustration of Capote looking like Porky Pig.'

'Well, it's called that because of a quote from Saint Teresa of Avila, who said that more tears were shed over answered prayers than unanswered ones.'

'Avid reader?'

'Maybe a little.'

'So what do you do?'

'I'm a sommelier.'

'Where?'

'Lake Tahoe.'

I glanced down at his wedding ring. The Indian in me was desperate to ask where his wife was, how old he was, what he was doing here and where he was going, but I held fire. The other part of me had no interest. At this moment this was just a sommelier with a mass of chocolate-brown hair, unusually dark blue eyes and a passion for books. The boy I was supposed to be taking care of had started to rub his eyes and yawn, so together we made up his bed, slotted away his backpack and switched off the light as he began to doze off. Once he had gone to sleep, we began whispering like parents.

'So this is pretty fun,' he said.

'What is?'

'This train journey is like a sleepover.'

'Don't be fooled, they're not all like this. The long ones can get tough.'

'What's the longest journey you've done?'

'Forty-eight hours from Delhi to Kerala.'

'Holy shit. The longest train journey I've done is the Amtrak from San Francisco to Los Angeles. It's about 11 hours, but it's really beautiful – most of the track is surrounded by vineyards, before you open up to the ocean and see pelicans swooping all over.'

'In that case you'll love taking trains here. I can't promise you pelicans though.'

He made up his bed and drew the blankets up to his armpits, before propping himself up on his elbow and turning to face me. 'Yeah? Tell me your top three trains.'

'OK, the Mandovi Express, which runs along the Konkan coast. You can hang out of the doors over the ocean and the food is fab – particularly the chicken spring rolls. Then Jammu to Udhampur, which travels over valleys and rivers around the foothills of the Himalayas. And then as far as swanky trains go, the Indian Maharaja was pretty special.'

'Is that like the Palace on Wheels or something?'

'It's newer, but takes a similar route through Rajasthan. I figured that there was no point in only jumping on the poverty bandwagon. I wanted to see the extremes of the railways.'

'Train fan?'

I laughed. 'I wouldn't ever have called myself a train fan before, but I guess I am now. But more of an India fan than a train fan.'

'Anyway, I'll let you get back to making notes.'

I shuffled under the covers, enjoying the rough tickle against my chin as the train rocked me gently from side to side. While flicking through my logbook, a pressed orchid fell out from the pages. I recognised it from the Indian Maharaja. Digging around my purse for a pen, I found a pinch of sand from Dwarka and the tuft of grass from Udhampur. As I wrote, I noticed the last of the mehndi from the Golden Chariot fading from my hands and was about to drift off when my companion piped up.

'Hey, do you have *Breakfast at Tiffany's* with you?'

'I do.'

'Do you mind if I take it?'

'Not at all.' I foraged around in my bag and produced the copy, which he slotted into a side pocket. He then pulled out a paperback of J.M. Coetzee's *Disgrace*.

'If you haven't read it, you should.'

Thanking him, I lay on my back and closed my eyes, trying to fit in a few minutes of meditation before going to sleep. Earlier in the day I had found Fiona Lanes on Facebook and sent her an apology for the horrid letter. It was 14 years overdue, but at least I had told her how sorry I was. I had also received a text from Ben, congratulating me on completing the journey. We had stayed closely in touch after I left the Lifeline Express, chatting on the phone most days, and I knew we would stay friends once we were back in London. And lastly, Passepartout had called that morning to say he was on his way back to Chennai and would meet me for a Thums Up at Imthiaz and Sweetie's kitchen table.

All was well.

Beneath the rocking of the train, the beat from my own body began to sound and I listened closely, unaware of the lights being flicked on overhead, the new family who had boarded and were now shuffling around, the babble of their voices ...'

I awoke in the same position I had fallen asleep in. Sunshine poured through the windows and warmed my face. I turned to the window and allowed it to heat my cheeks for a few moments, before I opened my eyes and saw that the blue-eyed sommelier had gone. We had talked on and off for six hours and he had left without a word. We had exchanged books, but not names. It was perfect. Everything may be impermanent, but he would always be the blue-eyed sommelier from Lake Tahoe with great taste in books. I did not want or need to know any more about him or where he had gone. This was the beauty of train travel. Travelling companions come and go. Some stay for the duration of the journey, but others hop on, then hop off when they need to. We enjoy their company while they are there and we wave them off when they leave. We do not pine for them, or stay angry that they snored. We sit back, enjoy the scenery and wait to see who fills their seat.

People come into our lives and they always leave. But what counts is the present. Twenty years ago I had hated Chennai and its people, but the bad ones had left. The clouds that rained down on my parents had moved along and, 12 years after losing touch with her, my brother had run into his best friend from that dreadful school and was now about to marry her. Yet I had chosen to hold the old images hostage. The past was just a series of memories. Why ruin the present for what had been, or what may never be? As Phileas Fogg had said, 'The unforeseen does not exist.' It was four months since I had returned to India. In that time these trains and their passengers had housed me, fed me, carried me safely and given us the chance to become reacquainted. Now that I had learnt to see things as they really are, I could see that India was no longer a stranger to me.

I gathered together my bags, Coetzee and my surrogate son and waited in the doorway of the train. Sunshine bathed the biscuit-coloured buildings as the train sailed past the backs of houses, threading through the heart of the city. In the morning light, it was like seeing Chennai for the first time. At 8:30 am the Charminar Express drew to a halt at Chennai Central. Pulling on my rucksack, I put my right foot down on the platform and watched as my flip-flop snapped. After 80 train journeys and almost 40,000 km – the circumference of the Earth – it had lost the will to live.

A plumper version of the boy's mother appeared on the platform and waddled over, grabbing his wrist as his cousins danced around him, full of questions. She smiled and shook her head from side to side as I waved at the little boy and ambled along the platform. Departing trains hissed, clanked and sounded their horns, no more my call to prayer. Halfway up the platform I spied a bunch of men shoving in the doorway of a passenger train. They squeezed between each other, elbowing, arguing and jostling before they turned and saw me watching. Breaking into sheepish smiles, they waved from the doorway. The train began to sail down the platform and out of the station as I waved back and allowed the crowd to sweep me into its embrace.

Snakes and Ladders

31 May

London had never felt so alive. I had flung open the windows and balcony door of my flat and the smell of an early-summer barbecue drifted in from next door's garden. A spiral of smoke curled its way up between the trees, green and glowing as the evening sun cut into the room at angles, bouncing off my computer screen. Reading the final line of chapter seven, I pressed print and sat back with relief.

It was one year since I had arrived home and I was a third of the way through writing this book. To my right was a stack of multicoloured train tickets, faded and wilting. A pile of hotel and restaurant receipts sat next to them, along with my large leather-bound logbook and six shabby notebooks barely holding on to their spines. Stuck to the wall was the pressed orchid from the Indian Maharaja – minus one petal. A cardboard box of books sat on the floor: before flying home I had posted my mobile library, which had arrived a couple of weeks after I did and still had about it a faint smell of camphor and dust.

What looked like a jumble sale was now my home. Most mornings I would manage half an hour of meditation – 45 minutes if I was lucky – before sitting down and sifting through the memorabilia, using each piece to reassemble the journey. On another wall was my map of India. Now the line of marker pen, which had once stopped so abruptly in Punjab before snaking mournfully down the centre of the country, ran all the way around, starting in Chennai and ending firmly back there.

I often found myself gazing at that map, remembering the snakes that had lain in wait, ready to strike. But for every snake, someone had always produced a ladder, whether it was the three gentlemen on the train from Delhi to Chennai, the Ambassador from Chandigarh to Delhi, or the sweeper on the platform at Londa. As Goenka had said, 'everything arises to disappear', and I'd now learnt that I couldn't control the roll of the dice, but I could at least put myself back on the board each time. Tracing the map with a finger, I wished that marker pen could have run through a few more states: Nagaland, Mizoram and Uttaranchal, for instance. As much as my questions about India had been satisfied, a new curiosity had been sparked, and I knew that I would one day go back.

On a separate computer screen a slideshow of photographs played on a loop, familiar faces appearing and fading into one another. I changed some of their names among the pages, but decided that others deserved to be recognised for their role in shaping my journey, which, in turn, shaped me.

Glossary

aarathi   Hindu ritual whereby light from an oil lamp is offered to the deity and then to the worshipper

Aavin   trademark name of Tamil Nadu milk producers

Archie Double Digest   double edition of the American comic

barfi   traditional Indian sweet made from condensed milk and sugar

beedi   thin, leaf-wrapped Indian cigarette filled with tobacco

bindi   bright, decorative dot worn on the forehead

Blue Label   premium blend of Johnnie Walker whisky

bogie   train carriage

carrom   table boardgame where players flick disks into four pockets

chappals   flip-flops

charpoy   traditional woven low bed

Chennai   formerly Madras

chowkidar   watchman

dacoit   robber or bandit

dhaba   local roadside restaurant

dhoti unstitched cloth worn by men, wrapped around the waist and legs

dosai fermented crepe made from rice flour

dupatta long scarf usually worn with salwar kameez (q.v.)

Femina women's lifestyle magazine

firang derogatory term for foreigners

gulab jamun deep-fried balls of cloyed milk in sugar syrup

Hakka a migratory community now settled in south China

Hrithik Roshan popular Bollywood film star

idli savoury steamed rice cake

jalebi bright orange, pretzel-shaped sweet

kara steel or iron bangle worn by members of the Sikh faith

karahi large wok

Kathak North Indian classical dance

keema pav street-food favourite of fried minced meat and bread

khichdi rice and lentils dish

koel Asian cuckoo

Kolkata formerly Calcutta

kumkum powder made from turmeric or saffron

kurta loose-fitting shirt worn by men and women

kwashiorkor disease caused by malnutrition

ladoo sugary, ball-shaped sweet made from chickpea flour

lungi sarong-like garment

Mirinda orange soft drink

Moksha final release of the soul from the circle of reincarnation

Mumbai   formerly Bombay

murukku   crunchy deep-fried snack

Naxalite   militant communist group operating in India

paan   betel leaf and areca nut

pagri   Rajasthani turban

pongal   savoury rice and lentil dish

prasad   food first offered to a deity then distributed to worshippers

puja   religious ritual to make offerings to a deity

Punju   derogatory term for Punjabis

rajma   red kidney beans in thick gravy

rupee   Rs.70 = £1

sadhu   ascetic or wandering monk

sahib   courteous term for a master

salwar kameez   long shirt or tunic worn over baggy trousers

sambar   spiced, lentil-based stew

sannyasin   ascetic

sapota   sweet, malty-tasting fruit with a kiwi-like skin

tamasha   bustle and excitement

Tatkal   scheme devised by Indian Railways for booking last-minute tickets

Thanjavur   formerly Tanjore

thukpa   thick Nepali noodle soup

Thums Up   leading brand of cola

topi   small hat, narrow at the front and back

uttapam   thick savoury pancake with toppings

Acknowledgements

I had no idea how many people would come together to shape the wonderful journey that began when I boarded the first train and ended at the last line of this book. To the cast of characters who wandered the train aisles, slept above me or sat by my side, I hope that I have shown my gratitude throughout the pages. In addition to Nicholas Brealey and his team, particularly Tom Viney, a core group deserves my heartfelt thanks.

While in India, Urmila Dongre offered me a permanent bedroom, delightful company and much-needed antispasmodics, as did Radhika and Krishna Das, Neil Sudhakar, Arun Chadda and Kavita Bhupathi Chadda. Sweetie and Imthiaz Pasha, my surrogate parents, thank you for your love, affection and occasional ridicule: without you I would not have survived and would still be queuing for tatkal tickets at Chennai Central.

Huge thanks go to Giles Heron, my next-door neighbour and chief proofreader, for coffee, *Community* and keeping me sane, and to Russell Goulbourne, whose eagle-eyed editing and brilliant wit and wisdom have made this a much sharper book than I could have hoped. In their own ways, Stephen Armstrong, William Dalrymple, Matthew Rosenberg, Milan Samani, Arun Rajagopal, Harald Haugan, Meredydd Lloyd-Jones, Charles Cumming and Michael Haydock gave me little prods and pushes when I needed them.

Chris and Lynn Palmer's impeccable timing was a godsend – and the same goes for Marc Sethi and Edward Price – much love and gratitude for your photography and friendship when I needed it most. Adam Benzine, Ramin Farahani and Sarah Warwick have weathered my strops and tears with hugs, humour and encouragement, but a special thank-you goes to my school friend Abizer Kapadia for designing the most beautiful website, without which this book would never have happened.

I will be forever grateful to my dear agent, David Godwin, for making that crackly phone call to Gangtok, holding my hand from start to finish while writing this book and proving to be a wonderfully wicked companion in my subsequent travels. Enormous thanks to you and Anna Watkins for enduring my visits and shameless pilfering from your bookcases.

Lastly, and most importantly, I want to thank my parents Rekha and Rajesh, my brother Rahul, and in particular my sister-in-law Sarita, for giving me nothing but love and whoops of joy, and delighting in my adventures as if they were their own.

About the Author

Monisha Rajesh was born in King's Lynn in Norfolk and grew up all over England. She read French at the University of Leeds and taught English at a high school in Cannes before studying postgraduate journalism at City University London. She has written for the *London Evening Standard, The Guardian, TIME* magazine and *The New York Times*. Monisha now works at *The Week* magazine and lives in London. This is her first book.

ALSO FROM NICHOLAS BREALEY PUBLISHING

Misadventure in the Middle East:
Travels as Tramp, Artist and Spy

Henry Hemming

"The brilliantly written account of a daring journey, by turns hilarious and poignant, and a timely antidote to current misconceptions about the Middle East. Essential reading."
—Jason Elliot, author of *Mirrors of the Unseen* and *An Unexpected Light*

Experience the beautifully written tale of a hapless young artist, a beat-up pick-up called Yasmine, and an extraordinary journey across the world. *Misadventure in the Middle East* creates a portrait of the post-9/11 Middle East that transports the reader into the human heart of the region.

When Henry Hemming sets out in his pick-up truck to make a portrait of the Middle East, he has no idea what he will find or how he will live. Using art as his passport, he spends a year traveling throughout the area; his extraordinary journey finds him accused of being both an Islamic extremist and a British spy, dancing in a dervish hideaway and attending a Fourth of July party with GIs in Saddam Hussein's Republican Palace.

As the young people he meets along the way share their dreams and doubts, Hemming discovers an unpredictable Middle East that is in no way accurately represented by the nightly news. And as the invasion of Iraq intensifies, he realizes that in order to finish his portrait, he must go to Baghdad to find a fabled artistic renaissance—a trip that could cost him his life.

ISBN 978-1-85788-395-4
PB £10.99
www.nicholasbrealey.com

ALSO FROM NICHOLAS BREALEY PUBLISHING

SEDUCED BY SOUTHERN ITALY
CHRIS HARRISON

Head over Heel:
Seduced by Southern Italy

Chris Harrison

A whitewashed fishing village, a shapely signorina and an infatuated young man—head over heels on the heel of the boot.

This is Chris Harrison's hilarious and captivating story of leaving his previous life for La Dolce Vita—or rather, the Southern Italian version of that seductive way of life, with its luscious foods, physical beauty and sun-drenched vistas.

On a trip to Dublin, Chris falls head over heels in love with Daniela, an Italian girl 'with eyes the colour of Guinness', and follows her to her small home town of Andrano on the coast of Puglia. Among olive groves and cobblestone lanes, Chris takes us on a moving, insightful and often hilarious journey into the heart of Southern Italy. Along the way he introduces us to a cast of eccentric characters: a policeman who rearranges crimes to suit the necessary forms, a doctor who prescribes patients his homemade lemon liqueur, and—the biggest challenge of all—Daniela's mamma, who's determined to convert Chris to the Catholic faith, supervise his choice of underwear and build a second storey on her stucco home where the couple might live happily ever after.

Can this relationship with Southern Italy possibly survive or will the sweet life turn sour?

ISBN 978-1-85788-521-7
PB £9.99
www.nicholasbrealey.com